CRISIS AT
ADOLESCENCE

CRISIS AT ADOLESCENCE

Object Relations Therapy with the Family

Edited by
Sally Box
with Beta Copley, Jeanne Magagna,
and Errica Moustaki Smilansky

JASON ARONSON INC.
Northvale, New Jersey
London

Chapter 5 was first published as "Some Thoughts about Therapeutic Change in Families at Adolescence," in *The Journal of Adolescence*, 1988, volume 9, pp. 187–198. Copyright © 1986 by the Association for the Psychiatric Study of Adolescents and reprinted by permission.

Chapter 12 is based on the article "Working with a Family as a Single Therapist with Special Reference to Transference Manifestations," in *Journal of Child Psychotherapy*, 1983, volume 9, pp. 103–118. Copyright © 1983 by the Association of Child Psychotherapists, and used by permission.

Production Editor: Judith D. Cohen

This book was set in 10 pt. Baskerville by Lind Graphics of Upper Saddle River, New Jersey, and printed and bound by Haddon Craftsmen of Scranton, Pennsylvania.

Library of Congress Cataloging-in-Publication Data

Crisis at adolescence : object relations therapy with the family
  edited by Sally Box . . . [et al.].
    p. cm.
  Rev. ed. of: Psychotherapy with families. 1981.
  Includes bibliographical references and index.
  ISBN 1-56821-094-9 (hardcover)
  1. Family psychotherapy.   2. Object relations (Psychoanalysis)
I. Box, Sally.   II. Psychotherapy with families.
  [DNLM: 1. Family Therapy—methods.   2. Adolescence.   3. Family.
4. Object Attachment.   5. Psychoanalytic Therapy.   WM 460.5.02 C932
1994]
RC488.5.P79   1994
616.89'156—dc20
DNLM/DLC
for Library of Congress   93-9010

Manufactured in the United States of America. Jason Aronson Inc. offers books and cassettes. For information and catalog write to Jason Aronson Inc., 230 Livingston Street, Northvale, New Jersey 07647.

THE LIBRARY OF OBJECT RELATIONS

A SERIES OF BOOKS EDITED BY
DAVID E. SCHARFF AND JILL SAVEGE SCHARFF

Object relations theories of human interaction and development provide an expanding, increasingly useful body of theory for the understanding of individual development and pathology, for generating theories of human interaction, and for offering new avenues of treatment. They apply across the realms of human experience from the internal world of the individual to the human community, and from the clinical situation to everyday life. They inform clinical technique in every format from individual psychoanalysis and psychotherapy, through group therapy, to couple and family therapy.

The Library of Object Relations aims to introduce works that approach psychodynamic theory and therapy from an object relations point of view. It includes works from established and new writers who employ diverse aspects of British and American object relations theory in helping individuals, families, couples, and groups. It features books that stress integration of psychoanalytic approaches with marital and family therapy, as well as those centered on individual psychotherapy and psychoanalysis.

Refinding the Object and Reclaiming the Self
David E. Scharff

Scharff Notes: A Primer of Object Relations Therapy
Jill Savege Scharff and David E. Scharff

Object Relations Couple Therapy
David E. Scharff and Jill Savege Scharff

Object Relations Family Therapy
David E. Scharff and Jill Savege Scharff

Projective and Introjective Identification and the Use of the Therapist's Self
Jill Savege Scharff

Foundations of Object Relations Family Therapy
Jill Savege Scharff, Editor

Contents

PART I

OBJECT RELATIONS IN FAMILY THERAPY

PART II

AT THE BOUNDARY OF FAMILY THERAPY

PART III

PSYCHOTHERAPY WITH FAMILIES

Preface

Since the first edition of this book in 1981, many things have changed. Not least, a number of our contributors have changed their names because they started or joined new families of their own.

There have been other new developments, some of them in the field of family therapy itself, which I have addressed in the chapter on recent contributions. There are three new chapters, one on the transference with a single therapist, one on the therapeutic process and change in adolescence—both previously published in journals—and the other, hot off the press, called "The Significance of the Outsider in the Family and Other Social Groups."

All the contributors in the book have, at one time or another, engaged in the same workshop at The Tavistock Clinic in London and have helped to develop the approach represented there. The members of the workshop met only once weekly, but this was in the context of their more intensive psychoanalytically oriented work in the rest of the clinic. We were, in this way, immeasurably aided by the dynamic influence of the clinic and the ready availability there of recent contributions, such as those of Bion, Meltzer, Rosenfeld and others, and their application to groups and institutions as well as to the kind of psychotic or narcissistic states of mind that often prevail in the families that we see. In sum, we think that the approach might most accurately be described as a Tavistock psychoanalytic approach or a Tavistock object relations approach. But since these major influences have undoubtedly been Kleinian and post-Kleinian, that fact also needs to be clearly acknowledged in the name and attribution of our identity. So in the end I have referred in the introduction to a "Kleinian object relations approach," and unsatisfactory though this seems, perhaps it is the nearest we can get for the moment.

Contributors

Sally Box practices and teaches psychotherapy and its application. She worked in residential and therapeutic community settings in England and the United States and became engaged in family therapy during the 1960s in California. After joining the Tavistock Clinic in 1968, she sought to integrate this interest with her developing psychoanalytic understanding of individual and group dynamics and, as Chairman of the Young People and Their Families Workshop in The Adolescent Department, she fostered a psychoanalytic approach to work with families.

Ronald Britton is a Training Analyst of The British Psycho-Analytical Society. Formerly he was Chairman of The Department for Children and Families, Tavistock Clinic and a consultant to several local authority Social Services and Child Care agencies. He was involved in the development of "Young Family Centres" as a form of Day Care for vulnerable and deprived families.

Susan Carvalho (formerly Zawada) graduated as a clinical psychologist from Birmingham University, then worked in the Children's Department of the Maudsley Hospital for three years, where she first became interested in family therapy. For four years she was Senior Clinical Psychologist in the Adolescent Department, Tavistock Clinic. She is now Forensic Clinical Psychologist, Regional Secure Unit, North East Thames Health Authority.

Beta Copley trained as a Child Psychotherapist and engaged in the practice and teaching of individual psychoanalytical psychotherapy with children, adolescents, and adults. She is interested in the application of learning derived from psychoanalysis to a wider field such as Youth Counseling, Family, and Group Relations Work. She has been Chair of the Young People and Their Families Workshop at the Tavistock Clinic. She is currently in private practice and is also a visiting teacher at the Tavistock Clinic.

Anna Dartington (formerly Halton) trained as a psychotherapist at the Tavistock Clinic where she is now a staff member in the Adolescent Department and currently Chair of the Family Therapy Workshop. She works mainly as a psychotherapist with adults and adolescents but is also interested in the wider study of unconscious processes in groups and institutions. She works as a consultant staff member on Tavistock group relations conferences and is involved in management consultation in the Health and Social Services.

Nonie Insall worked as a Child Care Officer and Social Worker in two different local authorities. She then decided to specialize in work with children and their families, spending four years in the Child and Adolescent Psychiatry Unit at Guy's Hospital. Later she moved to the Tavistock Clinic as a Senior Social Worker, where she undertook psychotherapy training. Since leaving the Tavistock Clinic and moving abroad, she has worked privately both as a psychotherapist and as a teacher of psychodynamic skills in China and the Far East.

Roger Kennedy is a Consultant Psychotherapist to the Family Unit, Cassel Hospital, and a Member of the British Psycho-Analytical Society. He is co-author of *Works of Jacques Lacan*, co-editor of *The Family as Inpatient*, and author of *Freedom to Relate: Psychoanalytical Exploration*.

Jeanne Magagna is a Consultant Child Psychotherapist heading the Psychotherapy Department for the Hospitals for Sick Children, teaches on various trainings in Italy and England and works as a family and individual psychotherapist with people having severe communication and eating difficulties. She is also the joint coordinator of the Child Psychotherapy Training Program in Florence, Italy.

Errica Moustaki Smilansky is a practicing psychoanalytic psychotherapist with adults and is working as head of psychotherapy training and professional development at the Psychology Department in Hillingdon

Hospital. She originally trained as a clinical psychologist at the Hebrew University of Jerusalem and subsequently as a psychoanalytic psychotherapist at the Adult Department of the Tavistock Clinic. Her earlier work at an adolescent inpatient unit stimulated her interest in research with families that led her to study and practice psychoanalytic family therapy as well as to engage in clinical research with families and couples. In that research, she explored the way family relationships can be expressed in spatial terms. She has also acted as organizational consultant to mental health institutional settings where she applied understanding of family dynamics to understanding and influencing institutional dynamics associated with the process of change and the defense against it.

Margot Waddell trained at the Tavistock Clinic where she is now a Consultant Child Psychotherapist in the Adolescent Department. She has been teaching and lecturing on several training courses in England and abroad for the past few years.

Arthur Hyatt Williams was born in Birkenhead, and his childhood was spent on the Wirral. Intending to be a biologist, he won a medical scholarship. He studied medicine at Liverpool, and became a psychiatrist in the Army. Thereafter he worked at the Cassel Hospital. He was (regional) psychiatrist for the southeastern metropolitan regional hospital board, and Consultant Psychiatrist at the Tavistock Clinic from 1962 until retirement in 1979.

Gianna Williams (formerly Henry) is a Consultant Psychotherapist and Course Tutor of the Postgraduate Diploma/MA in Psychoanalytic Observational Studies (Tavistock Clinic/University of East London). She has also initiated a number of courses in Observational Studies in England and abroad.

Acknowledgments

I and my co-authors would like to thank our colleagues, especially those in the Adolescent Department at the Tavistock Clinic, London, who have helped with the development of this approach and given us their encouragement and support to write the chapters for the book. We would like to thank Mrs. Anita Cotten, for all the interest, patience, and unstinting work she put into the book; also to acknowledge Gianna Henry Williams, Jonathan Smilansky, and John Steiner, who helped Errica Moustaki Smilansky to prepare the Glossary.

The authors join me in acknowledging all those of our friends and families who may have had to put up with various sorts of discomfort arising from our preoccupation with this book.

For reasons of confidentiality, it has of course been necessary to disguise the circumstances of the families discussed so that they will be generally unrecognizable to all except possibly themselves. It may be that even so, some families will think they recognize themselves and if so, we hope they do not mind.

Sally Box
Bristol, England, 1993

SECTION I

Object Relations in Family Therapy

Space for Thinking in Families

SALLY BOX

This book is about experiences of work with families and about some of the ideas that have grown out of these experiences in the light of a particular background of psychoanalytic theory and practice.

The emphasis on thinking highlights the importance we attach to the essential relationship between thinking processes and states of feeling. It stems from the notion that the available "space for thinking" in any one family, as in any individual, bears a crucial relationship to patterns developed for coping with mental pain and ways of responding to life experience; that it serves both as an indicator of the quality of mental life and also as the most necessary condition for its development.

There is an increasingly widespread interest today in how people learn and how they think. For instance, what are the conditions for thought, of an independent and creative kind, in contrast to reactions that are impulsive and without thought, on the one hand, or determined in a stereotyped way by unrelieved custom or unquestioned authority, on the other? More specifically, from the point of view of this book, what prevents family members from developing their own identity and becoming independent individuals, able to separate themselves from the others — both internally and externally — so that they are not further perpetuating a pattern of life "in the shadow of the ancestors"? (Scott and Ashworth 1969). These are some of the questions that arise from our work with families in the light of the psychoanalytic principles on which it draws.

While our focus is clearly not upon directly influencing specific ways of thinking and behaving, we are interested in providing opportunities for family members to shift old patterns and unblock pathways to new ones, so that their capacities for learning from their own experience may develop and their scope for living be correspondingly enriched.

The approach is based on two particular developments, (1) that of object relations and psychoanalytic practice derived especially from the work of Freud, Melanie Klein and others who have elaborated her ideas, especially W. R. Bion; (2) the application of this to the understanding of group relations following the work of Bion and others such as A. K. Rice, P. M. Turquet, and Elliott Jaques. The common feature in these is the significance attached to the part played by unconscious phantasy in the elaboration and development of human relationships. All of them emphasize the use of immediate spontaneous feelings for elucidating these "inner worlds of relationships" or "shared phantasies" as they emerge within the boundaries of the session.

To a large extent, therefore, the approach represents a number of shared views and questions about the nature of human functioning, which relate directly to the body of knowledge and the concepts that we draw upon for understanding and interpreting the behavior of our patient families.

For instance, the value placed on trying to discover the truth, in psychological terms, is based on the view that apart from its scientific implications this is actually important for mental growth and development. "Falling back on analytic experience for a clue," Bion writes in *Transformations* "I am reminded that healthy mental growth seems to depend on truth as the living organism depends on food. If it is lacking or deficient, the personality deteriorates" (1965, p. 38). By this I am not suggesting, of course, that we are attempting to discover the truth of ultimate reality, but that there is a psychic reality that can become more known and that efforts to evade it may be seen as the basis of much malfunctioning in the family. Hence the importance attached here to providing a chance for the family members to get in touch with what their feelings and reactions actually are, and to be able to think about them.

In *Learning from Experience* Bion discusses the relationship between the experience of frustration and the capacity to face reality, and reminds us how Freud recognized thought as being stimulated initially in response to the experience of frustration—"An infant capable of tolerating frustration can permit itself to have a sense of reality, to be dominated by the reality principle." Bion then draws the distinction between "procedures designed to evade frustration and those designed to modify it" (1962a, p. 29). It is a crucial distinction in helping us to understand what is happening in the families we see. Our concern about what conflictual or otherwise painful issues are having to be avoided is related to the realization that it is by their avoidance rather than their existence that such issues are more likely to block or sabotage growth and creativity. That is, we are not in the business of attempting to remove conflict and frustration so much as providing space for their recognition and integration as an inevitable part of life and, within manageable limits, as a possible basis for new thought.

Hence the work we are describing is about making space for unacknowledged and disowned parts of the family and for the behavior that masks them. We suggest it is through active engagement with these aspects of all the individuals in the family, as they emerge in their relationship to ourselves, that the possibility for their acceptance and integration can occur. Only so may the foundations be laid that make for the kind of modification and growth that must spring naturally and from the inside.

The family can be seen as a particular sort of institution with its own culture and specific modes of dealing with life. It is comprised of individuals whose behavior and experience we know to be affected by the system of interlinking relationships of which they are a part. At the same time the individuals also contain deeply embedded characteristics, or internal relationships, which we believe do not lend themselves to substantial change simply through an alternation in the structure of the family system, but need to be understood in action and to have their unconscious meaning interpreted. It is these dual aspects of working with the family as a unit and the individuals within it that constitute both the difficulties and fascination of the task.

All of us who work with families for any length of time are bound to be exercised by the qualities of extreme negativism, acting out, and other sorts of intransigence that we meet in many of them. Indeed many families are referred as families because none of the individuals in them is willing or able to use individual therapy. Until recently it is doubtful whether any analyst or therapist would hope to succeed in treating them individually even if they wanted it. It does not seem at all surprising, therefore, that people have sought totally new ways of approaching these problems.

The work of Minuchin or Palazzoli, for example, with the families of anorexics is particularly challenging in terms of the means and nature of the changes that are described. It is always difficult to know what we actually do when we are with families. There is a notorious gap between what people say they do and what they actually do! Moreover, one often finds oneself closer in style to some who profess a very different approach. For this reason alone, there is no substitute for description of what is said and done in the therapy sessions. We appreciate this principle in other books and have attempted to support it with the inclusion of direct clinical material throughout this one. Clearly evidence is important, however difficult to establish, but one cannot forever dodge the wider implications involved in different approaches and these seem much more complicated. For instance, while I think we would find ourselves quite in tune with the way the dynamics of a family are described and understood in some of the clinical examples cited by Palazzoli and even with some of the interpretive interventions she mentions, most of us part company with her on "epistemological" grounds—to use her own word—and in relation to the "ploys" and strategies that she advocates as an integral part of her approach (1978). At the same time we think there is a valuable heritage of literature and experience in which analytic principles have been applied to groups and institutions which has only just begun to be tapped. There is a long way to go in terms of the development of appropriate skills in applying these principles to families before we can be more clear about their limitations. At the moment we are more conscious of our own.

Some current preoccupations within the field of psychoanalysis—in relation to narcissism, narcissistic states and perverse relationships—are especially relevant for understanding and handling these phenomena. A number of relatively recent developments seem particularly helpful in bridging the gap between the understanding of individual and group dynamics and between intra-personal and interpersonal functioning. The concept of transference is a core one both in our work and in the book and has been central to psychoanalysis since Freud first introduced it in 1900. Ideas about the nature of what is being transferred, particularly in terms of the significance of phantasy and of the effect it has on the receiver are constantly changing and developing. We have inherited, for instance, elaborate notions of identification, important modifications on the original idea of countertransference, and developments about notions of projection culminating in the specific concept of projective identification with its rich offspring in Bion's model of container–contained (1967, pp. 67–70). The latter, developed through work with borderline psychotic patients, is of particular value to us in our work with families.

In her chapter, Margot Waddell discusses these psychoanalytic concepts in relation to specific clinical examples. After putting the family in its social context and touching on some of the issues involved in the change from couple to family, she concentrates especially on the implications of the processes fundamental to family functioning that come under the heading of projective identification. She explores first the way they operate in the family, then the way they are lived out in the transference relationship to the therapist.

The importance attributed to the part played by phantasy in the mental elaboration of events occurring in external reality clearly influences the significance attached technically to the work done with the transference as distinct from the actual external relationship between the family members. In fact this may be one of the major features that differentiates one type of approach from another, and accounts for some of the contrasting views described by Susan Carvalho in her chapter. She reviews the development of family therapy from its beginning to 1981, when this book was first published. She also describes different approaches and highlights the problem of evaluating outcome. (Indeed, with families, perhaps a more accurate picture might be gained over more than one generation, in terms, for instance, of the kind of mating and parenting experience the children are able to offer when they become adults.) The survey reminds us of our difficulty in getting to grips with the different values involved in different approaches and in the different views about human nature and human growth.

One of the issues about family work that we have not attempted to resolve is that of appropriate criteria for deciding between individual and family treatment. There are some indicators that are suggested in the book and some families who clearly could not accept any other way of being seen, if only because no one individual owns a wish for help on his or her own behalf. In general, these indicators would not differ markedly from those suggested by Frieda Martin (1977) although her actual way of working and her idea of an analytic approach differs from the one described here. Apart from these broad indicators, more specific attention is given in the book to drawing a distinction between a way of working during an initial exploratory stage and the way one would work with families in long-term analytic type treatment.

In her chapter "Introducing Families to Family work," Beta Copley compares three families in which she saw some or all of the members for exploration and worked with them about what kind of psychotherapeutic help they wanted and could use. She describes their functioning, as it emerges in the relationship to the setting and herself, and discusses her thoughts about the criteria it suggests for determining the next step.

Sometimes, the logical or only realistic next step is for parents to be worked with on their own — with or without a child in individual treatment. Sometimes one or more children are already in individual treatment and this may operate as contraindication for family treatment. But work with the parents raises particular issues of its own — many of which are familiar to those who work in traditional child guidance clinics. In the first part of their paper, Anna Dartington and Jeanne Magagna consider some of the problems of management involved in setting up treatment for a parental couple. They go on to describe, in the second part, the process of treatment in one case, elaborating on some of the relevant concepts, such as that of shared phantasy. They address specifically the issues of co-therapy with this couple and the use of the therapist's countertransference in relation to each other for understanding different aspects of the couple in therapy.

The theme of co-therapy is explored further in relation to work with the whole family in Arthur Hyatt Williams's paper, where he describes the long-term treatment of a family in which the adolescence of the two children heralded disruption of the tenuous balance in the family dynamics and was accompanied by violent outbursts that could be seen to shift from one member to another. The boundary between the family as "sanctuary" and as "prison" is discussed in relation to the problems for these adolescents to grow up and leave home.

Roger Kennedy and Jeanne Magagna describe the particular dynamics and reactions in a family where a murder had taken place and suggest from their work with this family how the process of getting in touch with the regret and remorse involved can, first, be defended against by characteristics of perverse sexuality, and then can bring with it the attendant dangers of a "life-risking psychomatic symptom which symbolizes an identification with the attacked murdered person."

In many cases referrals come to us with a long history of contacts with other agencies. In his chapter Ronald Britton relates the dynamics of such contacts and the enactment that is often evoked in the workers concerned with the dynamics of the families with whom they are dealing. He discusses the phenomena of the *repetition compulsion* in these terms, goes on to compare this view of the system to that of family therapists who base their approach on General Systems Theory, and considers some of the implications of the principle of *dynamic equilibrium* in terms of Freud's concept of the *constancy principle*.

In my own chapter, I have discussed, in relation to clinical material, some of the technical issues involved in providing a method that is suited to our overall stance of trying to offer people a chance to develop the use of their own experience and to draw upon it as a basis for thinking and choosing new possibilities or reviewing old ones. I have attempted to compare work with two different families in terms of each one's characteristic approach to containing anxiety in the family and to suggest that the differences are reflected in the differential experience for the therapists in their effort to provide containment in the treatment.

All these ideas represent a growing interest in what becomes of unbearably painful, conflictual, or otherwise unmanageable feelings that arise in an individual and threaten to overwhelm him. Whether the individual is himself able to digest, metabolize, and use the feelings as food for thought, or whether he must find some other way of managing is what determines the crucial outcome in every day-to-day crisis of this sort. Those familiar with the work of Melanie Klein may appropriately be reminded of the distinction between what she has called the paranoid-schizoid position associated with processes of splitting and idealization on the one hand and that of the depressive position associated with the capacity for concern, to symbolize and to tolerate pain on the other (Klein 1946).

In a paper entitled "Development of Schizophrenic Thought" (1956), Bion draws on these earlier analytic concepts to show the link between the individual's difficulty in tolerating frustration, the hatred of reality (internal and external) that is a function of that difficulty, and the consequent detrimental effect on perceptual processes. He shows in turn how the mechanisms of splitting and projective identification described by Klein, while a necessary part of development, can be used to defend against awareness of painful reality and at the same time to prevent such reality from providing the possible basis for the development of relevant thought.

Gianna Williams's chapter describes how one family began to shift from the paranoid-schizoid to the depressive end of the spectrum in the course of their therapy. She introduces the term *psychic damage* to discuss the kind of impoverishment and distortions that may be a function of the family members' efforts, individually and collectively, to defend against psychic pain. This and Nonie Insall's chapter both portray how the related difficulties of mourning are worked with in the context of the sessions and the ending of treatment. But in the family described by Insall the defenses are of a more primitive kind. The use of mechanisms of projective identification are more pervasive, and the way that members use each other to express aspects of themselves is reflected in their difficulty in appreciating the significance of the therapists as separate individuals. The process of the treatment described suggests how, from being somewhat chronically tied to each other within the family and to institutions outside it, the family used the limited time available to begin differentiating and working on the implications of being separate.

The chapters that we have added since the previous edition of the book will hopefully serve to make a bridge with this one, between that time and this. One chapter, following on "An Outline of the History of Family Therapy," is explicitly about some of the recent contributions that are most relevant to our way of working. In it, I have tried to compare these with our own approach, particularly in terms of key aspects, such as the therapist's use of his countertransference experience in the sessions.

The two new chapters in the second section share some common concerns in that both address the adolescent process and the role of the adolescent in the family. Apart from this, however, the centre of interest in each is quite different: Anna Dartington's chapter focuses in a most original way on the significance of the outsider role for adolescents and relates it to twentieth century European literature. This chapter also illustrates the understanding and management of adolescent disturbance that involved hospitalization. In the other chapter, I take up the issue of change in psychotherapy with families at adolescence and illustrate in some detail the effort to engage with this process in the early stages.

The transference work in long term family therapy is not strongly represented in the original edition. Beta Copley, in her new chapter, has described in valuable detail how she worked in the transference as a single therapist for over a year with one very difficult adolescent and his family.

We hope these new chapters will add to the substance of the book and provide more reference points and examples for others interested in this approach to draw upon, debate, or add to in the further development of it.

Finally, the key concepts are defined in the Glossary and Errica Moustaki Smilansky has added a section on each, describing their development in terms of analytic theory and discussing their relevance in terms of application to our work with families. In view of the importance attached to direct experiences with the family on the basis of the worker's understanding and interpretation of them, we have attempted to provide sufficient clinical material for the reader to think for himself. But it may well seem too much and certainly if read all at once would prove quite indigestible! Probably each chapter represents something of a meal in itself and about all that can be comfortably digested at one sitting.

In summary, while sharing some ideas in common with other family therapists, I think there are a number of features both in terms of philosophy and technique that differentiate this approach from most others found in the literature on family therapy, including other object relations approaches. That is, like others, we have been interested in understanding the dynamics of the family as a group, but unlike most, our interest is on actively interpreting the family's use of projection in the ways that its members perceive and engage the therapists. In this sense the way the family experiences the therapist and the way the therapists experience the family represent the crucial evidence and material worked on in the session. Attention throughout to the underlying meaning of behavior and to the processes of transference and countertransference in the sessions seems to be in contrast to most other approaches, especially those which are informed by a more behaviorist model.

These ideas form the background of the approach that constitutes the theme of this book. The rationale for such an approach is a matter for discussion throughout but clearly relates to our particular view of therapeutic processes. The attempt to create space for the family to relive conflicts as they emerge in the context of the therapeutic setting is related to the value we see in this as a basis for successful internalization. Such internalization is in turn seen as the key to the modification of internal structures or internal object relationships. It is this that constitutes the process of change with which we are concerned.

2

History of Family Therapy

SUSAN CARVALHO

Unlike psychoanalysis, with its one seminal originator, family therapy and theory did not grow clearly from the work of one or two major figures. Instead the ever growing movement of workers interested in working with families has as its ancestors a great variety of pioneers of different disciplines, backgrounds, and orientation. With such diversity of influences in the past it is not surprising that there is currently considerable heterogeneity in contemporary theory about, and treatment of, normal and disturbed families.

Certain psychoanalytic writings can lend credence to the notion that the family movement has its roots back at the beginning of the century. Thus, in 1909, Freud reported the treatment of "Little Hans," in which the father was introduced as the active therapeutic agent in the treatment of a phobia in a 5-year-old boy. Indeed, here Freud worked solely with the father to effect change in the son. In 1921, Flugel published *The Psychoanalytic Study of the Family* and, in the 1920s, the Child Guidance Movement began, where it was the standard practice for a worker to work with a parent, in addition to the primary psychotherapy being undertaken with the child. Several years later, in 1936, the ninth Psychoanalytic Congress discussed "Family Neurosis," and both Grotjahn (1929) and Laforgue (1936) wrote comprehensively on the notion that individual neuroses in a given family complement and condition one another. However, while it is clear that before the Second World War there was some evidence of theoretical and clinical awareness of the importance of the family, essentially both psychoanalytic theory and practice remained almost exclusively orientated toward the individual, a "one-body psychology" (Rickman, in Bion 1961).

The idea of trying to understand and change a family appeared at mid-century, at the same time as many other changes in both the culture and social sciences of post-war North America and Europe. One particular cultural phenomenon of immediate relevance to the present discussion was a reemphasis on the family, and especially on the importance of the nuclear family, following the upheavals of the war. Simultaneously, group therapy was developing (e.g., Bion 1961), social psychiatry was concerned with the effect of total institutions and the efficacy of therapeutic communities (e.g., Goffman 1961, Jones 1952). Also man and other animals were being regarded by behavioral scientists as inseparable from their environment (e.g., Skinner 1953). Psychoanalysis too was developing and changing. Having gained general acceptance as a treatment method during the 1930s, and having provided useful concepts and procedures for the mass need during the war, psychoanalysis became established, and was being taught in universities, informing therapists, educators, and parents.

Psychoanalytic thought also began to diversify, and here it is essential to pay attention to the divergence between developments in psychoanalysis on either side of the Atlantic. In some senses the British movements mirrored these other changes with the emergence of the stress laid on object relationships, the organism (in this context the individual) being seen, not in isolation but rather in interaction with its surroundings, as part of a unit (mother–child dyad, family, marriage, institution, group). Thus we see in the contemporary British School of Psychoanalysis a fundamental emphasis laid on object relationships and developments from object relationship theory, including the concepts of projective identification, transference and counter-transference, and containment, as described by, among others, Klein, Winnicott, Bion, and now, as applied to family work, in this book.

However, these advances in theoretical understanding and conceptualization are frequently ignored or misunderstood in the current family therapy literature, where the terms *psychoanalysis* or *psychoanalytic* are most often used to refer to a topographical model of psychoanalysis, with an emphasis on instinct theory, linear causality, and the discovery and working through of early repressed traumata. So, for example, a British writer, Walrond-Skinner will still write: "in some treatment intervention, such as psychoanalysis, healing and change spring from insight gained with the early traumata of certain childhood events" (1976, p. 21) and goes on to refer to "the remote [Freud] or extremely remote [Klein] roots of traumata" (p. 26). Such a proposition appears to be echoed by the majority of North American family therapists and theorists although it is, in fact, a misdefinition of the term *psychoanalytic* as currently applied. In this essay I would like to propose that this misconception accounts for a good deal of polarization and conflict that may well be redundant.

While psychoanalysis has been diversifying, it has also been questioned and challenged. Thus, as psychoanalysis was developing and becoming powerful and prestigious in the late 1940s, so various workers were becoming aware of some of its clinical limitations. An essential notion in the traditional medical model of psychiatry that carried over into the psychoanalytic world was that a disturbed individual could be plucked from his environment, have his intrapsychic problems resolved by providing insight and relieving repression, and then return to his natural social situation transformed and able to cope. However, therapists began to notice that individual change sometimes brought with it consequent changes in the family or social situation, and conversely, that family resistance could produce resistance to change in the individual. Often this was an accidental discovery, but workers began to try to grapple with the idea that family factors could be related to individual pathology and change. Simultaneously, various frustrations with the traditional psychoanalytic approach began to emerge, particularly in relation to the treatment of schizophrenia, and to the treatment of behavioral difficulties and delinquency in children, coupled with the problem of working conventionally with impoverished and deprived patient groups. All these factors led workers to consider the family as the particular focus of attention.

It is generally acknowledged that Ackerman, a child psychiatrist and analyst, was one of the first therapists to take the revolutionary step of bringing whole families under direct observation in interviews. During the 1940s he had become interested in the family as the focus of attention and wrote that we should see the family as a social and emotional unit, emphasizing explicitly the interrelatedness of family members, and describing work with the family as a treatment modality in its own right, rather than one of many choices of technique to treat an individual. However, throughout North America and Great Britain it appeared that gradually, various workers and institutions were making similar discoveries and having similar thoughts while essentially working independently of one another. Thus, for example, in 1949 in London, Bowlby published his short but extremely influential paper "The Study and Reduction of Group Tensions in the Family." In this paper Bowlby described several occasional conferences with the whole family, as part of his ongoing work with the individual at the Tavistock Clinic.

Concurrently, in California, Gregory Bateson and his colleagues were conducting a research project that was formulating and testing a broad systematic view of the nature, etiology, and therapy of schizophrenia. The theory of schizophrenia they presented is based on communications analysis, and more specifically on that part of communication theory based on Russell's Theory of Logical Types. From this theory, and from observations of schizophrenic patients, they derived a description of a situation called the *double bind*, a situation where it is hypothesized that "no matter what a person does, he cannot win" (Bateson, Jackson, Haley and Weakland 1956). Bateson and colleagues suggest that a person caught in the double bind may develop schizophrenic symptoms and they discussed how and why the double bind may arise in the family situation. This research, and the work it stimulated, was to have a fundamental impact on the whole field of family therapy and theory. It laid emphasis on the family as being the unit of dysfunction but also introduced the models and language of cybernetics and communication theory to the behavioral sciences and the therapeutic arena. The approach suggested that the interchange of messages between people defined relationships, and that these relationships were stabilized by homeostatic processes in the form of actions of family members within the family. The therapy that developed out of this view emphasized changing a family system by arranging that family members behave or communicate differently with one another. It was a therapy based not upon psychodynamic principles nor upon a theory of conditioning. The central issue was about how people were communicating at the moment that was the focus of attention.

By the 1960s the family therapy and theory movement had begun to surface and become institutionalized. Various landmarks emerged at that time. In the United States, for example, the Ackerman Institute in New York was founded in 1960, the journal, *Family Process* was published for the first time in 1962, and in 1964, the Philadelphia Institute was founded. In Great Britain R. D. Laing published *The Divided Self* in 1959, *Self and Others* in 1961, and *Sanity, Madness and the Family* in 1964. In the preface to the last book Laing acknowledges his debt to, among others, Bateson, Jackson, Shapiro, and Wynne, with whom he discussed his research into the families of schizophrenics in 1962. As Bartlett (1976) has shown, Laing "rarely includes the reciprocal action of the designated patient, much less the totality of the reciprocal actions of the family members as a system," ideas Dicks was beginning to attempt to elucidate in relation to marriages (Dicks 1963). None the less, as Walrond-Skinner writes: "Laing and his associates have been extraordinarily influential in developing an intellectual climate conducive to viewing psychological disorders from within a framework of dysfunctional interpersonal relationships" (1979, p. 4).

Since the early 1960s the family therapy and theory movement has expanded considerably, and it continues to do so. Various writers have attempted to differentiate the schools of family therapy that now exist. The first published attempt at such a classification is the paper by Beels and Ferber (1969), which merits some detailed attention by virtue of its now being regarded as a classic paper in the family therapy literature. For the purposes of the present paper the discussion of the Beels and Ferber paper will also serve as a vehicle to introduce, and briefly describe, several key schools of family therapy.

Beels and Ferber state that the therapeutic "relationship [in family therapy] has for its definite and agreed-upon purpose changes in the family system of interaction, not changes in the behavior of individuals. Individual change occurs as a by-product of system change" (p. 285). Further, they state that all the family therapists they reviewed would agree that "the first purpose of working with a family group is to improve its function as a family . . . to promote its growth and differentiation" (p. 285).

Beels and Ferber propose classifying family therapists in terms of how they individually present themselves to the family they are treating, that is, essentially in terms of how they intervene in a family. Thus they divide *conductors* from *reactors*, the reactors being further divided into *analysts* and *system purists*. Beels and Ferber state that the conductors (who are described as usually being powerful, charismatic therapists, and who include Ackerman, Satir and Minuchin) "conduct a meeting with a very definite end in view. They arrange with the family a new experience in the possibilities of relating to one another, and they are quite direct about setting that experience up" (1969, p. 293). The "very definite end in view" is decided upon by the family therapist and is colored by his or her own value judgments and notions about appropriate family functioning, and the majority of conductors appear quite unabashed about making clear their own belief systems.

The reactor/analyst group in which Beels and Ferber include Wynne, Boszormenyi-Nagy, and Framo, is described as being distinguished by a terminology and interest that is said to be more or less similar to that of a psychoanalytic tradition:

> . . . They believe that the individual carries within him a non-rational and unconscious truth which when encountered meaningfully in the therapy, will help to set him free. . . . For Boszormenyi-Nagy and Framo the heart of the therapeutic undertaking . . . is the uncovering of the distorted internal part objects of the family members, especially the internalizations and projections of the parents within the current family. [p. 295]

Beels and Ferber attempt to show how Wynne's concept of "Trading of Dissociation" relates to the Kleinian concept of projective identification. "Wynne writes 'here I refer to a system or organization of deeply unconscious processes, an organization which provides a means for each individual to cope with otherwise intolerable ideas and feelings' " (p. 305). They discuss how Boszormenyi-Nagy locates the prototypes of many defensively split-off and projected part objects in the parents' experience of their own parents and how he completes the three generational picture of this phenomenon which, it is suggested, often results in psychological disturbance in the third generation. Boszormenyi-Nagy describes his version of the therapeutic working through of the parents' attachment to (or denial of) the grandparent objects, as essential to the therapy. Thus the reactor/analyst group does indeed appear to use certain current psychoanalytic concepts and values in their clinical work, although it is clear that no solid psychoanalytic model underpins their theorizing.

The third group Beels and Ferber describe are called reactor/system purists. They, including Zuk, Haley, and Jackson, among others, take as a general basis for their theories communication theory as first developed by Bateson and colleagues. The therapist intervenes in the family's communications system, actively gaining control of it by various deliberate techniques, to affect change in the whole family system. Although grouped as reactors, Beels and Ferber make it clear that this group are also activists of a certain kind. These workers do not think that "the truth of the unconscious shall make the family free. The curative agent is the paradoxical manipulation of power, so that the therapist lets the family seem to define the situation but in the end it follows his covert lead" (p. 296). Beels and Ferber maintain that all reactors do have an end in view for the therapy, but that they gain control of the family in a way that is more indirect and complex than the conductors who make no bones about the matter.

Beels and Ferber's paper is over two decades old now. Where it is still useful, it is proposed, is in the way it draws attention to therapists' differences in styles and value systems. It also highlights how even these therapists who would maintain they do not control the therapy do in some senses exercise power over the joint work through their control of the setting and the communications attended to. However, the categories proposed quite clearly have had limited usefulness in providing a taxonomy of family therapy and theory, particularly since over the past decade the systems view has moved from being a minority point of view to a position of central importance in the body of family theory and practice. Additionally, it is difficult to place certain schools in Beels and Ferber's categories. Palazzoli and her colleagues (1978) would call themselves systems purists, but probably not reactors. Minuchin, too, would probably see himself as a system purist, but he certainly is also a conductor. The work described in the present book would fit most neatly into the reactor/analyst group. However, while there are certainly real theoretical similarities between the work described in this book and the works of those authors placed by Beels and Ferber in the reactor/analyst group, significant and important clinical differences exist, such as the difference in emphasis on the use of the transference and countertransference, particularly as experienced in the here and now, and in the degree to which therapists will be directive. Thus, while the paper remains a classic, the actual classification proposed no longer seems useful.

Martin (1977) recently and more straightforwardly suggests that family therapists, faced with the difficulty of working in a highly complex field and aware that it demands a new orientation, but without the necessary framework, have tended in North America to resort to one or two polarized theoretical and technical positions. On the one hand, she proposes, there are those North American therapists who have stayed with, and tried to utilize, concepts and techniques both from classical psychoanalysis, and she suggests, from object relations theory (such as Wynne, Boszormenyi-Nagy, and latterly Stierlin). On the other hand, there is the group she labels system purists, who "have tried to simplify matters and make them more manageable by discarding analytic concepts and turning to concepts derived from communications theory" (p. 55). As well as those system purists listed by Beels and Ferber, Watzlawick and Palazzoli should be included in this classification. Martin suggests that British writers such as Skynner and Byng-Hall tend to make their frame of reference a bridge between the two groups, "and are therefore less clear" (p. 55).

Walrond-Skinner (1979) suggests a

useful broad distinction seems to be between those schools of family therapy which concentrate on helping the family group to change by acquiring some insight into areas of its dysfunction [dynamic, Bowenian and experiential schools] and those schools of family therapy which concentrate on helping the family to change its patterns of behavior without increasing its awareness of dysfunctional processes [strategic, communicational and behavioral]. [p. 2]

Walrond-Skinner is essentially taking the same stance as Beels and Ferber in differentiating family therapists by means of what they actually do. The theory that informs these different schools is given less stress, Walrond-Skinner making it clear that she sees descriptive characterization of family therapists and their methods as being most useful at the moment.

Bentovim (1979), in contrast, states that "although it may not be a useful task to attempt to produce a superordinate theory of family interactions and intervention, it is necessary to attempt to begin to organize the increasingly large literature of family therapy and theory" (p. 324). He proposes a particular classification of theories based on the number of elements necessary for their construction, considering dyadic, triadic, and group theories of family interaction. The elegance of this approach is that Bentovim shows that at each level, dyadic, triadic, and group, theoretical concepts born in disparate frames of thinking can be related to each other and indeed when juxtaposed appear complementary rather than opposed to one another. Bentovim's contribution is important since he demonstrates that concepts arising from a wide variety of frames of thinking can be related to one another creatively. He has presented an interesting schema for such exercises which is currently of value, even if, as with the classification proposed by Beels and Ferber, the actual categories quickly become redundant.

It would be most surprising, in fact, if it were not possible to find rapprochement between the conceptual premises of the various schools of family theory. Medawar (1969) and others have argued that living phenomena, but in particular, human life, can be seen as a series of hierarchically arranged open systems, so that family therapists might speak of a hierarchy as follows: intrapsychic object systems, individual, family, work group, community. So, it is proposed that in discussing similar phenomena some writers have developed their own descriptive terminology, other have used the concepts of already existing theories, and others have taken up the language of General Systems Theory. The crucial difference among the various schools lies in the way theoretical understanding of the family as conceptualized by each school is applied in a clinical setting, and in the way each therapist chooses to intervene in each family.

At this point it is important to stress that the effect of any form of psychotherapy is difficult to assess. Frude (1980), commenting on methodological problems in the evaluation of family therapy, points out that this difficulty has sometimes led to the extravagant and erroneous claim that effectiveness is simply not proven. The measurement of effectiveness of family therapy does remain problematic for many reasons, but in particular because of the difficulty in defining effectiveness criteria, and the difficulty of designing studies that will adequately measure success against such criteria as defined. There is nonetheless a growing body of research, extensively reviewed by Gurman and Kniskern (1979), which gives empirical support for the belief that family therapy is a meaningful way to intervene therapeutically in a family. However, Gurman and

Kniskern (1978) question whether standard empirical criteria are sufficient for studying the outcomes of family therapy, proposing that indices based on patients' and therapists' objective assessments must also be considered. They point out that even the most concrete measures reflect a researcher's ethics and values, the implication being that any outcome criteria are full of value-laden questions, such as what it means to be a healthy family. These issues are highlighted in a study designed to compare insight and problem-solving approaches of family therapy (Slipp and Kressel 1978). The authors report that when asked directly whether the therapy they received was helpful, the insight treatment group reported greater satisfaction than the problem-solving group. In contrast, on various standardized measures of family functioning, such as rating scales, the problem-solving group showed higher levels of adjustment as defined by the scales. Such results clearly illustrate the difficulty in choosing meaningful outcome criteria in comparing or evaluating approaches.

The central point here is that there is not, and there probably never will be, any particular method of family therapy which has been scientifically and empirically proven to be *the* effective treatment methodology, although family therapy as a treatment modality has been shown to be clinically valuable. There is, similarly, no generally agreed upon aim of treatment. Choice of school of family therapy must ultimately depend upon the therapist's own preference for method of working, and reflect his or her own value systems, prejudices, and theoretical orientation.

It is clear that fundamental philosophical differences do exist between the various schools of family therapy that must be examined and evaluated. Madanes and Haley (1977) offer seven dimensions on which they propose therapists differ: past *vs.* present; interpretation *vs.* action; growth *vs.* presenting problem; method *vs.* specific plan for each problem; unit of one, two, or three people; equality *vs.* hierarchy; and analogical *vs.* digital. In the discussion of some of these dimensions, specifically past *vs.* present, and unit of one, two, or three people, Madanes and Haley are clearly making points against psychodynamic approaches to family therapy. As discussed earlier they are criticizing a standpoint that no longer applies in Britain, so that some of their arguments are irrelevant to the current discussion.

However, two of their dimensions are crucial, and will be considered in greater detail here. These are the dimensions of interpretation *vs.* action and growth *vs.* presenting problem. When discussing interpretation *vs.* action they write, "whatever the cause of the problem the therapeutic issue is what to do about it" (p. 89). The choice for the therapist is among facilitating awareness and integration through interpretation and containment in order to facilitate change (psychodynamic therapists), or encouraging change either by providing alternative, structured experiences within a family interview (experiential therapists), or by actively requiring new, prescribed behavior outside the interview in the real life of the family (directive therapists). Further, therapists differ in relation to their goals of therapy, that is, on the dimension growth *vs.* presenting problem. Madanes and Haley (1977) write:

> Some believe that therapy should solve the problem which the client offers and think that therapy has failed if this problem is not solved, no matter what other changes have taken place. Others, although they are pleased if the presenting problem is solved, do not have this as their basic goal but instead emphasize the growth and development of the person. Family therapists are divided on this issue with some focusing upon the presenting problem and some emphasizing the growth and development of the whole family. [p. 89]

In Madanes and Haley's paper their therapeutic position is clear. The main characteristic of their therapy is that

> the therapist plans a strategy for solving the client's problems. The goals are clearly set and always coincide with solving the presenting problem. The therapy is planned in steps or stages to achieve the goals. The therapist must first decide who is involved in the presenting problem and in what way. Next he must decide on an intervention which will shift the family organization so that the presenting problem is not necessary. This intervention takes the form of a directive about something the family is to do both in and out of the interview. Directives may be straightforward or paradoxical, simple and involving one or two people or complex and involving the whole family. These directives have the purpose of changing the ways people relate to each other and the therapist. [p. 96]

The focus is upon change by directives.

This approach is clearly antithetical to the approach illustrated in the work in this book. The therapist using Haley's model takes responsibility for deciding what change should occur in the family system, and how this should be achieved. Understanding, in the family, is considered irrelevant. One problem is focused upon. Should another emerge, a further treatment contract is negotiated. In contrast, the view expressed in this book is that therapy provides the offer of an experience that would allow the family to gain an increased capacity to tolerate psychic pain, such that they (the family) can then negotiate for themselves changes in the family if appropriate. The debate between the proponents of these two positions antedates the birth of family therapy, echoing, for example, the heated arguments between the behaviorist school and the psychoanalytic school from the mid-1940s until the present day. It is here proposed that workers with different philosophical beliefs will long have to coexist, practitioners grouping together with like-minded colleagues to refine and develop those particular approaches that they have found both effective and satisfying.

If different groups of workers adopt different philosophical stances, then so too the question has to be asked: do different sorts of treatment suit different sorts of families? Clearly families present for treatment with a multiplicity of areas of dysfunction, presenting at differing times in their natural history and in differing family constellations. There are some families for whom family therapy is contraindicated (see Skynner 1969, Wynne 1968).[1] Furthermore, it is proposed here that there are families who may experience therapies based solely on awareness, understanding, and the toleration of psychic pain as irrelevant, leading to their prematurely leaving treatment unhelped. It was out of such experiences, for example, that Minuchin developed his *structural family therapy*, adopting a communication model in work with deprived, disorganized, lower-class families where traditional therapy had made no impact whatsoever. Further, it may be that families with extremely entrenched pathology, often going back several generations, such as those families with an anorectic or psychotic member, described so vividly by Palazzoli and her colleagues, can most profitably be helped by an approach that actively and directively uses the forces deployed by the family *against* change, to produce change.[2] In addition, Martin mentions those defensively verbal middle-class families for whom interest in the meaning of their communications may well be anti-task.

However, there is no doubt that there are many families who have a wish or need, even if unexpressed, to understand themselves or understand how things became as they are: families with unresolved mourning, for example, families in crisis and in need of being contained before any change can happen, families stuck in particular pathological patterns of neurotic relationship, scapegoating families, many disparate groups where action or structural change are only part of the desired solution.

Family therapy is now established as a well-recognized treatment modality. Its limitations, indications, and contraindications clearly need clarifying. Each school's unique contribution values elucidation and con-

---

[1] This issue is addressed in Chapter 4.

[2] The reader will recognize that this view relates to a different set of values than those implied elsewhere in this book.

sideration. However, it is hoped that the future will also see more cross-fertilization of ideas and concepts, for all these developments can only lead, ultimately, to increased efficacy of intervention in families, and to greater sophistication in theories of family functioning.

Some Recent Contributions to the Literature

SALLY BOX

Since this book was originally published, and this chapter was written, family therapy has become more firmly established as an approach. Like psychotherapy itself, however, it still means very different things to different people.

In 1984, the eminent psychotherapist and researcher Samuel Slipp pointed out that "despite the rapid growth in family therapy . . . no encompassing theoretical framework has yet evolved" (p. 2). In his book, *Object Relations*, he provides an impressive overview of much of the family therapy and relevant psychoanalytic literature and sets out to integrate them into such a framework (Slipp 1984). I propose here to try to relate this to our own work, along with some other recent contributions on the subject.

It is interesting to note that having trained at Langley Porter in San Francisco, Slipp gained firsthand experience with many of the early family theorists and therapists in America, such as Don Jackson, Virginia Satir, and others, before becoming interested and involved with members of the British School and with Kleinian concepts. As a training psychoanalyst with this background, he was unusually qualified for the task he set himself.

He draws heavily on Kleinian and other object relations theory to make links between individual and family dynamics as well as between

25

directive family therapy and approaches that are more non-directive and psychoanalytically inspired. In this way, Slipp has clearly—though apparently unbeknownst to him—shared much common ground with us. In particular, he stresses the significance of projective identification for understanding the relationship between individual and family dynamics and the importance for the therapist of being aware of how these processes are operating at any one time.

In some ways however, he and we have followed separate directions. In the work described in this book, (1981) we have tended to focus our energies on developing a consistent way of working with the families that we see, starting with the actual interactions of the sessions with them, using the concepts mainly to help understand their feelings and functioning, with very little emphasis on formal classification or diagnosis. The object has been primarily to fine-tune our tools to provide an exploratory space in which decisions about treatment can be reached, especially in terms of what the family can manage in relation to what is offered. This assumes at least some wish and readiness on the part of the family to join in, and also that the requirement for formal psychiatric classification is not the primary emphasis in the context, though we have an eye open for the possible need for inpatient backing. Out of this have developed some criteria and guidelines for recognizing different types and levels of functioning in families and some of the trends and difficulties that we may anticipate in each case. Perhaps we could refer to the approach as phenomenological, compared to others which are more nosological, focussing on issues of classification.

As I understand it, Slipp's interest is in establishing an integrated system of family typology, intentionally relating his family types to psychiatric diagnostic categories. He describes interesting correspondences among four of these and the interactional patterns of the families in which they arise: schizophrenia, hysteria-borderline, depressive, and delinquent. He outlines details of the relevant patterns and suggests the part the child in each is likely to play. For instance, "In schizophrenia, the parents cannot deal with aggression openly . . . aggression is denied and displaced onto a child, who is induced through projective identification into the role of the bad maternal object, the family scapegoat" (p. 175); in families with a depressive patient, a child is pushed into the role of savior; in delinquent families, that of avenger; and those with borderline or hysterical personalities, the go-between. Slipp allows that these do not always exist in pure form and that variations do occur.

From our point of view, such variations would refer to most of the families we see. But perhaps one could usefully think of the categories as representing a particular tendency in each family.

Slipp explains how invaluable the countertransference experience of the therapist can be when appropriately drawn upon to help understand and work with the patient in individual therapy. In the context of family therapy, however, he gives less attention to the therapist's countertransference, at least for interpretation. He extends the use of the term to refer to the projective processes operating between the family members, when one member of the family, for instance, is induced to carry and express the feelings of others. But what the therapist is induced to feel and do Slipp sees more in terms of the dangers—of being sucked into the system and getting into a treatment misalliance. So in his view, while it is important for the therapist to try to register his countertransference, this is not presented as a major tool for interpreting in the family group sessions. In fact, in the case examples that he gives, neither transference nor countertransference interpretations in relation to the therapist seem to play a central part. This issue, with regard to differences between English family therapists, is also discussed by Copley in her chapter on the family's transference to a single therapist.

The strength and the special value of Slipp's contribution, as I see it, is in terms of the monumental job of integrating concepts from different theoretical standpoints into a framework for classifying and diagnosing family dynamics in a way that could also help the therapist to understand the implications of particular projective patterns as they crop up in the therapy.

A central aspect of our own approach has been the availability of Kleinian and post-Kleinian psychoanalysis and its wide application to the work with narcissistic and psychotic states in their many manifestations: in group functioning, with severely deprived children, as well as with other disturbed individuals and families. We have also drawn considerably on specific models for applying these to the understanding of groups and institutions, and this may account for some of the differences between the approaches. The work of group relations practitioners such as Rice, Miller, and Turquet offers a model that draws on field and systems theory as well as on direct experience of Kleinian psychoanalysis to provide such a framework. This is commonly referred to as The Tavistock Group Relations model and is a unique way of learning from experience about intragroup and intergroup dynamics, one in which the consultants' use of their own countertransference plays a key part.

The powerful experience of participating in such group relations events has provided a crucial element for most of us, both as individual practitioners and in developing our approach to working with families. Such models as this have undoubtedly supported the emphasis we place on the therapist's use of his countertransference for the interpretive work with the family group.

I think it is no exaggeration to say that this internal work that the therapist can do, to metabolize what happens to him in the sessions, has come to represent the central skill to be developed for working with the feelings in the family that cannot be borne or managed there, and for enabling their transformation.

Another important contribution to thinking about families since we first published this book is that of Harris and Meltzer. Their focus in this instance is also on describing and classifying families and they offer a model for thinking about the "functioning of the individual-in-the-family-in-the- community" (Meltzer & Harris 1986 p. 154). They suggest a notional model that describes different types of family organization. These are not intended, as they say, "to present a concept of the ideal and its variations," but rather "to attempt, a highly dynamic model which assumes some degree of flux as a constant factor in the life processes of individuals, families and communities." So the descriptions must be taken both as "the description of a momentary state, and as a general tendency" (1986, p. 160).

Meltzer and Harris describe many variations of family life based on the functions the parents are initially able to fulfill and how other members of the family may be able, at least temporarily, to fill the missing roles. The way the functions are held help to understand the dynamics and to think about how to respond clinically. They suggest eight different functions that can be seen to be fulfilled or not fulfilled by different individuals in the family: "generating love, promulgating hate, promoting hope, sowing despair, containing depressive pain, emanating persecutory anxiety, thinking, and creating lies and confusion," (p. 154). Awareness of the presence of these functions and of who is carrying them provides another useful guide to the functioning of any particular family. These ideas are drawn on by both Copley and Dartington in their chapters.

The four good functions are carried in what is termed a *couple family*, where there is at least in mind the idea of a functioning couple, though there are variations when maternal or paternal dominance features strongly. In what is described as a *gang family* there is by contrast a lack of genuine, deeply-felt introjective functioning with a consequently more shallow, self-seeking life style. The membership may tend to make use of each other and the community in a predatory, delinquent, narcissistic fashion.

Besides their own original ideas, Meltzer and Harris have been strongly instrumental in disseminating the psychoanalytic thread of ideas from Freud through Abraham to Klein and Bion. They represent a major influence in the development of Kleinian ideas and they describe their model as Kleinian–Bionic. They do not include examples of their actual work with families, though some aspects of the model lend themselves readily to clinical application and are clearly based on their own first-hand experience.

Not surprisingly, the approach represented in this book has prospered most in clinics and departments where there are practitioners with experience in psychoanalysis who are also interested in applying this to the understanding of group and institutional dynamics. In Europe, these practitioners are found in centers that have developed training courses and conferences based on Tavistock models, for instance in Denmark and Italy. Because of the basic psychoanalytic underpinning, the possible recommendation of analytic psychotherapy with individual children and adults is not divorced from the consideration of family therapy, and the latter then may be used as the approach of choice for the initial exploration or as an alternative mode of treatment in a particular case.

The most thorough and detailed new work along these lines is that taking place at the Washington School of Psychiatry. The writing of Jill and David Scharff bears impressive testimony to the development there of an object relations approach that has now been taken up by others in different parts of the United States (Sussal 1992). Drawing on many of the same sources, though with more emphasis on Fairbairn, they have described clearly and simply many of the concepts we share, adding their own ideas. In particular they introduce the new terms *contextual* and *focused holding* to distinguish between two aspects of the therapist's task corresponding to that of the mother with her baby. Roughly, these refer to the management of the environment on the one hand, and the more centred eye-to-eye understanding or deeper transference work that may develop within that, on the other (Scharff and Scharff 1987).

There are undoubtedly some differences in theory and corresponding practice between their work and ours, though it is hard to gauge the significance of these in the abstract. For instance, what is it that the patients are transferring, and what are they living out in the transference? I hope it is not just quibbling to identify the difference, for instance, between the notion of reliving the past, as the Scharffs conceptualize it, in contrast to our notion that the patients are, in effect, enacting the inner world of the present. In this view, the internal relationships, though derived from the past, are constantly changing and presenting different unintegrated elements, often via projection, to be explored and worked on in the transference. The difference in practice is, I think, one of emphasis but significant all the same — when and how, for instance, the intensity of feeling is kept within the transference relationship to the therapist and when related back to the past at a more conscious, verbal level.

Such debates as this could not take place at all without the clinical examples that the Scharffs so liberally provide, and they have no doubts about the central significance of both transference and countertransference.

Indeed, what is most exciting and significant about recent psychoanalytic work is the increasing inclusion in a manifest and considered way of the part played by the therapist and his or her experience in the sessions. The therapists are less and less presented as outside, observing and commenting on the family dynamics from the sidelines. Instead they are seen in the middle of the system, trying to metabolize their own experience and draw upon it in a disciplined way to better understand the family members and identify the underlying crux of their current distress. This represents a major tool in the work of interpretation that is central to this approach.

Drawing on Bion's seminal work on thought and thinking, we consider and try to illustrate in the book that our selection from all the material of what is the central anxiety or pain for the family at any one moment takes its credence from our own countertransference experience. Put in another way, the formulation of an interpretation of the key unconscious relationship being enacted here and now is a difficult piece of work and, at its most meaningful, includes within it the evidence derived from the therapists' awareness of their own feelings. This helps to discover the emotional sore spot for the family that is being communicated or expelled via projective identification to the therapist at any one moment in the session. We have illustrated this process in our clinical examples.

This conscious, purposeful, and trained use of the worker's actual experience, which has gradually become so central to our psychoanalytic approach, represents, in my view, something of a revolution. It is akin perhaps to similar radical changes that are taking place in other fields of scientific endeavor. It is exciting to find others struggling with these same issues.

3

The Family and Its Dynamics

MARGOT WADDELL

WHAT IS MEANT BY "THE FAMILY?"

When we speak of *the family* we are referring in a very general way to a group of people whose relationship to one another is determined by ties of kinship. Yet the assumptions behind any particular reference are bound to be highly specific within a given historical and cultural context. In our society, for example, the family might normatively be described as a socioeconomic unit organized around a heterosexual pair. Even more specifically, the meaning of the word *family* for any single individual will be inseparable from his or her experience of their own family. So that when we examine individual families and their modes of relating we find ourselves far from the normative definitions of the historian, sociologist, or anthropologist (in relation to whom any one family will seem as often the exception as the rule). We find ourselves nearer to a much more personal situation, relating to a group that may be characterized by the nature of the interactions between individual members, by the dynamic processes that underlie the more evident structural bonds, processes that can be seen to be so common, so specific, so recognizable as to be given a label—*family dynamics*.

While it is the case, on the one hand, that in Britain and the United States by the age of 16 only about 70 percent of children are living with both their biological parents, it is also true, on the other, that closer to 90 percent of children are born to couples, whether married or not, within a so-called conventional family situation. Thus the family therapists will often be working with single parent families, second families, re-formations of families, and other kinds of grouping. Yet the nature and development of the dynamic processes that prevail in such situations will usually be found to be functions of nuclear family interactions, early in origin (with important cross-generational links) and largely unconscious, but which may become conscious in the course of therapy.

The purpose of the present chapter is to provide an overview of a number of such family dynamics seen within a psychoanalytic framework, and to convey some sense of relevant aspects of the theoretical background to the therapeutic work with families described in this book. The detailed ways in which specific family dynamics, normally unknown or unnoticed, may be uncovered and explored, how we and the family try to understand them in the process of therapy, will be the subject of later chapters. The immediate intention is to review what it means to speak of family dynamics by bringing together different kinds of examples of family functioning. It seems appropriate, in the light of the theoretical framework for the work described, to view these processes to some extent historically, starting from the couple's shared object — the baby — and tracing the roots and development of familial processes from that point.

PROCESSES OF FORMATION

People enter the institution of the family by birth. It is at this point that what had previously been the dynamic of a couple relationship (itself influenced by internal parental figures) becomes part of an external reality. The institution, then, is already the composite of two others, the mother and her family, the father and his family. This is a simple, self-evident statement, yet in terms of the forming and maturing of a family, the birth of the baby has to be seen as a particular kind of event, for it marks the beginning of dynamics that may establish continuing and quite specific patterns of relationships in the future of that family. With the birth or perhaps even with conception, a triangle comes into being in the external world, which may already be part of an internal triangle or shared phantasy between the couple. It is, in other words, now an observable triangle, as opposed to one of which the reality is largely internal. Problems relating to triangles now become focused in problems of relating between people: the possibility of exclusion, of shifts in pairing, of victimization, jealousy, competition, as well as the more positive, newly shared, and intensely experienced bonds of parenthood.

The change from couple to family is likely to bring into play aspects of relating between the parents that they had not experienced with each other in the same way before. Their baby's birth may evoke in each not only caring, devoted, protective, deeply loving feelings, but also quite infantile and dependent ones, such that the apparent asymmetries between physically strong adult and helplessly weak baby will not be the only, or even the most important, formative differences.

For together with the infant's actual helplessness is his phantasied omnipotence. Together with the mother's mature physical and emotional competence are other feelings of inadequacy and dependence mobilized by the mother–infant interaction, the stirrings of early feelings in relation to her own mother. Such emotions may be experienced with an intensity that causes her to feel at times like a powerless infant herself.

Melanie Klein's theories of early infantile development provide essential insight into what may be happening in the family at this stage. The nature of the infant's earliest internalizations and projections has a lasting effect not only on his or her own psychic development but on the basic meaning of mothering, fathering, and parenting that operates within that individual family. This is, of course, a two-way process, in that the child is also liable to be an object for the parents' projections. The infant's earliest environment is largely determined by what his parents, usually primarily the mother, bring to the situation, and their capacities to separate out infantile and adult feelings. The feelings of the baby may make the mother feel competitive. Or the father may be undergoing his own quite specific struggles and changes. Earlier anxieties, for example, are often reevoked by exclusion, sensed or actual, from what has become the primary couple, mother and child. (The high incidence of extra-marital relationships at this time may not be simply a function of sexual unavailability.) The therapist's contribution may be to try to sort out some of these things, such as where the feelings come from, how they are being expressed, what significance they have, the nature of their impact on the family group and on the therapy group.

CONTAINMENT

In this very emotive situation one particular action or interchange may have a multiplicity of meanings. Cases of baby-battering, for example, often stem, at least in part, from the mother's desperation at her own inability to meet what seem like tyrannical demands from her child. In the large number of cases involving potential or actual battering, either parent may be temporarily overwhelmed with infantile rage by the experience of inadequacy. The parent's feelings may become mixed up with the baby's in such a way that the adult restraints are lost and physical violence is resorted to as an expression of impotence, fear, anger, and primitive anxiety.

Yet one of the dynamics we have become better able to understand is the normal capacity to bear some kind of anxiety. This is described by W. R. Bion (1962a). If the mother feels temporarily incapacitated, father, hopefully, will in turn be able to help bear the mother–infant couple's relationship. A typical situation might arise over feeding: mother has become tense and exhausted to the point where the baby is unable to suck. Noticing mother's distress the father, in apparently quite simple ways, may be able to provide crucial emotional and physical support. Holding the baby, reassuring mother and child, making a cup of tea or whatever, can express the way he is taking in the experience and thereby holding the couple until the mother's renewed strength and calm enables the baby to feed again. This illustrates one aspect of what is meant by *containing*—the capacity on the part of a parent or therapist to take in another's feelings for a time, thereby bringing relief and support, and to use this experience to help them appreciate more accurately what the other is feeling. An understanding of the importance and efficacy of this process has had a considerable influence on the way we work with families.

Sensitivity to the feeling in the group may enable the therapist, temporarily, to take over, to hold or contain some of the painful or unbearable aspects, whether of the individual or group, until they can be understood, worked through, and perhaps integrated again. A family's capacity to do this may vary from day to day and week to week. Nonetheless, over time, the general psychological impact of the baby's feelings on the parental couple is likely to be very powerful. The extremities of satisfaction and frustration experienced by the infant, the gratification of blissful fulfilment on the one hand, and the enraged, destructive impulses on the other, are the states of mind described in Klein's paranoid-schizoid position. It is this stage of object formation that is dominated by processes such as splitting, omnipotence, idealization, and denial.

Particular areas of interaction may acquire special significance. The degree of anxiety, for example, which such behavior generates will vary from parent to parent. So will the mother's ability to contain certain feelings and to be aware of the areas of identification and separation between her own needs and the baby's. Likewise the father's capacity to support the intensities of this interaction, to be a sustaining emotional presence, will be tested for the first time. These are all on a continuum of past dynamics in the parents' families, present ones being set in train, and others to come, the roots of which are being established in these early days of family life. Whether over time these dynamics are dealt with as problems within a functioning family system, or whether they take on a disturbed or pathological quality is, of course, very much related to environment in the more usual sense of the word. The kinds of life stresses that the group as a whole, or individual members within it, undergo, the general family circumstances, questions of finance, housing, jobs, friends, schools, community, health, all have crucial roles to play in the family's capacity to maintain some kind of equilibrium in their complex interrelationships.

THE FAMILY AND THERAPY

(The therapist's relationship with a family will usually begin at the point where problems have been acknowledged. This acknowledgment is often focused on one or two individuals, rather than experienced as a problem of the family group as such. The task is then to uncover what underlies the more obvious manifestations of family stress or group disintegration:to recognize the less easily distinguishable dynamics that may originate in the parents' own experience and be mobilized in the family group at a very early stage) It is important to emphasize what kind of uncovering is meant here. It does not signify the mere exposure of aspects of family life that have been kept hidden perhaps from consciousness as well as from observation, a process that may be experienced as very persecuting by the family members. A rather different process is involved, one in which the (therapist draws on his/her own feelings and reactions in the situation to illuminate and share some of the difficulties, as they are felt in the session, in a less persecutory way. The therapist's role is to bring insight into what is and has been happening within the individual psyche on the one hand — the intra-psychic mechanisms — and a sense of the nature and functioning of group phenomena on the other — the inter-psychic mechanisms.)

In this way the immediate therapy situation may be drawn on to illustrate family dynamics that have been going on over time. The vertex is that of the here and now rather than the historical.

Two brief examples will illustrate the process. The first demonstrates how the therapists, by observing and interpreting the way they were themselves related to, were able to make explicit family dynamics that originated in each parent's previous history but became focused in relation to the couple's shared object — their newly born baby. With the birth the case shifted from marital to family therapy. It had been noticed by the co-therapists in early sessions that both the husband and wife, but particularly the husband, would constantly try to engage one or the other therapist in a kind of pairing, to the exclusion of the other partner. The continuous attempts later by the baby in the session to involve one or the other parent or therapist in an insistent eye contact had the effect of distracting from what was going on with the parents. The baby was not only, in effect, doing the same as the parent trying to establish a pairing relationship at the expense of the others present, but was also expressing in the session a way of dealing with a constantly fended-off fear of being left out, rejected, excessively jealous or alone. It was not until the baby's behavior was pointed out and its relevance to the family group interpreted that the father was able to recall how intensively he had tried as a child to monopolize his father by holding his attention, how he would insist on pairing to the exclusion of sharing, and how this way of being had extended into his subsequent intimate relationships, particularly with his wife.

The behavior of the 6-month-old baby in this setting seemed to point to the importance, felt by each member of the family, of getting into a single pair relationship—the expressed need to hold one another's attention. In this kind of process lies a strengthening of the bases for development of the classic triangle already in the making, as we have seen, in the internal experience of the parents, and often the source, later, of overt jealousy, competition, withdrawal, rivalry, exhibitionism. As I have suggested, it is frequently the manifest behavior in such situations that is considered the problem. The underlying meaning is harder to recognize.

The second case also relates to the uncovering of processes that had been set in train very early in the family's history. This time, attention was drawn to the family's difficulties by violent acting out on the part of the only child when he became adolescent. The child, a 15-year-old boy, was initially referred on the grounds of his excessively aggressive behavior toward his mother, and because of the conflict stirred up in the marital relationship by the disparity between that hostility and the strikingly close and affectionate bonds between father and son.

In the course of therapy it was discovered that at the time of the pregnancy and birth of her child, the mother's image and sense of esteem was extremely low. Her feelings were reinforced by two major factors: her sexual relationship with her husband had been physically painful to her over a long period of time and, second, shortly before she became pregnant, she had had a dermoid cyst removed, the nature of which, containing as it did bits of hair, glands and nail, she found monstrous and repulsive. When the baby was born she experienced him as a mixture of the horrible and the perfect. The "good baby" she wished to give to her husband—indeed to a large extent handed him over to the father's care— for contact between the baby and herself was composed, in phantasy, of badness and disgust. The extent to which the monster/saint split, which originated in the mother's feelings, was later expressed in the boy's actual personality and behavior was very striking and became the focus for the therapeutic work. The course that the boy's development was taking was closely in tune with, and contributing to, the family splits, particularly his mother's phantasies.

I have taken this rather dramatic example as an extreme representation of a dynamic that is easily recognizable in family interactions—the way in which family members enact certain roles or develop certain character traits that have been in some sense unconsciously assigned, fixed, and colluded with from very early on.

The family itself is often well aware of some of these characteristics and on one level may be quite conscious of the nature of the relations between them. Indeed, with families seen in treatment, these manifest roles often constitute, in one form or another, the presenting symptoms. In other words, the family may experience them as the problem that has been brought to therapy to be removed or cured—for example, the under-achieving child, the phobic adolescent, the overanxious mother, the impotent father. Statements such as "she's the quiet one," "he's a noisy rascal," "he's doing brilliantly," "she won't lift a finger," are as common as sibling rivalry, cross-generational competition, jealousy, and similar easily recognizable phenomena. They are part of normal family functioning. Their precise nature may never be particularly noticeable or so significant as to constitute family pathology as opposed to the normal ups and downs of family life. (For an early established family dynamic may operate quite normally and only later become problematic, possibly precipitated by some crisis or a developmental stage in one of the children's lives, which apparently has no relation to the problem.)

THE FAMILY AS A GROUP

The difficulty is to determine what lies behind the disturbance, what certain psychological traits and modes of behavior in the individual may mean to the group, what is implied for the individual by the group's functioning, what is the family's hidden agenda.

Individual and group functioning are not separable in any simple sense. One of the most important factors, which has become clarified by psychoanalytic work with families, is the way in which the mechanisms of the individual psyche find expression in family group terms, and how, by treating the family itself as a kind of psychic entity or unity, the unconscious processes may be revealed. The individual may, as a mechanism of defense against anxiety, in an attempt to preserve the integrity of the ego, make a split between good and bad objects. Sometimes, in the infant's behavior, such a process is referred specifically to the breast as a kind of prototype of this splitting—the baby tending to see one breast as idealized and the other as bad.

In the same way in the family, unity, either of the marriage or of the group, may be preserved by splitting good qualities into one family member and bad into another. In object-relational terms, the group splits off its own angry, bad, irresponsible parts into one member who then becomes designated as a bad object. In such cases a lot of the blaming, however unpleasant and potentially damaging, may be quite explicit and conscious. But slight shifts in the balance of relationships may precipitate a pathological situation that requires therapeutic help to resolve.

In the families of disturbed children it is often the case that the child has become the embodiment of certain family conflicts that have not been overtly expressed, only covertly, and often unconsciously, through the child. The ultimate example of this process is explored in Edward Albee's play *Who's Afraid of Virginia Woolf?*, in which all the couple's conflicts, hatreds, bitterness, inadequacy are split off into a child who, it emerges, does not even exist. If, by looking at such splits in the therapy situation, the underlying anxiety—be it separation, fragmentation, madness, sexual deviance or whatever—can be stated and understood in comparative safety, the starkness of the splits may be greatly reduced and the victim of them may be enabled to get better.

An example, which in the light of these processes suggests that family therapy might have been more appropriate than individual therapy, is provided by a family of two small girls. The elder daughter, Sally, came into therapy when she was 6, highly disturbed and antisocial. In the course of her four year individual treatment she improved considerably. During that time, however, it was possible to observe a familiar phenomenon. As Sally got better, her younger sibling, Jane, became increasingly violent, fearful, and out of contact. It was as if the family disturbance was being located in the most vulnerable member, so that first one child, then the other functioned as a scapegoat for the family disharmony. It seems that, upsetting as it was to contemplate each child as a case for treatment, it was in some sense easier to do so than to confront the extent of the disturbance in the parental relationship. As so often when the defensive stakes are high, this family was too threatened to consider being seen as a group, but could tolerate the idea of therapy for an individual child. Zinner and Shapiro (1972) put the issue very succinctly: "a variety of parental coercions interact with the child's own requirements to fix him as a collusive participant in the family's 'hidden agenda' " (p. 523).

PROJECTIVE IDENTIFICATION

In the foregoing example the family dynamic of mental conflict takes the form of the group's conflicts being located in the individual, who, for reasons of her own pathology, acquiesced in the assigned role. Recent thinking in family dynamics and psychoanalytic work in an object relations mode has shown that in many disturbed families the reverse process also occurs. That is, what appears to be a group problem or an interpersonal conflict within the family may be the consequence of one member's intrapersonal conflict becoming a group concern. The psychological mechanism determining both processes is the Kleinian notion of projective identification. This concept can be perceived as emanating from individual analysis, but it has become central to our work with families both in terms of the unconscious processes in operation between family members and in such a way as to enable understanding of the family dynamics through the therapists' experience of the family and the family's of the therapists.

Klein herself gives an account of the mechanism in her paper "On Identification" (1955) in which she states that not only destructive and bad parts are projected into others, but good parts as well, for instance, for purposes of communication, or for safekeeping. She describes projective identification as bound up with developmental processes arising during the first three or four months of life, as a mechanism for defending against anxiety—by splitting off destructive or bad parts of the self—and as a fundamental influence on object relations. Interpreters of Klein take up the term *projective identification* to describe how the object may be perceived with characteristics of the self, and the self be identified with the object of its projection (e.g., Segal 1964).

The mechanism provides an explanation for feelings and interactions that are familiar as part of normal functioning. One may, for example, feel one is like somebody as a result of attributing one's feelings to him. In this case the motive might be one of communication; feelings may be transferred for the purpose of being understood. But the same process with a different motive might function as a means of control: in attempting to make another person experience what one is feeling, one might be trying to take possession of him. It may be used, as we have seen, as a way of expelling or disowning bad thoughts and feelings—by getting other people to think and feel and take responsibility for them—defensively in other words, perhaps with the purpose of avoiding excessive conflict within the individual ego, or between the partners of a fragile relationship. In any such case it is clearly important to establish what the motive is, but at the same time to recognize that there could be more than one, that the projective identification may be serving a multiple function.

In family therapy we have found that awareness of the role and function of projective identification both in the family setting and in relation to treatment itself is crucial. One kind of family, for example, might use it as a means of expelling and disowning unwanted parts of the self. It might be found, as in one family, for instance, that the mother has an intensely close and loving relationship with a son, whose frequently surly and uncooperative behavior is a source of constant battles with his father. While consciously disapproving of, and upset by the tensions between the boy and his father, the mother is, perhaps, at the same time gratifying, through her rebellious son, her own frustrated desires to revolt against her father. Indeed in her choice of husband she has found a man in many ways similar to her father. To neither of them is she able to express any aggression.

Alternatively, we can see the mechanism operating in a different situation, the kind of family in which one child is attractive, successful, popular, kind, and the other difficult, socially isolated, bad-tempered, average to mediocre in work, occasionally delinquent. (See, for example, the Smith family referred to in Beta Copley's Chapter 4.) Over time, the split may get reinforced — all good qualities are invested through a process of idealization in the girl, all bad through denigration in the boy to the detriment of each.

A third kind of example may be given in slightly more detail, this time of the pattern operating the other way around — from the child to the parent figure. This family had separated, regrouped and separated again. Dan, the oldest of the three siblings, was 11 when his parents parted. His mother began living with an older man of whom the children, especially Dan, became very fond. At the same time, being the oldest, Dan was in some sense expected to be the strongest of the three children and a support to the other two, losing in the process a reliable support for himself, in that both his parents were preoccupied with forming their new relationships. After four years or so his mother's second relationship also broke up and she set up home with a third man and became pregnant soon afterwards. At this point, Dan, unlike the other two children, opted to stay not with his father (with whom close contact had been maintained), nor with his mother (with whom he was also on very good terms), but with the man of his mother's second relationship. On examination it became clear that a strong element in this choice was that Dan's frustrated need for protection from his own parents meant that he was projecting his own protectiveness, previously felt towards the younger children, into this surrogate parent. With these feelings somehow lodged in the adult, they then elicited for the boy the very kind of protectiveness that he himself had lacked. The object of his dependence was, in fact, a person who was himself usually very dependent and unreliable and who, unlike the other adults in the situation, never became a biological parent.

In the first two instances, problems occurred when the mechanisms, adopted to maintain a kind of uneasy family equilibrium, themselves failed. Not only destructive feelings and impulses, but also more positive, indeed idealized, abilities and talents were respectively parceled off into individual members of the family in such a way that a particular mental structure became overrepresented in a single individual. In these cases the function of the projective identification was clearly primarily defensive and concealed unworked-through anxieties, needs, and repressed feelings on the part of the parents. It may often be the case that over time the child's experience of himself will be affected by the ways in which the parents have treated and perceived him — in turn a function of their own internal processes, needs, and anxieties. The third example relates to a much more constructive use of projective identification in the family group. By attributing part of himself to an adult man, the boy in this complex family situation was finally able to enjoy the protectiveness thus elicited.

PROJECTIVE IDENTIFICATION AND FAMILY FUNCTIONING: A CASE HISTORY

A more extended example will provide a clearer sense of how these kinds of unconscious identifications develop in a family over long periods of time, resulting in deep disturbances that may, as in this case, manifest themselves in quite serious individual pathology. As we have seen, the disturbance of one family member may often be evidence of the family's need to maintain unity as a group, or as a couple, with the kinds of consequences we have been looking at. Such was the situation in the Lang family. John was referred by the school counselor because of his fear of looking like a homosexual. The counselor knew that there were long-standing marital problems in the family and felt that they might be willing to come all together to discuss their son. This working-class family consisted of mother, father, and John, aged 17, and two younger brothers. In the sessions father and mother did almost all the talking and John remained the largely silent but firmly designated index patient. It was his problems that were the parents' repeated complaint: he was totally preoccupied with his uncertainty about whether or not he looked like a "pouf." Everywhere he went he heard people calling him a pouf or a queer. He could hear people saying these words from car windows or as he roared by, helmeted, on his motorbike. He had become unable to go to school or, at times, even out of the house except when wearing his helmet. He was slovenly, dirty, rude, unhelpful, provocative to his younger brothers, obsessed with his bike, and obsessed too with his inability to turn off appliances (lights, cookers, taps, etc.) or to lock up properly. Sometimes it would take him five minutes to leave the house. He would have to check and recheck, or get one of his friends to do it for him.

Early in the treatment it became clear that there were many other problems in the family besides John's. His were simply the most dramatic and most immobilizing. Yet whenever the cotherapists attempted to make this explicit the parents would resort to what became a familiar smoke-screen of bitter marital rows. The rows usually focused on sexual anxieties and mutual accusations and recriminations, particularly by father against mother. The most recurrent charges were over the close friendship she had had with another woman when the children were young, to the exclusion of father (as he maintained), and over the extreme proprietary feeling (which he stoutly defended) toward his former wife, from whom he had separated two years earlier. Mrs. Lang defended herself, asserting that the closeness of her friendship with her woman neighbor was the consequence of neglect by her husband, and the charges of her having other relationships were figments of his imagination. The one good relationship in the family—repeatedly stressed by Mr. Lang—was that between father and John.

Toward the end of the family sessions, the emphasis began to shift slightly from John to father, and in particular father's own sexuality. For instance, an occasion was described in which father and John went out together to see if father could actually hear John being called a pouf. Crossing the road, John said he heard someone say "pouf" to the pair. One of the therapists enquired how it was possible in a situation like that to know to whom the word referred. This comment introduced a new dimension to the therapy—a more generalized awareness of problems of sexual identity pervading the group. The nature of sexual roles and identities in the family began to come up in other quite specific ways. For example, in one session mother gave an unusually distressed account of an occasion when she had asked her husband to make a rabbit hutch for the children. He had not done so but when he found his wife finally doing it herself he accused her of trying to be a man. The apparent simplicity of the anecdote belied the family's intense anxiety, which lay quite close to the surface but could not be expressed directly.

John later came for individual therapy and poured out his dislike and contempt for his father—feelings that had not been expressed in the family sessions. A major element in this hostility seemed to lie in his feelings that his father looked effeminate. The word he repeatedly used to describe his father—"a joker"—could, to all intents and purposes, have been "pouf." He felt that he physically resembled his father, had similar speech patterns and mannerisms, and had indeed been close to him throughout childhood, sharing interests and identifying strongly until two years previously. It was then that his problems had begun. This seemed to coincide, in terms of material from the family sessions, with a trip by mother and children to Spain, during which John had seen his mother flirting with a hotel waiter. It also emerged that it was at this time that mother, having discovered that father had been having a number of affairs, insisted on living apart. She had accepted him back once in the intervening period but separated when he again started having sexual relationships. John's expressions of contempt and disgust for his father's behavior were extreme, and sessions were spent venting his anger and scorn. Meanwhile, however, his original symptoms began rapidly to disappear.

Such phenomena are clearly multidetermined and not subject to simple explanation, yet the processes of projective identification are strongly in evidence. It seems that the largely unconscious, or at least preconscious, fear of the father about his own sexual identity may have been split off into his closely identifying son. The only remaining manifest glimpses of the pathology in the father were the obsessional preoccupations with his wife's potential infidelities, his exaggerated characterization of her friendship with another woman as homosexual, and his own promiscuity.

An aspect of this case which should have been given more emphasis at this point is the extent to which John may have been a ready receptacle for his father's projections. It has been indicated that projective identification is an unconscious process that takes place between two people in either internal or external reality. This can, in some cases, actually involve collusion, but it may not necessarily go as far as that. Some differentiation has to be made between receiving and colluding with the projections. It is important not to see the object of the projections as necessarily passive. The point is that the object, the second person as it were, may be involved to a varied extent, according to the readiness or vulnerability with which he receives the projections. In John's case it may be that unconsciously he felt that he had to replace his father at the point of marital breakdown, and that in the process his oedipal feelings were reevoked. As eldest son he could identify with father as seducer, perhaps the waiter in Spain trying to put his hand on his mother's bottom (for so the story went). If, then, John identified with one aspect of his father's sexuality—the sexual relationship with his mother—it may unconsciously have seemed necessary to him to defend against the danger of closeness with mother, lest he experience the relationship as incestuous. It was thus, perhaps, less frightening to him to hear from others accusations of his homosexuality, for, however painful, this protected him from the far worse oedipal anxiety over his relationship with his mother. If some version of these hypotheses were right it would be easy to see how readily John might receive his father's projection. Possibly his obsessive rituals were also rooted in this area of unconscious sexual guilt — the necessity of checking and rechecking turned off ovens, lights, and so forth, being an unconscious need to verify that the feared seduction of mother by son had not in fact occurred.

In these descriptions the focus has been on the role of projective identification within families. To have discussed the issue in this way is to suggest, misleadingly, that there is a separation between the two functions of projective identification mentioned earlier — in relation to the family situation and in relation to the transference in the treatment. In the family work we have been developing together, the two are hardly separable. For it tends to be through the therapists' awareness of how the family is experiencing them, as well as what they are themselves being made to feel, and their ability to interpret that, that insight is gained into the dynamics going on in the family itself. For it is through a sense of the ways in which the family is engaging and relating to the therapist that it becomes possible to uncover the underlying meaning of the disturbances.

As will be seen in analytic work with families, countertransference has a central role. In a direct sense the countertransference may consist not only of the therapists' reactions to the family and their problems, but also of feelings that belong in the individual or the group as a whole but have been projected into the therapist by means of the process just described. Less directly, the mechanism may also play a part, in the therapists' feelings about each other, evoked especially by the family's perception of the sort of couple they are. These feelings may change significantly according to the kinds of projections that are being made: the nature and meaning of coupleness, or the lack of it, within the family.

The ways in which these changes may occur in a single session and how the therapists in that session work with the mechanism of projective identification are illustrated in detail in other chapters. However, a more general example of the way these processes are worked with over time may be provided by an exploration of the notion of containment in a family therapy setting. It often becomes clear when a crisis of some kind is taking place in a family — in terms of marital tensions, children's problems, illness, or even death — that the family's ability to cope, to contain the anxieties evoked by these situations, is importantly related to the parents' own experience of containment of the kind discussed earlier in the chapter, both in childhood and in their current adult relations. The degree to which adult intimate relationships may bring into play powerful feelings of dependency, frustration, anger, or whatever — especially in the context of the birth of a child — has already been suggested. Such feelings are derived in large part from earlier bonds in infancy and childhood, and are reevoked in particular situations.

The following example of specific therapeutic interaction, drawn from a paper by Sally Box (1977), demonstrates especially clearly how family disturbances may be uncovered through close attention to the dynamics between the family and the therapist involved in the case. The example shows how the problems of containment, reflected in the experience of the therapist, may offer a key to the central dynamic of the family situation. It is an interesting case in that it provides a study of a frequently unrecognized issue — the masking of emotional disturbance by physical illness, retardation and Down's Syndrome in a family.

The paper describes a young woman, Jenny, who came for treatment in a crisis, culminating in fears about suicidal impulses. In the initial exploration with her, it gradually became clear that she was struggling with a number of conflicting feelings around the fact that she had a mentally retarded sister, Mary, about whom she felt both a strong sense of duty and enormous resentment. She had tried unconsciously to deal with those feelings by becoming the main caretaker of a physically crippled young college friend. But in the face of her friend's dependency she became afflicted with the same guilt-ridden and, on some level, murderous feelings that she had long experienced in relation to her sister. Her response was to want to regress to being helpless and cared for, like her sister. A decision was made to include Jenny's parents for a few sessions and the therapist immediately felt intensely affected by a present, but as yet unspoken, weight of emotion. She drew upon this to recognize aloud the enormous burden being passed from one to another in relation to Jenny's sister. It then became possible for the family to share, for the first time, their previously unexpressed concerns and anxieties on each other's behalf, and also the different sorts of pressure each had been under over the years. It emerged, for example, that when, during a year when her mother had been unwell, Jenny was virtually in charge of the house and particularly of her sister, she had come under increasing pressure from an aunt to hospitalize Mary. In the event of Mary actually being sent away, Jenny had suffered acute feelings of responsibility of which her parents had hitherto been ignorant. It also slowly and painfully emerged that mother too had powerful feelings of guilt and responsibility about Mary, stemming from her sense of having been unready to have a baby and her inadequacies over nurturing her in the early stages. Mary's institutionalization had presented a crisis for her as well as Jenny and also for father. All three had difficulties visiting Mary and had never been to see her together, or had her home for a visit. What was discovered in the course of the sessions, and in the talking that went on between Mary's parents, meanwhile, was that her father did not hold his wife responsible, as she had feared, for her reluctance to bring Mary home for a visit. On the contrary, he shared it. They went on a joint visit to see Mary and found that they could even enjoy it when shared in that way. Sally Box's paper (1977) concludes:

> As may happen in some cases this couple seemed able to make considerable use of the few sessions they had. What had evidently been a taboo area, now became a matter of mutual interest and concern to be explored together. They felt they had work to do but already experienced great relief. Also, and almost immediately, Jenny was able to function again comparatively normally. Although she continued treatment for herself, there is little doubt that the weight of the burden she carried was lessened when her parents could open themselves with each other to entertain their part of it. [p. 16]

It is possible in this case to draw a parellel between aspects of the therapist's function in work with parents and of that of the parents themselves in providing a modicum of containment for the painful emotions of their children. The example is intended to show how, in the course of the family's development, this function had gone awry. It describes how the therapist attempted to provide a containing space and to offer an experience of helping the family face and bear something of the violence, guilt, and despair that they brought to sessions. As Box says, "It is clearly not a matter of therapists soaking up all the pain themselves and being left with it, but rather of working on it inside themselves in order then to give it back verbally so that their clients have a better chance of integrating and managing it for themselves" (p. 16).

CONCLUSION

Since the time when therapists are likely to have contact with a family is at the point of crisis or breakdown, it is with the material behind the family "myths" that they will be primarily concerned—with the analysis, that is, of the different kinds of defensive behavior adopted by the group and with the anxieties and unconscious processes that underlie them. The most relevant concepts in thinking about these processes and working with families, turn out to be strikingly similar to those prevailing in early infancy. These concepts are splitting, denial, idealization, denigration, and projective identification. This suggests that dynamics of family functioning may significantly conform to some of those more primitive mechanisms.

Through examining at length the nature and functioning of what may be taken to be the centrally useful concept in this work—that of projective identification, along with concomitant concepts of containment, transference, and countertransference—an attempt has been made to elucidate the ways in which it is possible to get in touch with the more fundamental, obscure, unconscious dynamics within a family. Kleinian theory originally developed out of clinical experience with individual children who were at an even earlier stage of development than Freud had considered. In applying these notions to group functioning, Bion (1961) has emphasized that similar primitive processes are at work. Both these areas draw on fundamental family dynamics, but in individual and group therapy the family itself is not actually present as a unit in the therapeutic work. In the psychoanalytic approach of this book, insights learned from the study of the child and of the group come together in the family, which is after all the locus of the dynamics on which psychoanalysis is based.

SECTION II
At the Boundary of Family Therapy

4

Introducing Families to Family Work

BETA COPLEY

In initial explorations with clients, knowledge of two different kinds develops. On the one hand we begin to learn something about the family itself, what the problems are, and how the members relate to one another as the family dynamics unfold. On the other hand, alongside this, we try to learn about the family's hopes and expectations of the clinic and begin to experience the use that is being made of us. In other words, there is appraisal from the point of view of the transference and countertransference. These two strands are not necessarily experienced separately from each other in the course of the session.

In this chapter I look at the interweaving of these two aspects of the work as a means of thinking about the nature of family interventions and indications for their use. I also propose to give detailed examples of how the interaction with the worker may help a family to develop its commitments to further understanding. In the examples I give there was no one motivated to seek help as an individual or as a couple, so only further family work of some kind was possible.

Mr. and Mrs. Smith came to the Counselling Service of the Clinic, saying they did not know what to do about their daughter Mary's behavior; they added that she herself refused to come. Mrs. Smith had made the appointment for herself and I had not expected to see the father as well. Mother was a neat, middle-aged woman, who initially seemed emotionally aloof and full of complaints about her daughter; Father seemed more relaxed, puffing away at his pipe and speaking rather softly in a fairly offhand way, as if his intervention was absolutely expected, but at the same time giving a feeling of detachment. Mother spoke of what she presented as the basic problem, namely, Mary wanting to drop out of school where she said that, despite previous good academic achievement, Mary's work had fallen off. I explored this a little with them, but went on to query whether there were other areas of difficulty. I also asked if they both, in fact, viewed the situation the same way, Mother having done most of the talking.

In doing this I was attempting to make more sense of my somewhat puzzled feelings about the incongruity of Father being at the interview, while at the same time giving the impression of being very much at home there.

I went on to say that the appointment as I understood it had only been made for one parent and wondered if there were feelings that were relevant both to this and the fact that they both came. They looked at each other, and although they did not respond directly to my question, Mother, with some backup from Father, went on to speak about Mary keeping bad company. They spoke of how she stayed out late with a group of young people and complained that they did not really know what she was up to. I wondered about their anxieties in this respect, and they said they didn't know whether or not she had sexual relationships. On further discussion some of the family background emerged, for example, that the parents worked as insurance agents and were not at home as much as the children. They had added that there was also an older daughter, Sheila, whose image gradually unfolded during the interview as the good one of the family. She was said to have a good relationship with Father and on my instigation we had an inconclusive but potentially useful discussion as to whether it was the father who treated her differently or she who behaved very differently to her sister in the family, or a combination of both.

I tried to explore with the Smiths their views about Mary's "bad friends," from which it emerged that Mr. and Mrs. Smith felt the problems were due to "split parents" and a "lack of respect for parental authority" among the friends with whom Mary mixed. I commented in low key, that they were talking about "split parents" and a "lack of respect for parents" and wondered if this struck chords in their own family in any way. They then said with some embarrassment that there had been some kind of split between themselves about two years ago. I asked gently about this and was told that this had to do with Father having a relationship with another woman. However, they told me, rather quickly, that this was all completely finished now and had been sorted out, although there had been considerable differences between them.

The above interchange seemed to bring the parents more into the interview as people with relationships of their own, as opposed to merely aggrieved parents complaining about their daughter's behavior in the outside world. It thus became possible to look more at the interrelatedness within this family. One could say at this point that we were on the boundary of possible entry into some kind of family therapy.

Mother brought out some concern that they might have made mistakes, though Father tended to make light of this. They spoke of Mary's jealousy of her sister and also of the latter's good relationship with Father. I referred to the "lack of respect for parents" they spoke of among Mary's friends and wondered whether there was anything like this in the home too. Mother spoke with feeling about how Mary would talk on the telephone to her friends at length, complaining about her mother in a denigrating way, as well as being directly insulting to her. She said that Father did not intervene and that she felt very unsupported.

I am trying to illustrate here how the parents had projected onto Mary's environment feelings of disharmony and inadequate parental functioning that had originally arisen between themselves. After being helped to give some recognition to this, they became more open to further explorations of the family relationships.

As the interview progressed a basic disagreement between the parents became more apparent: Mother resented what she felt was Father's indulgence toward Mary and Father criticized Mother for rigidity and having too high standards; for example, Mother felt Father condoned Mary's coming home late while Mother tried to enforce what she felt were more reasonable hours. Earlier in the session one of the anxieties expressed was that Mary might leave home completely and stay with these young people they had mentioned earlier. They then related with some diffidence what they called occasional stealing by Mary of insurance money they sometimes brought home. They felt driven to lock their takings in their bedroom and this led me to ponder aloud if they felt their marital situation was really being raided by Mary, and they agreed.

What had by now emerged was a picture of a family to some extent at odds with each other, the parents feeling not only that Mary was falling into bad ways and might leave them as well as school, but also feeling raided and invaded by her. We were also in touch with marital discord and with Mother's feelings of being unsupported as a mother. In addition there was a picture of another daughter who was presented almost as "too good," raising in one's mind the possibility that one might find that Mary was being seen as "too bad." It was possible to share this perception with them and suggest that a reasonable way into this situation would be for some kind of family intervention in which the family could come together and look at some of these issues. Despite their having said at the beginning they did not think Mary would come to the clinic herself, they accepted fairly willingly and thought they would be able to get both children to come. The parents, after having been helped to think about their own feelings, had been able to move in this brief intervention from complaining about a daughter who was said to be unwilling to come to the clinic to being willing to examine their own difficulties and those they had with their children. This latter view of themselves may have enhanced the parental authority that would enable them to feel they could bring Mary. The invitation to bring the "good sister," Sheila, may also have contributed to their ability to come as "good parents" with a "good" relationship to at least one child.

The family did come for family therapy with two of my colleagues, a man and a woman, as co-therapists. They were thought to make good use of it and it is interesting to note that the conflicts between the parents and Mary were fairly rapidly resolved.

I would like now to turn to the Brown family, members of which I saw twice in the setting of the clinic Counseling Service.

Initially all I knew was that a mother, Mrs. Brown, was coming about her daughter, of 16. I was surprised when I got to the waiting room to find the mother with a very young-looking adolescent standing behind her, making odd movements with her mouth and shuffling with her feet. Somewhat perplexed, I asked if they wished to be seen together. Mrs. Brown said Aileen might as well hear what we said, did I mind? I suggested that they come to my room and we could talk, wondering to myself if Aileen was meant to listen to Mother and me talking about her. Mother immediately launched into an account of her difficulties with her daughter. Aileen was thought not to have done well in her examinations and might not be kept on at school. There was also trouble at home. She and her husband could talk to Aileen as much as they liked, but she would not listen. Mother continued forcefully and emotionally that it got her health down, "making" her have ulcers and headaches. She had to go to the doctor, she said. Aileen had been a bit better since the doctor had a talk with her, and the latter had suggested that she might benefit from a talk with somebody else, for example, here. Was this right?

I felt that I was wanted by Mother to be some kind of medically prescribed "talker" who would forcefully "cure" Aileen, although she had some doubts as to whether I would fulfill this role. I also felt that I was to be some kind of built-in action paragraph in relation to the school, though not clear what. In addition, I was very aware of Mother talking to me about Aileen in her presence, while the latter sat silently, looking rather like a 12-year-old. Trying to give attention to the feelings of both and to phrase what I was made to feel in some way that could be useful to them, I recognized with Mother that she felt very upset. I then turned to Aileen and asked her what she thought about this, and also wondered what she felt about coming. She said she did not mind really. I wondered if she shared her mother's views about the various problems. Aileen replied that she felt treated like a child younger than her years. I said I was in a difficult position because I was being asked by Mother, I thought, to give Aileen some kind of talk, really a talking to, that was meant to produce considerable change and make her better. However if I could or would do this, Aileen might feel I was treating her as much younger than her age.

It had seemed to me necessary to interrupt the flow of Mother's complaints in order to bring Aileen into the interview as a person. The next step was to try myself to hold on to and then share with them what I perceived as their very different stances. If I had not done so I think I would have been in danger of colluding with Mother's projections and so rendering myself useless to the family. I went on to explain that this was not the way we worked, but queried with them what they knew about the kind of service they had come to, and clarified how a joint exploration of problems, as opposed to provision of solutions, was offered. I also explained the Brief Intervention nature of this particular service.

In brief or exploratory work it also seems to me sensible not only to attempt to understand with clients something about the initial hopes, expectations, and fears that they bring, including what is being projected onto the agency, but also to give some realistic information about what could be available. Apart from trying both to give them some indication of what I felt they were expecting of me and to clarify what could be offered, I hoped that if I could in any way hold on to and show them their opposing views it might be possible to bring what working capacity there was in them into the session.

I made some further allusion to Mother's view of Aileen not listening, which she felt ended up in illness in her, and Aileen's view perhaps of being talked about or at rather than with, for example, in Mother's conversations with the doctor, the headmistress and myself. Aileen then said that she did feel people talked about her too much. I asked her if she could enlarge on this but she suddenly left the room to go to the toilet.

Mother and I sat uncomfortably for a moment or two. Mother then said she did not think Aileen was taking the interview seriously and, I felt, put pressure on me to agree, as if we were two adults talking about a small recalcitrant child. In support of the method of work I had outlined, I began to put something to Mother about the complications of Aileen being out of the room, but the latter came back in quickly and I referred back to the situation before she went out. She, however, said she had forgotten. It occurred to me that she may have attempted in a concrete way to evacuate her feelings down the toilet, but I did not feel it appropriate to raise such a view at this particular time. I also thought it important to get into the open what she might have felt had been happening between Mother and me in her absence as well as what had actually happened. I therefore reminded her that before she had left the room, we had been referring to her feelings about people talking about her and perhaps she felt that her mother and I had been doing just that during this time. She replied "yes" with considerable gusto. I also made clear that in our work I thought that communications would have to be shared openly, and obtained Mother's permission to repeat what she had said to me.

Aileen then gave a long account about the school situation. She said that people, particularly other children, talked about her at school, and that she was not really interested in other children at all. This led on to her saying in her somewhat stilted manner of speech that she considered that education was not for the purposes of socialization but to enable one to take one's place in employment in the adult world. She then complained about the childish behavior of children at a school she had attended for five years and from which she had been suddenly withdrawn by the parents, though apparently in some disagreement with each other about it at the time. There were then references to the adult bridge club nearby which Aileen attended; how she came home late and how the parents worried. This culminated in Aileen saying in a pseudo-adult voice that there was no cause for any parent to be worried and in any case it was not their business; she really felt more like an adult than a child anyhow. On my exploring ideas about the future, Aileen talked rather grandly, about wanting to go to college with a view to going on and improving the world. She also said she would like to live in a room on her own where she could cook for herself, feed herself, and be entirely self-sufficient. "With no parents?" I asked. "Yes," she said. "What are parents for?" asked her mother. This led me to wonder aloud about the father and to query the disagreement between the parents about the previous school. Mother went on to say, "Oh yes, we've had lots of quarrels," and Aileen replied in reproving pseudo-adult tones, "You shouldn't quarrel, you really shouldn't quarrel; it's a habit you really ought to stop, it's not good for anybody."

Somewhere in this discussion I pointed out the ongoing dispute in the family about the nature of adulthood and how it affected relationships between parents and children. I went on to say that it might be useful to look at the areas in which quarrels arose, to try and understand more about the feelings involved. I also pointed out that there were two of them here and we were talking about quarrels or differences that were said to arise among three people and went on to suggest that maybe Father should take part too. (They had told me that Aileen's older sister of 21 had married and left home and that an older brother was away in the north so there was no question of inviting them to come too.)

After some discussion this was accepted, whereupon Mother turned to me with a confident air and said, "Confidentially, before Father comes, I had better tell you . . . " I interrupted her and again took up my reluctance to receive a confidential communication in a threesome, indicating that this topic had already been broached in a twosome, and perhaps also was an issue for the family. She acquiesced and said, but no longer "confidentially," that Father had had a stroke last November but did not like having it mentioned. He had not quite accepted it and it was very difficult because Aileen wrote him horrible notes. These, on inquiry, included "I hate my father" and "my father is cruel." Mother added that it was a cruel thing to have to come down to breakfast and to find such a note when you have had a stroke. I said, "Yes, but maybe hate is also a difficult feeling to deal with" and Aileen said "Yes."

The interview ended in a more relaxed way and I think we all thought something had happened in this session. Probably the major feature was my function of holding on to and thinking about Mother and Aileen's opposing and seemingly undiscussable views, without, I hoped, being pushed into collusion with either of them. A setting as a basis for some further exploration may also have been provided.

Father came to the next session and he too made strange movements with his teeth and body. There was quite some animosity apparent between him and his daughter and Mother complained that he did not exercise enough discipline. I also felt she did not give him much space to do so. We explored such themes as Aileen feeling infantilized (which had already come up in the previous session) and Mother feeling upset because Aileen had threatened to hit her when she was old, claiming Father would no longer be able to protect her. To this Aileen protested with a highly "reasonable" air that she was only defending herself because Mother kept "looking at her at mealtimes." This somewhat strange point illustrated Aileen's view that Mother was "getting at" her and controlling her by looking at her. It was now possible to relate this to Mother feeling that she was being made by Aileen to have ulcers and headaches. I commented on how powerful communications within the family of a nonverbal nature were felt to be.

All three members of this family continued to vociferously express their viewpoints about a number of family disputes with an air of speaking the self-evident and only possible truth. It seemed very clear that it was not only Aileen who "did not listen" to the feelings of others. Yet what from the beginning could be seen to be a disturbed family had managed to come to the clinic, do a bit of work, and evince some interest in the proceedings. They seemed at least momentarily relieved at having some discussion of their unhelpful polarization, and having some of the infantile/adult confusion given some recognition by me. This did not amount to much more than bringing to their joint attention that there seemed to be very differing views among them as to who might be being adult, and who infantile, but as each one felt absolutely "right," this seemed to be a very painful area for them all. They may also have been helped to listen to each other, however briefly. That there was some response to my attempted containment, as opposed to the seemingly usual pattern between themselves of reacting to these interchanges, made me wonder if it might be possible to work further with them. Against this there was the concreteness of their thinking, the presence of projections, probably on the basis of part object relationships, that were felt to have strong physical effects, such as being causative of physical illness in Mother. Altogether there seemed to be a predominance of what could be called paranoid/schizoid ways of thinking with much of the so-called "adult" behavior of all of them probably being an indication of pseudo-mature adulthood based on projective identification (see Waddell, Chapter 3, this volume; Smilansky, Glossary). There seemed to be no indication for attempting individual work, because none of them seemed moved by curiosity about their inner world, nor wanted to be seen as patients. I did, in fact, refer them on for further family work, but in the view of the therapists who attempted to work with them in some depth, the family experienced this as attacking and although initially interested, withdrew after a number of interviews.

Looking back on the case it seems to me that the points about family psychopathology that I have outlined in the last paragraph were a contraindication for attempting this latter work, namely, longer term family therapy using transference interpretations. It seems to me now that the work done with them in the Counselling Service was primarily that of containment. This concept as used here originated in the work of W.R. Bion (1962a); it is elaborated by Waddell in Chapter 3, Box in Chapter 5 and Moustaki in the Glossary. In family work it seems to me that a worker can open him- or herself to the full impact of the communications coming from different family members, however bizarre, incompatible, and painful, and attempt to give them some space within themselves. The worker, having borne and thought about them, can then relate them back again to the family in a more bearable form.

Although I did offer the Browns some aspects of a containing experience attempting to give attention to, hold, and relay back some of their contentious interchanges, I now think that I overreacted to what I experienced as some use of what we did together and passed them on too quickly in an attempt to utilize some mobilization of energy for work. On reflection, I think it would have made more sense for me to have continued with them for a few sessions more, largely on the basis of an explorative and containing experience. I could have offered the possibility of a follow-up some time later if this had seem appropriate.

As I elaborate when discussing methods of work below, I use my own feelings in the countertransference as a guide to understanding with such families. Although with this family I picked up early on Mother's wish for me to talk to Aileen as a means of controlling her, I now think I did not pay enough attention to the notion of my being felt, by Mother in particular, as a powerful therapeutic tool "prescribed" by her and the GP to fulfill a particular requirement in her mind. This may have led to my having responded with some degree of therapeutic zeal to the idea of a further referral. With hindsight, I might have been more alert to the lack of feelings in the transference or countertransference of me as an "object" with personal qualities; this lack was another factor that did not bode well for the family being able to sustain working in depth.

Although I would not call the foregoing accounts Family Therapy, they may be worth thinking about as examples of therapeutic work with families. This kind of work can, I think, be thought about as a useful entity in its own right, as well as a possible introduction and entry, where appropriate, into more formal family therapy for the families concerned.

METHOD OF WORK

I would now like to gather together some thinking about aspects of the method of work that I use and its relation to psychoanalysis. In individual long-term psychoanalytical psychotherapy my main working tool is the transference relationship to myself, which I attempt to gather in from the beginning of therapy with the purpose of using it to allow understanding of, and change in, the internal objects of the patients. In other words, in the session I am constantly attempting to relate material to myself in the transference. This would obviously, seem inappropriate in brief work, whether individual or family. In the latter, while not making the exploration and interpretation of the transference the main working tool, it does seem essential for the therapist to be constantly aware of its development, with a view to taking it up when necessary.

In this kind of work I see actual interpretation of the transference as appropriate in three kinds of instances that can, in fact, overlap, as they do in the examples that I go on to give. In the first instance, it serves to draw attention to material in relation to oneself as a means of illustrating something in the clients' external lives in a way that they might be able to use. For example, with the Browns I took up the possibility of Aileen feeling I was someone who was talking "at" her, as in Mother's conversations with the doctor and headmistress. Secondly, it may be necessary to comment on something in relation to oneself to avoid a block in the session, that is, a negative transference reaction} the same example in relation to Aileen applies. (The third instance is the use of oneself in the here and now, quite often in the form of a representative of the agency, as a means of relating to what the clients are hoping for, fearing, or experiencing, this time with the aim of making the current experience usable by them.) Taking another facet of the same example, when Mrs. Brown quoted the doctor in a way that made me feel I was expected to take powerful action in relation to Aileen in order to give relief to her ulcers and headache, it was appropriate to take up what was hoped for from me. Although technically a transference reaction, it would seem to be inappropriate to take it up with emotional impact in relation to oneself, but better to try to understand their expectations of me as the person they happened to encounter in the agency. The initial interchange with the Brown family is, in fact, an example of what can be called pre-transference phenomena, in other words feelings that related to me not as in a particularly personal interaction, but rather based on the family's projections onto the agency before coming.

Here of course the countertransference is relevant, because one gets in touch with such projections by way of what one is made to feel. I felt, for instance, that I was to be a prescribed, forceful cure for Aileen. You may have noticed that in the cases that I have presented I have drawn very much on my own observations and feelings in the countertransference as a method of working and understanding. I am using the term to describe manifestations in the worker arising from interactions with patients and clients; the concept is further expanded by Margot Waddell in Chapter 3 and Errica Moustaki Smilansky in the Glossary. To give another example, at the beginning of the first case, the Smiths, I both observed and experienced Father as a passive listener somehow "in" the situation, yet not actively involved. This experience helped me to feel it was appropriate to try and open up the parental relationship and explore the relevance of Father's passivity to the difficulties reported in relation to Mary. It is clear that the use of the countertransference is a major tool in all our work.

Longer-term family work offers more opportunity to help a family in depth by using transference manifestations as a tool of family work. In this context I am referring to transference as the infantile feelings arising in the family experienced in relation to the therapists. Although aspects of transference in relation to the institution also arise and can be taken up, as in the earlier examples I have given in the context of briefer work, the transference can also be interpreted with reference to the therapists as they are felt to be perceived by the family in the here and now, say, for example, as a parental couple. This approach also calls for the development of family interpretations, allowing insights into how the family uses the therapists. This is illustrated in the following case of the Manner family.

It seems to me that when one is thinking about the appropriateness of offering the longer-term work to a family, one might think not only about the dynamics of a family, but also about their capacity to work, making use of transference understanding as, for example, the Browns probably could not, though the Smiths and the Manners could.

I should now like to illustrate how, using such criteria, we decided to offer ongoing therapy to the Manner family.

Mr. and Mrs. Manner came to the clinic asking for family therapy for themselves and their 19-year-old daughter Olga. A male co-therapist and I saw the three of them together. The parents explained that they had had family therapy in their own country, Denmark, and had been recommended to continue this during the period when the parents were on a work assignment in England. Olga had a long history of illness and had had various forms of therapy. Her current difficulties were said to include the inability to leave home or to take a job, and living very much as part of her parents' lives. Her parents expressed perplexity about how to view this, fluctuating between seeing her as ill and needing to be with them or as being lazy and requiring what they felt to be quite harsh treatment. Olga was unwilling to attend therapy on her own, though she was the one that the parents claimed needed it. We saw them first for a family exploration. Without a commitment to ongoing therapy. Early on the parents told us firmly that therapists were equally good anywhere and maintained that we were no different from our Danish predecessors.

Areas of fusion and non-differentiation within the family seemed apparent both from what we observed and from the history; we were not differentiated from the previous therapists. Although there may have been some external similarity to the Browns in expectation of the agency, this did not appear to be just a somewhat concrete pre-transference requirement that we should fulfill a role for them, but also a clinically useful manifestation of their difficulties in separating and differentiation. This became apparent in several ways. They, for example, in the exploration, were able to become interested and curious about us, both in relation to our style of therapy and as people; this gave us scope for beginning to examine with them areas of differentiation between the two of us as a couple and also between us and their previous therapists. In the countertransference we had fluctuating perceptions of being experienced at one moment as a conglomerate entity fused with the institution, or at another moment, more separately, though still as part of the Tavistock.

In the first family meeting we explained that we would soon be taking a prearranged break. The family was unwilling to believe that we ourselves could have made a decision to take a holiday so soon. They preferred to lay this event entirely at the door of the institution, seeing us simply as a part of it, and thus unable to decide such issues for ourselves.

The fact that one could see, feel, comment, and elicit interest in relation to ourselves, albeit at that time denied, encouraged us to believe that we could work in the transference. With so much fusion present in this family, it seemed very appropriate to try, where we could, to interpret in a way that was meaningful for the whole family by means of family interpretations. In an attempt to develop family interpretative work in this way, I find that I draw on the experience of group work as developed by W. R. Bion (1961).

In an early session, for example, the therapists made interpretations that the parents assiduously translated "for" the daughter, the index patient. The latter could speak some English but was basically inactive in therapy at that time. When we talked about this, Olga rejoined that the therapy was for her (despite the fact that she had not wanted to be an individual patient), implying that her parents were doing their job correctly. We in turn interpreted for the family that we were felt to be the parental-therapist providers of mental food, Mr. and Mrs. Manner acting as the "ears" or "hands" to take it from us and put it in the "Olga mouth" of the family body.

Working with this family, then, we tried to provide ourselves as a basis for first understanding, and later disentangling, family interactions. In this way we also made available the possibility of introjecting and identifying with unfused, differentiated objects. Observations of the family dynamics and our perception of the transference and countertransference manifestations in the first few meetings led us to offer the family ongoing therapy in which we used the transference relationship as a basic method of work. The therapy ended nearly two years later, shortly after Olga, who was then in full time work, had left home and was about to be married.

SUMMARY

In this paper clinical examples have been given of families with whom it seemed possible to engage in some form of family work. Problems referred to by these families or elucidated by the therapists included:

Difficulties experienced as occurring directly in family relationships	⎧ Smiths ⎨ Browns ⎩ Manners
Splitting, projecting, and scapegoating	⎧ Smiths ⎨ Browns
Fusion and non-differentiation	Manners
Families where a potential patient might not otherwise come	⎧ Smiths ⎨ Browns ⎩ Manners

This, of course, is not intended to be a comprehensive set of criteria. It has not been appropriate to examine the alternative of individual therapy in this paper. Interestingly enough, however, although it was not the intention to find such examples when collecting this material, it does overlap considerably with some of the indications given for family therapy elsewhere in the literature, for example, S. Walrond-Skinner (1976); F. E. Martin (1977).

I think these interventions illustrate that when deciding how to proceed (it may be useful to look not only at a family's symptomatology and internal dynamics, but also at how the family relates to, and is experienced by the workers in the transference and countertransference) An attempt has been made here to illustrate how one may decide about alternative kinds of family interventions and their possible usefulness. One could perhaps postulate at this stage of our thinking two somewhat different, but overlapping, areas of work with families.

1. Intervention with a family, or some family members, involving chiefly exploration, clarification, and containment, with possibility of some work in such areas as projections and splitting. Such work would rely particularly on the use of observation and the countertransference with limited use of transference interpretations, but, in my view, should pay considerable attention to the family's expectation of the agency. It might be brief, would not necessarily require any conscious commitment to therapy, but might give relief from family stress and allow some movement to take

place within the family. This could well be sufficient for the needs or kind of involvement a family was willing or able to make or that an agency could provide. A family may also be helped by work done in this way to undertake further work (e.g., the Smith parents moving into family therapy with their children). For some families, based, say, in the paranoid/schizoid position, more interpretative therapy may be perceived as too persecuting and/or unfulfilling of expectations that may be manifest in the family (e.g., the Browns).

2. Family therapy, very likely longer term, where one is attempting to develop the use of interpretations geared toward the family meaning of what is being discussed, with the benefit of the interpretation of a transference relationship to the therapists as a working tool (e.g., the Manner family in this chapter and other families elsewhere in this book). Working in such a way offers a family a chance not only of alleviating external distress but also of unraveling the distortions of its shared internal world. Hopefully it may also help one to experience and learn more about the use of a psychoanalytic approach in thinking about families, which might have further application in short as well as long term work.

Engaging in the Process of Change with Families at Adolescence

SALLY BOX

> *Before enlightment chop wood and carry water; after enlightment, chop wood and carry water.*
>
> Buddhist saying

INTRODUCTION

A psychoanalytic approach, in contrast to a behavioral one, is about different states of mind. Change on this basis is notoriously difficult to discern and even more difficult to demonstrate in practice.

In an earlier paper (Box 1978) I attempted to describe the basic tenets of our approach, and it is interesting and perhaps salutory to write about it again now some years later. What is there new to say? What has changed in the meantime? I am reminded of patients or students struggling to identify what they have learned and how they are different after the experience of the therapy or the course. Such notions provide the occasion for exploring the nature of change in the adolescents and their families whom we see with reference to recent psychoanalytic work that has become especially meaningful in the meantime.

In that earlier paper, I discussed the significance of a consistent setting, of understanding and working with the processes within it, and the therapist's use of his own experience there. These remain essentially the same. The difference may be that as this framework becomes more established, there is more room for maneuver within it; new influences and new experiences add depth and provide the basis for the occasional leap in understanding. Perhaps more significantly, one becomes a little less dominated by notions of what ought to be and a little more in touch with what is. This might also be true for our patients.

The quest for identity associated with adolescence is really a life-long quest, but it is particularly relevant to the whole family at the stage when the younger members reach physical maturity and older ones middle age. The "crisis" of adolescence and the "crisis" of mid-life then reverberate with each other and hard-won earlier patterns are inevitably disrupted. Perhaps the most painful part of the process for everyone is the challenge to cherished images of themselves — both as a family and as separate people. Aspects of emotional life that had been disowned are liable to force themselves to the surface and demand attention, and the shifts produced by this upheaval are not necessarily in a positive direction. Old ghosts may reemerge and secret fears be realized in action as unconscious relationships in the family are unknowingly enacted, like an immutable family fate, because they cannot be consciously acknowledged or known about.

If, however, these inner relationships can be known about and engaged with, it may become more possible to differentiate between the essential aspects of identity that can bear examination and are worth fighting for and those that have to be hung onto in the face of contrary evidence for the sake of an image of a self-protective kind. I am thinking especially of the prevalence of narcissistic defenses, used when the family is preoccupied with pursuing a particular image; I am interested in attempting to identify and consider some of the problems of working with these in the families referred to us for help.

Recent psychoanalytic work on psychotic, borderline, and narcissistic states is particularly relevant. (Chasseguet-Smirgel 1985a,b; Joseph 1975; Rosenfeld 1965a,b; Steiner 1977, 1979). It can help us to differentiate the quality of communications in the family, especially nonverbal communication and to distinguish between signs that indicate a shift toward greater integration and those that represent a hidden attack on understanding. Also it may enable us to think more clearly about the different ways the family has of managing uncomfortable feelings and dealing with emotional pain. For the light shed on this — and indeed so many other aspects of both group and individual processes — I shall refer especially to the contribution of Dr. Wilfred Bion.

But first a brief example.

THE C FAMILY

A common self-image of families seeking help is that of a normal happy family. Having to come to the clinic is itself an upsetting threat to this idea and there is often a great struggle to protect the image, even (or especially) as the adolescent's behavior is belying it.

One such family, residing in England from abroad, was referred about the behavior of Jane the younger of two teenage daughters. Jane was described as being rude and difficult with her parents and having a boyfriend of whom they disapproved, "ignorant and from a lower social status." The parents in the family clearly put a premium on politeness, courtesy, and cooperation as well as their concern about class and status.

It emerged that both children had had "unacceptable" boyfriends and both had had pregnancy terminations which, with the help of the GP, had been kept secret from their parents in order to "protect them." This notion of protection was a pervasive aspect of the family life and one which the GP seemed to have been constrained to join. The therapists also were aware of great difficulty in confronting issues in the family and they shared a feeling of walking on egg shells, of great fragility and vulnerability. It was felt that to crack this smooth veneer would produce some disaster.

At the same time the family was paying a high price for it. The girls, unable to voice their own questions and fears or to manage the unacknowledged aggression around, were implicitly introducing all these through action—fights, and unsatisfactory, potentially disastrous liaisons. But more specifically, it emerged, they were unwittingly enacting roles derived from an earlier drama, still heavily invested in the parents' phantasy, particularly that of their mother. For she told us how her father—a "bad character"—had left her mother when she was little. Everyone including her father's own parents had apparently been very disparaging about him and he seems to have become something of a legend. What was clear but less conscious was her continuing preoccupation about this irresponsible but apparently sexually exciting figure in her inner world, which the girls were now reintroducing through their illicit liaisons.

As the family became more available in the treatment we gained glimpses of the more manifest process by which this had happened: one of the girls said, about her parents' response to her relationship, "They overreacted so very much I think if anything it kept us together, it kept us really close," and her sister said, "The more they put pressure on—'You're not going out with him again'—the closer I felt to him; the more problems we seemed to have between each other, the possibility that we might be broken up, that pushed us together."

To quote from the original write-up of this family: "It seemed likely that far from disregarding all the warnings, the girls had rather specifically realized their parents' worst fears. They had acted out some of their very pressing preoccupations about sex, particularly about sex with undesirable men." In this family, then, aggressive feelings had been almost totally denied and split off, apart from occasional violent eruptions from the usually meek father, and had been linked in phantasy with bad and dangerous sex.

DISCUSSION

Freud demonstrated the phenomenon in individual development of the "return of the repressed." In families, we can see how unacceptable aspects of behavior and feelings may be split off from consciousness in one member but retained in the unconscious life of the family to erupt in unexpected ways through other members.

This is not an uncommon phenomenon, particularly to family therapists, but the process by which it occurs is more obscure, and I think it useful to consider it in the light of some relevant concepts, both for its theoretical significance and its implications for treatment.

Different therapists use different terms to describe families in which the members are enmeshed with each other in this way. In this family we can see how the girls, in their struggle to free themselves, are demonstrating the extremely dependent nature of the relationships that exist between them and their parents. Their comments suggest clearly the way their parents' preoccupations and anxiety serve to reinforce their counter-dependent behavior and the extent to which this is based on a lack of differentiation among them all.

It is confusing that this term *dependence* is also used to refer to the quite different phenomenon of acknowledging dependence on someone else as a separate individual and recognizing his or her capacity to help. It is exactly this capacity that represents such a problem for many of our patients, especially those in whom narcissistic preoccupations predominate and for whom the idea of needing or caring for anyone else is seen as demeaning. ("I can manage on my own . . . I am self sufficient . . . I am not a child," etc.) In these families, it is this idea of feeling like a child, or a patient, that has to be resisted—omnipotent phantasies are clung to in the interests of fending off the painful feelings of limitation associated with full recognition of *difference* and of separateness. (The little boy cannot be Mummy's mate as Daddy can; Mummy does not have a penis as Daddy does; Daddy cannot have babies as Mummy can.) To avoid such recognitions and all the feelings of jealousy and rivalry involved implies denial and splitting. Also, protests to the contrary notwithstanding, it implies enormous dependence on the others who have become the repository for those unwanted feelings or aspects of the self.

Melanie Klein coined the term *projective identification* to describe this way that conflictual or unmanageable feelings are denied and expelled, being then perceived and identified elsewhere) particularly in the mother or some part of her body. She pointed out that while this is a necessary process in all normal development, the result, when it is carried out excessively may be an "overstrong dependence" on those who represent these projected parts (Klein 1946).

Such processes of splitting and projective identification clearly have important implications for our work with families. They belong with the more primitive state of mind that never completely disappears, forming the background from which our most immediate responses tend to spring throughout life.

Klein termed this the *paranoid-schizoid position* in contrast to the later developing *depressive position* where the leading anxiety is about the safety of the others and one's effect on them, initially of course, the mother or parts of her. It is the working through of the depressive position that finally enables an increasing ability to integrate different aspects of the self and thus relinquish the need to control others. It ushers in the capacity to care for the others as separate individuals rather than perceiving and treating them as extensions of oneself. But the achievement of this is liable to be tenuous at the best of times and normally there is a constant fluctuation between the different states of mind. The balance between them in any one family is a crucial determinant of its functioning. Wilfred Bion (1970) gave us the notion ps $<$ – $>$ d to represent the movement back and forth, and he elaborated greatly on the factors that influence this.

In the book *Learning from Experience*, Bion (1962a) considers some of the different ways that people have for dealing with anxiety and emotional pain. Building on the work of Klein, he draws the distinction between procedures designed to avoid pain and those designed to modify it. He suggests that the key factor in the outcome determining this is whether there is an available object, felt by the infant to be the breast, but in fact the mind really, which can register and bear the anxiety, the destructiveness, and the distress, and can help the baby feel they are manageable and can be borne. It is this that in Bion's terms enables the experience to be contained, to be held in the mind sufficiently for it to be made sense of and gradually integrated into the individual's other experiences. He called the function that enables this process to take place *alpha function*, and highlighted the significance not only of obviously painful experience but also of the impact of a new idea for instance, because of its disruptive effect and because of the demand it makes on the individual to relinquish his established ways of viewing things. Elements of experience that cannot be tolerated are referred to as *beta elements*, having to be ejected outward either into space or, more hopefully, via projective identification into a potential receiver, "a container," such as the mother, her breast, or perhaps another member of the family. But if the mother (or whoever) cannot perform the necessary alpha function, cannot work on the experience and "transform" it, then what becomes of it? She may try to ignore it, producing a sort of boomerang effect; or alternatively she may become possessed, or taken over by it. Bion spoke of "playing a part in someone else's phantasy." This is clearly what happens to children, as in the previous example, when they become the vehicle of their parents' projective identification, or the containers for the phantasies derived from their parents' unmanageable experiences. And if we are at all receptive (not the boomerang type!) then it happens to us as therapists.

But in order to avoid the kind of misunderstanding that often arises in relation to this function of containment I want to emphasize the active component of it, for this often gets lost in favor of a more passive, spongelike notion of the therapists' or parents' task, one which involves a denial of aggression rather than a managing of it, or in the case of the therapist, a readiness to interpret it. Otherwise, and I think this is very relevant to our family, the message conveyed is that it cannot be managed—that it is unmanageable. For the less it can be known about consciously, along with the associated fears, the more scope there is for unconscious phantasy to grow and get a grip on the life of the family.

In sum, we can envisage how the inner world of each of us contains a cast of characters and relationships that have not been assimilated and that retain their capacity to tyrannize and to enthrall. They push us to identify and engage complementary characteristics in the external world in a way that can be quite enslaving. Eric Berne brilliantly illustrated this phenomenon in *Games People Play* (Berne 1964) and I think we can now understand a little more how and why it happens. We can contrast it also to another way of relating, one based on appreciation of the others for their own characteristics rather than those that we have projected onto them from ourselves. In the process of therapy, if it is effective, these inner world figures become modified. The setting of the therapy provides for them to become activated but this time in the relationship to the therapist.

THE THERAPEUTIC TASK

The task of the therapist, then, is to be available to play a part in his patients' phantasy scenario but, rather than enacting the projections as he is implicitly invited to, it is to monitor his minute by minute experience in order to try to understand what is the part he is being required to play and to transform it. This is also the best route to the patient's inner world.

(In the work with the family there are feelings and aspects of their experience that cannot be tolerated anywhere, and it is these we as therapists will experience. So we are struggling with three main elements: (1) what the family is telling us and bringing us consciously, (2) what they are showing in their behavior toward each other, and (3) perhaps most significantly, the experience they give us in the process and what we can learn from this about the unmanageable aspects of their inner world that most need containing.)

To the extent that the therapist can provide this function, they not only help those particular split-off feelings to be integrated and assimilated, but also they provide the basis for a beginning internalization of the function itself. I'd like to try to illustrate these elements from a family whose vulnerability was such that it was difficult for any of them to acknowledge or allow a wish for help. Like the earlier family, this one was also struggling with the collapse of a powerful image—a rather different image to that one, but serving a similarly defensive function. While the prevailing atmosphere in the first family was one of idealization, the atmosphere in this one was one of denigration.

FAMILY D

The family was referred by a therapist who had seen the younger daughter, Janet, following a serious suicide attempt. He had concluded that a family approach might be more appropriate because of the separation difficulties that had emerged in the consultation, and also, it seemed, because of the marked lack of any clear motivation on the girl's part.

Besides Janet, aged 17, the family consisted of Father and Mother and Betty aged 28, living away from home. In order to convey something of the quality of the interaction in the sessions, I will describe a few brief extracts.

Initially it seemed that only the elder daughter, Betty, thought that there was some use in the idea of coming together as a family. Janet said it was never her idea and she didn't agree with it, but she would go along with it. Mother said that Janet should make up her own mind about coming and Father cut across to say "Well we are here now, what have you got to tell us?" This emerged as a characteristic mode that had the effect of quite drastically reducing possibilities for either the expression of feelings or any concern and reflection about them.

The therapists' initial countertransference reactions were either to feel flattened into a rather stunned silence or to be stung into a rejoinder, and this was what usually happened in the family. At first when it was enacted by the therapists, one of them was gloomily silent, the other pointing out rather sharply that we had not actually heard from the family about the problem yet. This only invited further attack from Father along the lines that we should know all about it from the colleague who'd referred them, and wasn't there any communication around here, and so on.

Gradually as this continued, however, the therapists began to pay more specific attention to the style of the interaction, and to their own countertransference. A feeling of futility and failure prevailed. Our efforts were being met with evident rejection. Perhaps this was how the more powerful and important communication was taking place, both about the family expectations and about the feelings that the referral represented. The therapists were certainly being given a taste of what it is like to feel a disappointing letdown perhaps as the family members felt in relation to each other. One therapist commented now on the way that Father seemed to be voicing for all the family an issue about disappointed expectations. This was being shown in terms of their wishes and hopes about coming to the clinic: what they wanted was advice, what they should do to make things better. The therapists were simply not living up to their expectations and, in this way, should feel themselves to be failures.

The therapists here were accepting and identifying with the projected feelings of failure that the family found so intolerable for themselves. The interpretation seemed to open things up and allow the issue of expectations to emerge more clearly. Gradually, the girls started to speak about the expectations their parents had of them, particularly their father. His response to Janet was, "I don't expect anything of you, I don't want anything of you, you seem to imagine that I do. I'd be happy if you just went off to America or Africa, it wouldn't worry me." The girls demurred, and Janet said, "You want to know everything that is going on." Father said all he wanted was peace, there were other things to do in his life besides worry about them.

This repetitive theme was indicative of the strong need in the family to appear above caring too much and to avoid vulnerability to any sign of rejection. If there was any rejecting to be done, no one could do it better than him, Father seemed to say. Janet shared with her father this wish to convince everyone that she did not care too much. Mother, although denying any particular expectations of Janet, also clearly indicated her enormous disappointment with her daughter via a kind of muted tirade about her not passing her school exams when she could have, and instead leaving home with a boyfriend. They had accepted that, Mother said; they didn't try to fight it but they weren't prepared to have her back just when she felt like it. And then there had been the overdose—Janet was so unhappy—well, she'd tried to accept that too, now Janet was home again, and she just felt she must try to ignore everything and accept her the way she was. As the session continued it seemed increasingly clear that the particular blot that Janet and her suicide attempt represented on the family landscape was this powerful demonstration of unhappiness and vulnerability in their midst that could no longer be avoided.

Janet seemed to be literally the sore spot in the family, and her presence a constant reminder of all the disappointment they each felt about the way things had actually worked out for them. It was the awareness and the exploration of these kinds of feelings that the family was trying to hold at bay and defend against in their session, desperately longing that somehow we could cure the sore spot and change its representative, Janet, in front of their eyes—quite magically really. Similarly, any expression of concern or alliance with the needy part of them was liable to be experienced as extremely persecutory, and this was related, I think, to the projected feeling that any such interest was bound to be of a narcissistic kind, not motivated by genuine concern for the other, the child, or in this case the patient, but rather by a predominant interest in boosting the therapist's idea of themselves as good parents or good helpers, and so forth.

It may be, in fact, that, despite the talk of all of them being free to go their own way in this family, to be what they want, to find themselves, the thing that actually went most against the grain was someone spoiling the family notion of being witty, good to look at, good to be with, successful, and so on. Certainly the idea of feeling rejected, unhappy, and unsuccessful seemed to be quite insulting really, and feeling fat even more so. Her father clearly indicated his feelings that this daughter was a fat, ugly blob on the family landscape. It was rather as if Janet had done all this specifically to attack the image and the hopes and the expectations that her family had of her.

It was not long before the family again produced symbolically this same dynamic in their relationship to the therapists. It is the therapists' response, I suggest, that can provide a new element in the pattern, and enable a change in it. And just to finish I will try to describe this by way of the last example of the family's pattern of communicating its preoccupation, particularly around the theme of rejection, and the therapists' efforts to respond to it.

End of the Exploratory Phase

It was the fifth exploratory session that was tabled as the one in which a decision was to be made in relation to embarking on treatment after the break. In the previous one the interaction had opened up and in terms of both process and content was more evenly distributed. There had been a number of issues bringing Betty's feelings into focus more, including her jealousy of Janet. Father had joined in much more and revealed his affection for Janet, and Mother had actively shown her resentment toward her husband for his flip attitude and tendency to opt out. She had argued fervently in favor of having things out in the open, in contrast to his preference for keeping things quiet and avoiding disturbance or upset. But the shifts in the family were evidently being accompanied by distress and great anxiety.

Betty opened the session with a barrage against coming, depicting the therapy as destructive and dangerous and making a clear attempt to refocus attention on Janet. "I get on fine with my parents. It's just Janet. If she finds it so comfortable here why doesn't she come on her own?" While Janet in tears says, "But you said you wanted to get on better with me." Betty's fears seemed to be as much for her parents as for herself, for it emerged that, while Janet had felt better, Mother had become isolated and also extremely angry with her husband. She supported Betty's move to stop coming, openly voicing her fear that to continue could break up the family and the marriage. There were plenty of things wrong with the family, she knew, but until now they had managed to keep it together, and she was afraid of what was going to happen if it started coming out now. Mother had apparently, not for the first time, mentioned leaving home, and even this could not evoke any response initially.

Once again the therapists were feeling a sense of hopelessness and, in relation to the idea of the therapy—they don't want it, they can't use it, we may as well accept that and let them go. But one could also see this as a communication of a pattern. And eventually the therapists took it from that point of view. They spoke of the difficulty for the family to bear the feeling of anger and helplessness and isolation represented by the mother's threat to leave. They linked this with Janet's suicide attempt. The theme seemed to be that of opting out on the one hand, and reciprocal feelings of great failure on the other for those being left. This was now being played out between the family and the therapists in relation to the decision about coming here for sessions. Here the therapists are the failures, the no-good parent therapists. Mother responded to this, speaking of her own great sense of failure that had made her seriously contemplate leaving home. Janet, now very worried, said to her mother, "How do you think Dad would feel if you left?" Mother implied that she didn't think that he'd care. Janet turned desperately inquiring to her father. "I'd help her pack her bags," he said. Mother, almost in tears, said "There!" and Janet, "You don't believe him, do you?" But Betty and her father were both now seriously making a case for letting people go, as if this would be doing them a kindness. "If people want their freedom you should let them go."

Again the therapists initially felt speechless, but this seemed to be exactly the issue in relation to coming to see them, and that is what they interpreted. When the family talked of leaving, spoke of how fed up they were and how useless the therapy was to them, should the therapists then say, "Well if that's the way you feel, if that's what you want, so we'll help you pack your bags?" Or should they understand that it is more complicated than that; there's another side to it. They commented on the great uncertainty, as it had showed in relation to Janet when she left home and Mother when she contemplated it, as to whether anyone would mind. Could they still be wanted here? Could the therapists recognize the part of them that wanted to continue despite all their negative feelings and protests about it? In fact, there was time that could be offered for the therapy to continue after the break.

Now at last, it was possible for the family to respond differently, and it was Father in particular who started working to arrange a time with us, even speaking of converting the still resistant Betty.

In this way the family brought and communicated their sensitivity to threats of rejection and showed how they strove to defend against them. If the therapist can recognize in what way he is the subject of the patient's projective identification and allow himself to be a refuge for the split-off feelings, he may be able to draw on them to help him to understand via this very immediate experience some of the painful and conflictual feelings that cannot be borne and have to be projected. Hitherto unmanageable feelings may then take on a communication value and become "transformed," to use Dr. Bion's word, from being made indigestible elements flying about in the atmosphere, so to speak, to a message with form and shape that can be shared and perhaps reintegrated.

This process in itself is meant to provide an experience for the family, another dimension, which very gradually can be internalized in terms of the developing capacity of alpha function and containment within themselves. But such work in the countertransference does require the therapist to continue working on understanding his own emotional world and his own propensity to enact the projections with which he is identified rather than either recognizing them, or alternatively bearing the uncertainty of waiting in the hopes of something becoming more clear.

6

Reenactment as an Unwitting Professional Response to Family Dynamics

RONALD BRITTON

The notion that is expressed in the title of this chapter is that (contact with some families may result in professional workers or their institutions becoming involved unknowingly in a drama that reflects a situation in the relationships of the family or within the minds of some of its individual members. This is not recognized but expressed in action.)As the action appears to be that of professionals going about their business, that is, interacting with the family, colleagues, or other agencies, the fact that these transactions are shaped by an underlying dynamic is unlikely to be perceived. This may eventually call attention to itself by its repetitious nature or by the impasse that seems to follow a variety of initiatives. Indications of the presence of a prevailing unconscious process influencing professional responses may be the intensity of feeling aroused by a case, the degree of dogmatism evoked, or the pressure to take drastic or urgent measures. In other cases, in contrast to this, the professional "symptoms" are inappropriate unconcern, surprising ignorance, undue complacency, uncharacteristic insensitivity, or professional inertia.)

This last characteristic is illustrated in the case of a boy referred to a child guidance clinic by the school he attended, or more precisely, rarely attended. A new teacher at the school had reactivated concern about an old situation. In the past the school welfare officer had been very troubled about the boy who appeared to be neglected by his mother, with whom he lived alone. The welfare worker had involved the Social Services department in the case, as the boy could not learn at school and seemed undeveloped emotionally and socially. A regular arrangement was made for a woman social worker and the mother to meet to discuss the problems of both child and parent. The outcome was the perpetuation of this arrangement for a long time with its purpose lost and its effect negligible. Frustrated by her own lack of impact on the school attendance, the welfare officer had effectively ceased to be involved in the case. Like the boy's father in the early years of his life, she left the scene.

The psychiatrist at the clinic, having gleaned this information, felt his best course of action was to consult with the social worker already involved with the family, a common clinical approach. Thus began a protracted, desultory, "consultation" with the social worker, in which the "work with the family" was discussed. For a time the school showed signs of considerable frustration at the lack of new developments but then seemed to lose interest, leaving the two professionals still involved with the case in a relationship very like that of the boy and his mother, or the boy and his school, which was repeated with the mother and the social worker. There seemed to be in all the situations related to the case the emergence of a characteristic pattern of object-relations, that is, a pair staying together in an unsatisfactory, nonprogressive relationship from which frustration was nevertheless excluded and instead felt by the person whose failure to make an impact eventually led them to withdraw or depart.

A configuration like this could be discerned in a number of interpersonal contexts. It could also be a description of an intrapsychic situation in which freedom from frustration and its consequences was achieved by the elimination of any real desire or expectation from the individual who thus became the cause of discouragement of others who were provoked by this inertia into attempting to kindle some desire for change. Here we seem to be dealing with repetitious actions that transfer a pattern of relationships from one situation to another in which new participants become the vehicles for the reiterated expression of the underlying dynamic. The repetition compulsion may be a dynamic in the sense of being a compelling force determining events, but in another sense it is essentially static. The basic situation remains unrealized and unchanged while new versions of it proliferate. The cast changes but the plot remains the same. This is well described in the psychoanalytic literature as occurring in the lives of individuals; here I am referring to a similar phenomenon in the lives of families and groups.

A number of psychoanalytic concepts are implicit in this account. One is the recurrence of a specific pattern of events and relationships. This phenomenon referred to as the repetition compulsion was first described by Freud in a paper published in 1914 called "Remembering, Repeating and Working-Through". He linked it to the established idea of transference, which he said "is itself only a piece of repetition . . . of the forgotten past, and not only on to the doctor but also on to all the other aspects of the current situation . . . the patient yields to the compulsion to repeat . . . in every other activity and relationship . . . at the time." In the same paper he described the tendency to replication of unconscious ideas in action rather than thought for which the term *acting out* was subsequently adopted.

My characterization of a process in the case described above whereby frustration is denied and extruded from the relationship of the couple and provoked in a third party can be seen as an example of *projective identification*. Melanie Klein (1946) coined this term to describe a phantasy of the self or more often parts of the self entering into the identity of another person; if this is preceded by denial of those aspects in the subject then they are perceived as attributes of the object of the process. Thus in this case the third party appears to be one who wants change or development and the couple feels no urge to transform or clarify its situation. The situation could be described as an omnipotent unconscious phantasy that those aspects of themselves that would experience such desire, and its associated frustration and helplessness, can be split off and located in someone else.

However, there is more to it as the behavior and experience of others is actually influenced by the process. Wilfred Bion (1974) commented on this and together with other analysts who followed Melanie Klein has enlarged the use of the term to include the effect on the recipient of such projections.

> I am not sure [he says] from the practice of analysis that it is only an omnipotent phantasy; that is, something that the patient cannot in fact do. . . . I have felt and some of my colleagues likewise that when the patient appears to be engaged on a projective identification it can make me feel persecuted, as if the patient can, in fact, split off certain nasty feelings and shove them into me so that I actually have feelings of persecution or anxiety. [p. 105]

This would then link the notion of projective identification with that of *countertransference*, an older term defined as "the analyst's unconscious reactions to the individual analysand — especially to the analysand's own transference" (Laplanche and Pontalis 1973). As these two authors point out, some take the countertransference to be what in the analyst's personality is liable to affect treatment, others to that brought about by the transference of the analysand. Though this is an important distinction (implying as it does that the analyst has a special responsibility for the former) in practice, in the consulting room the two may not be separable since the one plays on the other. As Lagache (1964) points out, the transference and countertransference are reciprocal parts of a whole, involving both of the people present.

One way that the analyst may remain unaware of his countertransference is that he, like the patient, may act it out, instead of experiencing the psychic situation. A good deal has been written about the way an analyst may increase his understanding of his patient by scrutiny of his own irrational feelings and impulses in the analysis. Rosenfeld (1965a), like Bion, has emphasized that projective identification may be a form of unconscious communication from the patient. It may be, however, that it is in his behavior with the patient, including his choice of interpretation, wording, tone, and timing, that the evoked countertransference may be evident, as a reenactment of an unconscious object relationship in the analysis. Betty Joseph has drawn attention to this, emphasizing that "the more the patient is using primarily primitive mechanisms and defences against anxiety, the more the analyst is . . . used by the patient unconsciously and the more the analysis is a scene for action rather than understanding" (Joseph 1978).

It is a recurrent discovery that processes described as occurring in the microscopic world of psychoanalysis have relevance outside it. I believe this to be the case with the concepts just described: Freud in first describing repetition compulsion said, "The patient yields to the compulsion to repeat — in every other activity and relationship . . . at the time" (Freud 1914, p. 150).

I would like to paraphrase this in relation to the ideas expressed above and say that the more primitive mechanisms and defenses against anxiety are being used, the more is every professional contact likely to become a scene for action and for the professional to yield to the compulsion to repeat or reenact an unconscious situation. The term *countertransference* is commonly used to describe the feelings the analyst becomes aware of, or what he sees to be his emotionally determined expectations and apprehensions in contact with his patient. I would like therefore to use the words *complementary acting out* to denote the counterpart to countertransference in deeds rather than words; that is, the enactment by the analyst of a reciprocal object relationship to that acted out by his patient. By extension I propose to use this term to describe unconsciously determined action (or inaction) by professionals when this is evoked by their involvement in certain cases.

I have been impressed by the way this may continue beyond the immediate contact with the family and seem to infect the relationships of colleagues or different agencies. In some cases the pattern of response of education departments, schools, social services, or doctors takes on uncannily the shape of the family; quarrels are pursued between workers who seem as incompatible in their views as are the parents; highhanded intervention by senior colleagues echoes the domination of a family by the intrusions of an opinionated grandparent. In another case a succession of professional agencies not only failed to accept responsibility but uncharacteristically failed to communicate with each other or acknowledge other workers' existence, thus echoing the family pattern of a child who had been at different times abandoned by both his parents, long since separated, who related to him independently without acknowledging each other's existence.

Such examples have become familiar in examining the circumstances of situations referred to the Tavistock Clinic for help when there is disagreement, stalemate, or what are felt to be intransigent problems. The sphere of action, however, need not be so obviously related to emotional difficulty or disturbed behavior. The nature of complementary action may only become evident when a particular configuration is seen to recur in varied forms. The formulation of this may give a meaning that the separate acts, by their apparent diversity, have obscured. Thus, in the example I am about to quote, the way I choose to present the facts already represents my view of the case, as a coherent attempt to dispose of a psychological difficulty through a particular kind of action. It is clear that the events were perceived at the time as a series of situations unrelated to each other and demanding action in their own right. It is therefore evident that my view may be mistaken and might appear arbitrary or fanciful. As a hypothesis it can only gain strength if it has predictive value.

The case concerned a girl, her family, and a hospital. It was characterized by a preoccupation with removing some presence felt to be dangerous to the girl. She was recently sexually mature. One organ under suspicion was removed lest it contain the malignancy that had previously killed her grandmother. A second organ, known to be diseased in her mother, was suspected of causing the girl's symptoms and was excised only to be found quite healthy. The girl attempted to remove life itself by suicide. The hypothesis, that an unconscious phantasy was operative, that something malignant and female must be gotten rid of, seemed plausible. If this hypothesis was correct, this imperative, though unconscious, belief influenced the decisions and behavior of the girl, her parents, and a number of professional advisers at different times. One way of expressing this underlying phantasy would be to say that there was a powerful anxiety that something catastrophic would follow from the development of a mature, female, sexual presence (or in the psychoanalytic sense the emergence of a dangerous, female, "bad" object). In this family, you might say, there was a shared phantasy that there was something threatening about femininity, that women contained the seeds of destruction or malignancy. A family history of women of two earlier generations spending time in mental hospitals lent credibility to this version.

The working hypothesis gained support, however, by subsequent developments. Further mystifying symptoms provoked a superficially different but basically similar response within the hospital staff. The malignancy was now located not in an organ or tissue but in the girl's relationship with her mother. Specifically it was thought that the food produced by mother provoked the disease. The solution was again removal, this time of the girl from home, into care. I would emphasize here that this apparently new initiative, which in a psychodynamic sense is so repetitious, came from the professional staff as their response to the situation with which they were in contact. If they were steered by unconscious forces, these forces were operating in them, called forth as it were by their experience with this family.

The quality of this story provoked the feeling that these events belong in a dream. In a sense that may be true. To return to Freud's (1914) notion of acting out, he says, "The patient does not remember anything . . . but acts it out. He reproduces it, not as a memory but as an action" (p. 150). We can substitute for memory in this definition all other forms of mental activity. Hence action seems not simply a substitute for memory but for "realization." If we follow Bion (1970) in seeing the endeavor to contain emergent states within the "mental sphere" as a constant struggle for individuals and groups, the case can be seen as a failure of "psychic containment." First, within the girl whose phantasies were not expressed in thoughts or dreams, but in the development of hypochondriasis and the location of a feared disorder in a body organ. Second, within the family whose anxieties were not expressed in ideas but enacted in the dramas that spilled over into the hospital. Finally, in the professionals drawn into the case who took atypical drastic steps rapidly more than once and were stirred into repetitive action rather than reflection, even though very concerned about the case.

Bion's view (1967) is that thinking is a development forced on the psyche by the pressure of thoughts and that a breakdown in the apparatus for thinking or dealing with thoughts may lead to a psychopathological development. He suggests "that what should be a thought becomes a thing in itself, fit only for evacuation" (p. 112). We might add, "and dramatization." He links this capacity for thinking to the dominance of Freud's "reality principle", and its failure as a regression to the pleasure principle. This, in turn hinges on the achievement of what Melanie Klein (1935) called the *depressive position*. As Hanna Segal suggests (1964), "in the depressive position then, the whole climate of thought changes . . . capacities for linking and abstraction develop" (p. 63). She points out that "psychic reality is experienced and differentiated from external reality, the symbol is differentiated from the object . . . in contrast with symbolic equation in which the symbol is equated with the original object giving rise to concrete thinking" (p. 63). I believe that this latter state, characteristic of the paranoid-schizoid position, is linked to a greater tendency to action rather than thought a more wholesale acting out as Rosenfeld describes (1965a) and a greater tendency to evoke action in others.

The implication is that families whose mode of mental operations are characteristic of the paranoid-schizoid position (Klein 1975) rather than the depressive position are not only unlikely to see themselves as the agents of their own disturbances but are likely to evoke unconsciously determined action in those around them. The process of projection or projective identification within the family leading to the perception of one member as the source of difficulties is familiar as the scapegoat phenomenon and may lead to referral of this person.

In many other cases, however, the principal manifestations occur around the family rather than in it. The members of a family whose relationships are experienced in the main in the paranoid-schizoid position as opposed to the depressive position are likely to feel persecuted rather than guilty, ill rather than worried, enmity rather than conflict, desperation rather than sadness. They are liable to be triumphant or if not, to feel squashed and to see others as either allies or opponents. Their tendency to take flight (by moving, changing partner, changing schools, etc.) is linked to their belief that psychic experience can be split off and left behind. By the same token there is a sense of being hunted and a fear of being cornered.

For people with these characteristics a place like a clinic where problems are focused on seems threatening and even the collation of information is felt to be unwelcome. It is not surprising therefore that they shun clinics, avoid meeting teachers, and become the chronically unsatisfactory cases of social services if, as is by no means always the case, they are in the lower social classes. If the family is among the more affluent or educated groups the dramatis personae tend to be different but the kind of happenings are similar. The professionals then may be solicitors, private medical advisers, family friends or relatives, colleagues or partners at work, divorce courts, Members of Parliament and so on. The risk of their becoming unknowingly involved in an enactment is as great with even less likelihood of its being recognized.

It is the recognition of these provocative or paralyzing effects in such cases that at least gives pause for reflection. This often produces the painful discovery of the limitations of help or the constraints involved in the situation. In turn it may lead to the possibility of taking uncomfortable but necessary steps or accepting small, significant changes rather than cherishing unrealized hopes for a transformation. The thesis that is argued here is that realization, and change as a consequence of realization, rather than change as an alternative to realization may prevent patterns that cross not only individual but generational boundaries.

THEORETICAL DISCUSSION

The clinical phenomenon described in this chapter is of the reproduction among professional workers and agencies of a pattern of object relationships that resemble those of some families with which they have contact. The repetitious pattern or event may take place between family members, family members and professionals, professionals and professionals, professionals and social agencies.

It is argued in the chapter that the phenomenon of repetition compulsion first described by Freud (1918) may be analogous to this and that an essential element in this concept is replacement of recollection (or any form of mental realization) by a blindly repeated pattern of events. In the instances referred to, the events transcend the individual's and his family's lives and reverberate among those associated with them. It is suggested that some of the processes grouped under the concept of projective identification, first used by Melanie Klein, may underlie the phenomenon. Since it appears to occur even where there is no direct contact (as may be observed in groups who simply discuss these cases) the mode of operation would seem to be by identification and replication, mobilized by something psychic analogous to resonance; that is to compare it to the physical phenomenon by which vibrations in one object can induce sympathetic vibrations in another at a distance, for example, musical instruments. This would seem to be a feasible metaphor if the assumption was made that certain basic internal object relationships are ubiquitous. Freud speculated in "The Wolf Man" (Freud 1918) that a knowledge of the primal scene might be phylogenetic, thus implying that a rudimentary form of the Oedipus complex would be an innate. It is implicit in Melanie

Klein's writings that some basic phantasies are innate concerning good and bad objects for example, and the primal scene. Roger Money-Kyrle with his description of "imageless expectations" and Wilfred Bion with his notion of "innate preconceptions" make this explicit.

In the passage of Freud's referred to above where he considers the possibility of instinctive knowledge as a hereditary endowment, he uses the German word *instinktiv*, where the word he usually used that is translated into the English as "instinctual" is *triebhaft*, which is open to the substitution of "drive." This is of some significance in view of the later development of the concept of unconscious phantasy, particularly in Kleinian writing. Susan Isaacs (1952), in her definitive paper, "The Nature and Function of Phantasy," considers unconscious phantasy as the mental expression of instincts; all impulses, all feelings, all modes of defense are experienced in phantasy (p. 83).

Authors influenced by Melanie Klein, such as Bion, Jaques, and Menzies, have described how groups may share such phantasies and collectively react to them. In his paper "Social Systems as a Defence against Persecutory and Depressive Anxiety," Jaques (1955) describes institutions as having beneath a manifest structure and function an underlying "unconscious function." He sees this as the maintenance of shared beliefs and activities which collectively defend against basic anxieties. He describes this as based on shared projections, that is, "when external objects are shared with others but used for common purposes of projection, phantasy social relationships may be established through projective identification with a common object . . . further elaborated by introjection" (p. 482).

Thus in the first example in this chapter the fundamental anxieties associated with the Oedipus complex would be mobilized in the phantasies of those in contact with the case. Then the defensive configuration mobilized of a sterile couple and a defeated third party, enacted unwittingly. While repetition prevailed and unwitting reenactment continued, realization could be avoided, constancy maintained, and conflict averted. In the second case described, change is threatening the family in the form of the emergence of a sexually mature young woman and provoking basic anxieties about such an object or past object. "Malignancy" is suspected and the "malign object" sought in various anatomical organs before being perceived by the professional group as the mother herself. Here the shared phantasy of a dangerous, disordered, female object was collectively defended against by action designed for removal.

Events involving families, and the elements of society in contact with them, in such cases as I have described, are thought about by many family therapists in terms derived from General Systems Theory, Cybernetics, and Information Theory. General Systems Theory (GST) was founded as a general science of organization and wholeness by Ludwig von Bertalanffy in 1940; it has a great deal in common with Cybernetics, a subject that dates from 1942 and was named in 1947 by Rosenbleuth and Wiener to describe the science of control and communication in the animal and machine. It emphasized particularly that the laws governing control are universal and do not depend on the classical dichotomy between organic and inorganic systems. This is expressed in GST in the concept of *structural isomorphism* or with an assumption of *dynamic equilibrium* (Schanck 1954); that is the maintenance of an overall steady state by any fluctuation in sub-elements being compensated so the system remains in total balance.

Systems may have recognizable subsystems and the improvement of one of these to the detriment of the system as a whole is described as *sub-optimization*; hence the warnings from some family therapists about treating individuals and from some sociologists about treating particular families rather than society. The ascending order of systems inside larger systems like Chinese boxes is often referred to as "hierarchies" and the rules governing patterns of behavior that is reproduced at different organizational levels are called "recursive." This is a term borrowed from linguistics to describe language rules that can be applied an indefinite number of times in generating sentences. The phenomena that I have referred to could perhaps be described as recursive in this sense.

It is not my intention to describe the application of these theories to family therapy in this chapter or to place the concepts that I am endeavoring to describe in relation to a systems approach to families. There is, however, one fundamental question raised by the notion of dynamic equilibrium whether applied to individuals or families, which has a place in psychoanalytic theory and I would like to pursue that as it influences the way the social system (whether it be a family or an institution) is perceived.

This notion of dynamic equilibrium is enshrined in a very influential systems approach to sociology in the work of Talcott Parsons in the 1950s and the related school of structural functionalism. This is a mode of theorizing in which particular features of social structures are explained in terms of their contribution in maintaining a self-equilibrating system as a viable entity. I find it of particular interest that sociological critics of this approach object to it on three particular grounds: (1) that it is tautologous, (2) that it explains stability and not change, and (3) that it ignores essential conflict. Critics of other schools who particularly make this last point are known as "Conflict theorists" and may in general be either pluralist or Marxist sociologists who regard conflict as inherent in society.

It is of interest to a psychoanalyst because it covers similar ground to that which Freud explored in the 1920s in particular in "Beyond the Pleasure Principle" (Freud 1920) and "Civilization and its Discontents" (Freud 1930). In these two books he reexamines his earlier ideas about the basic forces underlying man's behavior and social relationships. He had previously followed the idea that the basic determinant was the "pleasure principle." This he derived from Fechner's "constancy principle" or "tendency towards stability." Activity was therefore directed to restoring an earlier state of things. It looked like movement but sought quietude: the dominance of the pleasure principle was opposed, he had suggested, by the reality principle. He realized therefore that if this—which we could perfectly describe as dynamic equilibrium—was the only force, the elementary living entity would from its very beginning have no wish to change. If conditions remained the same it would do no more than constantly repeat the same course of life. He linked, therefore, the compulsion to repeat in the behavior and experience of people with this tendency which he described as "the inertia inherent in organic life." "The dominating tendency of mental life . . . is the effort to reduce, to keep constant or to remove internal tension due to stimuli—a tendency which finds expression in the pleasure principle." (1920, pp. 55–56).

This he named the *death instinct* since he saw its ultimate goal as returning in ways "immanent in the organism itself" to inorganic existence. He was careful to point out that self preservation and mastery were component instincts whose function it was to ward off any other possible ways to death and were themselves manifestations of this status quo seeking instinct. There was only one inherent source of opposition that existed because it was a living system and that was the urge to reproduce. The disturber of the peace, therefore, in the case of the human being, was Eros, his capacity for object love, which in the individual stood in opposition to his narcissism. As Freud put it, object instincts were in opposition to ego instincts.

In "Civilization and its Discontents" he went further, more clearly equating the life instincts with the disturbers of the peace within the individual and the death instincts with a "primary mutual hostility of human beings," which he saw as perpetually threatening civilized society with disintegration. The satisfaction, he thought, that derived from the exercise of this destructive urge lay in the fulfillment of the ego's old wish for omnipotence; aim inhibited, "moderated and tamed." He saw its satisfaction lay in control over nature.

Freud therefore came to see conflict as inevitable and expressed in ambivalence toward love objects who were both the source of desire and dissatisfaction, the origins of hope and the end of omnipotence. Melanie Klein later was to describe in the depressive position the attempts of the individual to resolve this basic ambivalence to the primary object and its consequences. An object relations theory that incorporates this basic conflict and its attendant persecutory and depressive anxieties sees social conflict as inevitable and social institutions as attempting to contain them.

As Freud described it, the compulsion to repeat unthinkingly was an expression of that tendency to constancy, to inertia, which he thought innate. The countertendency—to experience, to seek, to relate—he associated with the life instincts and the urge to change. We could argue therefore that the struggle to realize rather than repeat takes place within this basic conflict and that an element of discomfort, strain, or anxiety is inevitable in the process. When professional workers therefore are called upon to resist unconscious collusion in order to become aware of the existence of an underlying dynamic configuration, they will find themselves going against the grain of their own emotional inclinations.

7

The Significance of the Outsider in Families and Other Social Groups

ANNA DARTINGTON

In this chapter I explore some ideas about one profound human dilemma, that of the tension between the person and the group. We are all fundamentally alone with our own experience and at the same time, willingly or unwillingly, but inevitably, an integral part of human groups: at work, in families, as citizens and members of the wider society. I am drawing on my own various experiences as a psychotherapist in the psychoanalytic tradition, working with individuals and families, as a student of English literature, as a supervisor of health service profession- als, and as a consultant to groups of workers who wish to explore their internal dynamics and their relatedness to wider organizations. Inevitably I am also a person influenced and conditioned by my own twentieth century European experience, post-Empire, post-war, post-Marxist, post- Freudian, post-modernist and, politically speaking, overfed, undernour- ished, and anxious.

I have chosen to concentrate on the idea of the outsider, a relative term, so I need to clarify my use of it. I am thinking of the outsider as one who is part of a social group but who, for a variety of reasons, takes a position on the fringe or the edge of that group. The role of the outsider must be clearly distinguished from that of the outcast. The outsider is *of* the group and definitely performs some function *for* the group. Of course he or she may become an outcast but only if he or she becomes too much of a threat to the cohesion, structure, and belief system of that group.

I have been influenced in my choice of the term *outsider* by a book of that name written by Colin Wilson in 1956. The book is a somewhat erratic but fascinating analysis of the themes and preoccupations of European literature in the first half of the twentieth century, a period of literary history that retrospectively became known as Modernism. This is a general term relating to a number of experimental tendencies in the arts that came to prominence at this time. In European literature it is associated with the writings of T. S. Eliot, James Joyce, Virginia Woolf, Joseph Conrad, Franz Kafka, Jean-Paul Sartre, and Albert Camus, among others. Modernist writing took root in a dramatic social context, a European war in which thousands died anonymously and seemingly obediently, a massive social revolution in Russia and the successive periods of Stalinist and Nazi dictatorships. Naturally enough these writers became interested in the fate of the individual in the face of a mass movement or a coercive social system. Most of them experienced themselves as socially or philosophically marginal. Many were exiles from their country of origin, some were politically active on the radical left, most were influenced by Freud's ideas about the unconscious mind, and all were experimenting with new and more immediate methods of communication in poetry, prose and drama.

So the outsider might be the writer himself, the character in the book or play, or the reader who identifies with the desire to be more simply truthful and more himself despite the social consequences. Anyone who has worked in a group of people who, in the service of understanding group dynamics, attempt to put aside social convention and explore their authentic responses to each other, will know how difficult this is.

In the preface to the English-language edition of his novel *L'Etranger*, Camus wrote:

> . . . the hero of the book is condemned because he doesn't play the game. In this sense he is a stranger to the society in which he lives, he drifts in the margin in the suburb of private, solitary, sensual life. [1942, p. 7]

The outsider is well placed to observe the world. The marginal position is a potentially creative one because the intellectual and emotional distance from familiar experience makes a space for a new viewpoint or an original thought to take shape.

My own view is that in the service of ordinary healthy gradual separation from the original family group, an adolescent must take up a position of temporary outsidership. In the establishment of his or her own identity the adolescent needs to embrace skepticism. He or she must look anew and look askance at all the rules, values, and behaviors that have previously been taken for granted.

The move toward skepticism is an attempt to find a space for thinking one's own thoughts. Before this level of independent thought can be achieved there is usually a period of counterdependence during which a clumsy and reactive type of obstinacy is explored.

As I was writing this chapter I heard an exasperated mother of a 14 year old boy talking on the radio as follows: "He was always a happy-go-lucky kid and never any problems with things like writing his thank you letters but suddenly he has become a monster, he won't wash, he won't get up on time and has become a militant vegetarian." I am not quite sure what this mother meant by militant vegetarian but I heard it as "refusing my food."

Of course it is easy for other family members to minimalize the immature politics of the counterdependent phase. I have often noted, sometimes with amusement, that the younger children in the family can be particularly smug and superior about this "dirty baby person" that their elder sibling has become. However these early restless strivings toward a truly separate individuality soon become something that is far more threatening to the family group, which is the careful scrutiny of parental attitudes in relation to parental authority, the right to govern, if you like. The developing scepticism of the 15–18-year-old seems to concern itself primarily with the unveiling of hypocrisy in all its subtle forms.

At this point I would like to quote from Colin Wilson's (1956) book *The Outsider*. He is speaking about one aspect of the outsider's state of mind:

> The Outsider's case against society is very clear. All men and women have these dangerous, unnamable impulses, yet they keep up a pretence, to themselves, and to others; their respectability, their philosophy, their religion, are all attempts to gloss over, to make look civilized and rational something that is savage, unorganised, irrational. He is an Outsider because he stands for Truth. [p. 13]

If we take "Truth" to be not so much an intellectual conviction but what is felt instinctively to be true or real, then this is, I think, an accurate description of the subjective experience of the mid- to late adolescent in relation to his or her environment. Of course he or she may well have quietly decided in earlier childhood that the parents were to some extent suspect. The difference is that the adolescent is now powerfully in touch with his or her own "dangerous unnamable impulses," has some considerable comparative experience of the adult world, and the vocabulary to articulate troublesome perceptions and anxieties. What he or she perceives is likely to be part projection, part acutely accurate observation. The important thing is not so much who is right, who has the truth, but the extent to which the family can agree to differ.

The outsider is not one who seeks gratuitous rebellion or romantic isolation for its own sake, but because he wishes to construct his world view from a reliance on his own experience rather than from what he is told by others; he must take the risk of being at odds with others in his social group.

Readers who are familiar with the writings of the psychoanalyst Wilfred Bion will recognize this as a central theme of his work. In citing this, I am not only paying a debt to him, but acknowledging that the processes I am describing here in the context of the adolescent in the family, are generalizable to all social groups and to the struggles of individuals who wish to live and work with others but wish to avoid the mindlosing quality of institutionalization.

My work as a family therapist takes place in two significant contexts. One is that of philosophy, that is, I am working within the psychoanalytic tradition. What this means is that I am working not only with what is going on, but why it is going on, and in the service of the why, the meaning, I am interested in the fantasies of the family about itself, its ancestors, its belief system, its values, fantasies, also about me, my co-therapist, and our relationship, which will include questions and thoughts about *our* belief system, the therapists' "family" in a sense. The first thing, quite rightly, that they will want to know is are we sane, or sane enough, or are we so tied to one way of seeing things that we cannot tolerate their diversity. In other words they may wish to be reassured that we are sufficiently inside our own belief system, that is, know what we are about but also sufficiently outside of our own belief system, so that we are available to new thoughts. That is a wealth of imaginative reference to consider and that is why it takes time and why it is useful to have two family therapists working together who can think together between the sessions and refer together openly during the sessions if necessary.

As an insider I am greatly assisted by the theoretical background of Kleinian object relations theory and Bion's idea of unconscious basic assumptions in groups. As an outsider I try to work with my subjective experience within that general theoretical context.

The other significant context of my work is place. I work in a department that provides a service for adolescents and their relatives. This means that families come to us feeling they are in trouble because an adolescent is in pain and creating pain. In my own experience this is usually, but not always, the first child in the family to reach adolescence.

A recent referral letter to the Adolescent Department was sent by the family doctor. In it the doctor says,

> I would be most grateful if this 19-year-old could be assessed for the possibility of some form of psychotherapeutic intervention. John has just failed all his A levels, having failed to do any work for them whatsoever. This is in spite of the fact that he was absolutely desperate to leave home.
>
> John appears to suffer from intermittent panic attacks, in between which he may cry for hours on end and become incapable of coherent speech. He denies that he is suicidal, but is finding it impossible to do any work. His parents don't know what to do with him. He hopes to break free from them but currently is completely unable to, as he has no job and is not studying.
>
> John's father is a very high powered scientist who has in fact had "breakdowns" at times of professional stress. The mother is a teacher, and is very distressed by her son's lack of academic success and lack of motivation to do a job.

This is a quite typical referral and I have chosen it because it highlights the inside/outside dilemma of John's very well. One can feel the loneliness of his distress and the bitterly painful disappointment and noncomprehension of the parents. There seems to be a complete breakdown in communication in this family and the doctor clearly wants us to know that there is a powerful belief system in operation in this family that relates to the primacy of intellectual work and achievement. We could speculate in a rather simplistic way that what is going on here is that John is rebelling against the family belief system. Though it is likely that this is a part of the picture, what comes across is John's paralysis of motive, his absolute inability to move into negotiation, with his parents, or outside to the world of friends, work or college, that is his inability to become actively angry inside the family, or to do "his own thing" actively outside it. It may be that John finds himself caught in a contradiction, that to please his parents he must sacrifice the one thing he feels he has, the capacity to be different.

I would like to put John's dilemma alongside the autobiographical writings of one of the modernist writers Franz Kafka. In 1919, when Kafka was 36, five years before he died, he wrote an autobiographical note about his family life entitled "Letter to His Father." In this short extract Kafka recalls the guilt and shame that he felt because he could not be the man that he was convinced his father wanted him to be.

You encouraged me, when I saluted and marched smartly, but I was no future soldier, you encouraged me when I was able to eat heartily or even drink beer with my meals, or when I was able to repeat songs, singing what I had not understood, or prattle to you using your own favorite expressions, imitating you, but nothing of this had anything to do with my future.

I was weighed down by your mere physical presence. I remember, for instance, how we often undressed in the same bathing hut. There was I, skinny, weakly, slight; you strong, tall, broad. Even inside the hut I felt a miserable specimen, and, what's more, not only in your eyes but in the eyes of the whole world, for you were for me the measure of all things. But then when we stepped out of the bathing hut before the people, you holding me by my hand, a little skeleton, unsteady, barefoot on the boards, frightened of the water, incapable of copying your swimming strokes, which you, with the best in intentions, but actually to my profound humiliation, always kept on showing me, then I was frantic with desperation and at such moments all my bad experiences in all spheres fitted magnificently together. [1925, p. 10]

One is struck by the pathos of these recollections and the powerlessness of this sensitive boy who could not disappoint his father by becoming himself, despite the fact that he clearly does not want to "play the game" as Camus put it. It was only later in his adult situation of self-imposed solitude that Kafka was able to fully articulate his own experience. His famous novel, *The Trial* opens with his chilling sentence: "Someone must have slandered Joseph K; because one morning, without his having done anything wrong, he was arrested" (1925, p. 1).

Over the twelve years or so that I have been working with families I have observed that in some of them, outsidership as I am defining it, that is, as a phase of necessary skepticism, is felt to be quite impossible. In these families it seems one is either right inside the family business or right out, an outcast in fact. The conflict seems to be to do with the families' unconscious conviction that: (1) the wish to separate is synonymous with hatred, (2) the families' reserves of love will not survive this hatred, (3) family catastrophe will ensue.

The unconscious phantasy of catastrophe is felt, to use Bion's term, as a *nameless dread* (Bion 1962), something akin to the terror of complete fragmentation. Readers who are familiar with Melanie Klein's work will recognize this state of mind as associated with the "paranoid-schizoid position" (Klein 1946), which is characterized by primitive mechanisms of defense, such as a splitting of internal experience and the denial of external reality.

I would like to share some experiences I have had with two families, whom I will refer to as Family A and Family B. Both were referred to the clinic by their general practitioner. Both were families of four members: mother, father, and two teenage daughters, one approximately two years older than the other. Both families had requested psychotherapeutic help out of desperation as a kind of last resort when the older daughter, who was the ill one, was around 18 years of age, and the younger daughter around 16.

The similarity in the structure and presentation of the two family groups, while in no way constituting a formal research sample, provided the opportunity to study contrast and comparison in the context of some shared assumptions of the families and our own.

I will present a picture of each family separately before returning to the common aspects that relate to the theme of this chapter. Where possible I will highlight the transference and countertransference experience, what we might call the psychoanalytic road to the family subtext. This is more clearly verifiable when working in co-therapy. With both these families I was lucky to be working with an experienced psychoanalyst and trusted psychiatric colleague, Jorge Thomas, whom I knew well enough to be able to share open discussion of our experience and to tolerate and examine disagreement between us.

Family A with daughters Alice 18 and Angela 16 were referred by the GP who wrote:

> I would be grateful if you could possibly see these parents. They have a daughter Alice who is now nearly 19 who has had behavioral problems for three or four years. These initially took the form of obsessions and complex ritualistic behavior. She herself has been seen by a psychotherapist in North London and was referred to a Psychiatric Department. However she has been disillusioned by her dealings with psychiatric services and has now refused to consider further referral. She is at present at private college taking "A" levels.[1] She still has some obsessions but her main problem is sudden and irrational outbursts of anger when she becomes particularly violent toward her mother but most especially her father. She has one younger sister of whom she is extremely jealous.
>
> Her parents are both very worried that it is going to lead to uncontrollable physical violence either on the part of Alice or possibly her father in self defense. She has actually tried to attack him with a knife. They don't want Alice to be forcibly restrained and as it seems impossible to persuade her to accept further help at present, I wonder

---

[1] These are advanced level of exams in Britain, usually taken at school or sixth form college, one or two years after ordinary level exams, and necessary for acceptance at University.

whether it would be possible for them to be seen at the Tavistock. I feel the adult psychiatric service in this area is not geared to cope with the specialized needs of this family and I would be grateful for your help and advice.

We wrote, inviting the whole family. Mrs. A. acknowledged our letter and sent a ten-page history of Alice's problems. The main points of the letter were as follows: Alice had developed obsessional rituals since age 14. Her rituals are concerned with washing, eating, and the fixing of objects in her room. At times when her parents had interfered with her rituals to get her to an appointment or to school she had kicked them and growled like an animal.

She had some behavior therapy in which her therapist persuaded her to go to the hairdresser without three days of praying, which had been her custom. This had been a disastrous experience and only seemed to prove to Alice that all her rituals were indeed necessary.

Despite her problems Alice passed 7 O levels exams at age 16.[2] Now she has stopped attending college. She says she has a respiratory illness. She is constantly blowing her nose and spitting but no physical cause has been found. Mrs. A. ends her letter: "It is because we can't talk to Alice about these problems without her losing her temper that we desperately need experienced counseling to help us through the intolerable situation."

The parents came alone for the first session. They were professional people, the father involved with legal work, the mother a local counselor involved in community work, but she had had to give this up to look after Alice.

They looked worn and tense and proceeded to give us yet more information in painstaking detail. When we asked where Alice was now, they said that she now spent her time in her room and refused to come out. Mrs. A. was taking up meals on a tray and leaving them outside Alice's room. Alice had started communicating with them by passing notes under her door.

The interaction among the four of us had a distinctive quality. I found it hard to think and the room that we saw them in seemed much smaller than it actually was. I recognized in my own mind that their daughter was probably very ill, but felt that an exploration along these lines in this first session would feel like a full frontal attack on their apparent goodwill and painstaking efforts to tolerate their daughter's

---

[2] These are "ordinary" level exams taken at about the end of compulsory school age and before leaving or continuing on into the sixth form. 7 O levels implies a good standard and the possibility of a further academic career.

bizarre symptoms and behavior. They seemed to be very proud of their efforts to manage the situation and related to us rather as if we were management consultants. Mr. A. used the language of the boardroom at one point saying "We would like to feel you could endorse our strategy." When I suggested that it did seem very difficult to talk about their feelings about their daughter's illness or indeed about coming to us for help, they replied briskly that they had been to busy to reflect on their feelings. Having briefly caught sight of the pain behind this defensive remark, my colleague verbally acknowledged the possibility that it felt humiliating to come to the clinic, if, as it seemed, their shared culture was one in which people should be able to manage by themselves. There was no immediate response to this but at the end of the session Mr. A. said as a parting remark that one of their relatives had been a founder member of our clinic.

After the session Jorge and I considered our own position. We both felt that a tragedy was being presented as some sort of behavioral problem requiring a corrective. The parents had not asked our opinion, nor did they seem interested in it. They appeared to want us to join them and accept their diagnosis of the situation, which was that love and patience would eventually win the day. It was a fierce, almost evangelical position and they had partly come to the clinic to have this position authorized by the psychotherapeutic establishment. This left us alone with the onerous task of addressing the unspeakable possibility of psychotic breakdown and of hospitalization. In the second session Mrs. A. handed us some of the notes that Alice was writing to them. This is a short extract:

> You don't have the right to "tread on me" just because I'm your offspring. That is something you *HAVE* to learn for the sake of a happy family, it's no good loading all the disagreements on my back and saying, "well she's different to us, she'll have to go." You're supposed to be an intelligent human being you should know that life doesn't work like that, if you don't have relatives that are clones of you and your ideals you can't just throw them out, just as you can't throw out all your workmates in an office if you don't like them. We are stuck together and I will always be a part of you even if you put me on a rocket and sent me to Mars — which you can't anyway, you can't push me around or *OUT* when you feel like it. There is such a thing as public opinion and you'd find yourself with a lot of "*HEAT* and *BAD PRESS*" if you did try to do that, yes, *even though I'm 18*!

Mr. A. said there was something important to tell us — that when Angela had been born, Alice was very jealous. One day when Mrs. A. was nursing Angela, Alice had demanded to join Angela in mother's arms. Mr. A. had prevented her and Alice had had a terrible tantrum and had held her breath to the point that Mr. A. thought she would die. He had been terrified and had never forgotten this. Mrs. A. said that she had wanted to do everything right as a mother and had always carried Alice everywhere in her arms as a baby, so of course it was understandable that Alice could not bear to be displaced by Angela. I said that as they told the story they seemed strongly identified with the rage of their frustrated baby and the parents acknowledged that they too disliked the uncertainty of any waiting situation. This linked with the countertransference experience, which was that the family wished to incorporate us and carry bits of our functions and insights away inside them. Our interpretations were either welcomed hungrily or spat back immediately. We came to recognize that when Mr. A. responded to our comments with the exclamation "Exactly!" something was being devoured with a savagery that could only be to do with some very primitive terror about having nothing.

As time went on it became clear that this family had cultivated a tyrant in their midst, a tyrant who was now 18 years old and had virtually taken over control of the household. Alice had a cough, she was convinced that she had a lung disease, she demanded an endless supply of tissues. If they did not come from Mark s & Spencer she spat on the sheets or the floor. Mrs. A. was becoming her servant, Mr. A. her protector. We were reminded of Herbert Rosenfeld's idea of the narcissistic gang in the mind. Speaking of his work with individual patients Rosenfeld (1971) states:

> The destructive narcissism of these patients appears often highly organized, as if one were dealing with a powerful gang dominated by a leader, who controls all the members of the gang to see that they support one another in making the criminal destructive work more effective and powerful. However, the narcissistic organization not only increases the strength of the destructive narcissism, but it has a defensive purpose to keep itself in power and so maintain the status quo. The main aim seems to be to prevent the weakening of the organization and to control the member of the gang so that they will not desert the destructive organization and join the positive parts of the self or betray the secrets of the gang to the police, the protecting superego, standing for the helpful analyst, who might be able to save the patient. [p. 249]

Meltzer and Harris, (1986) recognizing that some families had an observable tendency to operate like this, put forward the notion of a "gang family," a tightly closed system that is characterized by omnipotence, brooks no dissent, and in consequence no skeptical outsidership. However this formulation has to be understood as a shared state of mind to which a family has a tendency to revert. It does not imply a fixed or permanent state of affairs.

Family A. came to see us every week, soon bringing Angela, the younger sister. She, at 16, was underdeveloped, closely identified with her mother, had little social life, but was working conscientiously at school with the intention of applying to study psychology at Oxford, and told us that she was afraid of leaving home.

Four weeks passed during which Jorge and I tried to understand what Alice might be carrying for the whole family. At this time we felt ourselves to be the container for their fears. It was necessary for us to spend time together between sessions attempting to distinguish between the family's projections and our own intuitive view of Alice, who seemed to be becoming psychotic. Since Alice had consistently refused to come and see us, Jorge decided that it would be appropriate to mobilize his psychiatric role and he advised the parents to speak to their doctor to obtain a domiciliary visit from a psychiatrist. They were terrified and appalled by the idea that they would willingly allow Alice to be taken from them to a psychiatric hospital. "She would never forgive us and anyway she would refuse to go," they said.

Three weeks later the inevitable crisis happened. Alice had threatened to jump from a window if they did not supply a favorite food. It was 11 P.M. and the shops were closed. Alice barricaded her door and took up a position on the windowsill. The parents called an ambulance and the ambulance crew called a psychiatrist. Alice was admitted on a section, which her father reluctantly agreed to. During her four months in the hospital, she came regularly to the family sessions, being brought by escort and ambulance.

These are some notes that I wrote after the sessions that Alice first attended with her family.

As they came into the room Alice was a vibrant, powerful presence. She spoke straightaway wanting to explain that she had wanted to come to see us before but had been ill with a respiratory condition. She talked with no pauses and the tension rose in the room as her monologue became accusatory. She seemed to want to tell us how her parents had been ill-treating her and to create a kind of courtroom situation. I felt very trapped by this takeover of the session and I said something to Jorge in front of them about there being absolutely no space for thinking in the room and that maybe we would have to allocate time if everyone should have the opportunity to speak. Alice continued to interrogate her father, accusing him of arrogance and of brainwashing. Jorge brought them back to their current situation and the circumstances of Alice's admission to hospital. She told us that she had only pretended to jump out of the window. It was only to make her parents get her a respiratory consultant. Then Alice looked at us

and said that her father had physically attacked her. Mother interrupted to explain that she had asked Father to break the door down to
get into Alice's room, that it was necessary. Alice looked at her father
with murderous hatred. Father smiled, half embarrassed, half hurt,
but also trying to keep his temper. He explained to us why he called
the doctor but now Alice could not bear him to speak. Like a bitterly
rivalrous sibling she tried to stop him from getting our attention.
Mother looked tense and said how painful it was when they took Alice.
I felt that her baby had been torn away from her and my image in the
room at the time was of a body in a coffin going behind the curtain in
a crematorium.

Angela the younger daughter was overcome with emotion,
sobbing like a child. She said she had been away when it happened, she
should have been around to support her parents. She seemed fearful,
like a child who feels her parents might be lost or damaged. Alice
seemed to find Angela's expression of concern intolerable and said
angrily to Angela "You should consider *my* feelings."

So we saw the primitive tyrannical aspect of this family in action, but we
also saw a glimpse of something else in Alice, her potential as a very
attractive, highly intelligent young woman and we could understand that
there might have been high hopes for her, hopes that were now unbearable
to recall. This session was almost an enactment of the story they had told
of Mr. A. holding the screaming toddler Alice, who threatened to stop
breathing if she was not allowed to displace baby Angela at mother's breast.
What she now called her respiratory illness seems to link with her
breastfeeding as a baby, and we could only conclude that in this family a
belief or myth had arisen in which separation was tantamount to dying.

It is also possible to see this kind of dynamic or basic assumption in
groups of people who are not related. Gordon Lawrence (1979) says of his
experience as a consultant to work groups that he has observed a number
of identifiable group myths, one of which he calls the Robinson Crusoe
myth. This is

> . . . a myth about omnipotency where the members feel that they are
> in control and command of the whole environment and nature.
> Usually there is an atmosphere of exploitation and control where
> everything is done for the members' own benefit or the group's own
> benefit without thinking about the others. It is some sort of group
> selfishness where the outside bodies, or even members in the group,
> can be treated like things or possessions. [p. 10]

My co-therapist and I often felt ourselves being treated like possessions. In
the process of working with them but as outsiders in their group we were

often distrusted and sometimes hated for expressing opinions at variance with theirs.

The psychiatric hospital was of doubtful help to Alice. She was given some mild tranquilizing medication, which gave her some potential space to think, but she refused any individual psychotherapeutic help and continues to do so. What she did gain from the hospital was the opportunity to exist and to socialize outside her family. She had some behavior therapy to help her limit her ritualistic coughing and spitting, and it was this capacity of the hospital to contain and set limits that probably helped her the most.

She was discharged home, despite our suggestion that she might spend some time in an aftercare hostel. However she was now able to leave the house to experiment with some part-time work, and recently to spend some months abroad with friends, phoning home to her family weekly, mainly with demands that they send her money.

Angela did go up to Oxford, although returning every weekend for the first term, fearing always that something terrible might have happened to her parents. Currently she is having some counseling at college, her family continues to attend at intervals, and the parents are gradually beginning to look at some of their own differences and disagreements.

We subsequently heard from Mother that her father, whom she loved, was a tyrant and it was a long time before Mr. A. was accepted by him as part of the family. Mr. A. told us that his sister always felt that their father preferred him and she had never been able to forgive her father for this, even after his death. These reported vendettas and grudges of family history seemed to confirm the nature of the anxieties in the family about a destructiveness that can never be mitigated or repaired, an eternity of hell in the imagination. The situation inside Family A was sometimes experienced as a claustrophobic jail. At other times the hell was projected into the world outside the family, which then became, in phantasy, full of fear and danger. Perhaps the only way to leave home in such a family is by omnipotent manic flight or violent evacuation.

Family B came to us in an even later stage of crisis. The doctor wrote:

> I would be grateful if you could see this family for counseling as soon as possible. Their eldest daughter, Barbara, who is 19 years old, was admitted to the psychiatric department of the X Hospital in February of this year with a diagnosis of schizophrenia and she remains in the hospital held on Section 3 of the Mental Health Act. Since Barbara's admission to the ward I have been giving Mrs. B. regular counseling, mainly of the supportive nature. We have both, however, now come to the conclusion that the family needs some more experienced and in depth counseling than I am able to give. This especially applies to Mr.

B., who has had very little support from outside the family over the last 10 months. Rebecca is, I believe, receiving some counseling from a teacher at school (she has successfully managed to get through her GCSEs over the summer despite her sister's illness). Mr. and Mrs. B. both work full time. Over the summer Barbara has been spending quite a lot of time away from the hospital for overnight stays at home and these have been particularly traumatic for Mrs. B. as many of Barbara's paranoid ideas are directed toward her.

Mr. and Mrs. B. enjoy a very close and open relationship and have been able to support each other throughout this difficult time. About two months ago Barbara was almost at the stage of being well enough to come home when she had a relapse and that idea had to be shelved. There are now plans for Barbara possibly to attend a Richmond Fellowship Unit.

I feel that his family needs counseling in not only accepting Barbara's illness and its very likely poor prognosis, but also in exploring the family dynamics that her illness has revealed.

The parents came alone for the first session. They were successful professional people, articulate, sensitive, and warmly concerned about their daughter. In their case their anxiety was expressed differently. It was Barbara's possible return home that they feared, and they were worried too about the effect of Barbara's illness on their younger daughter Rebecca.

They too had an early memory that they urgently disclosed. Mrs. B. spoke of a visit to the Natural History Museum. They were in the room where the enormous life-size effigy of the blue whale was suspended above them. Barbara was 4 years old and suddenly became completely distraught. She lay on the floor under the blue whale and screamed, rolling about, refusing to be picked up and filling the vast room with what they described as considerable terror. Mrs. B. wept as she spoke about it, remembering her bewilderment, her embarrassment, and her sense of absolute helplessness.

Mr. and Mrs. B. brought their younger daughter for the second session. They greeted us with big smiles, which we experienced as something to do with a wish to reassure us.

These are a few notes that I wrote about the opening of this session:

I introduced us to the younger daughter mentioning her name, Rebecca. She quietly corrected me saying, "No, Becky" which was the name she used in the family.

Jorge, my co-therapist said "So what thoughts after the last session?" All three of them looked puzzled and this seemed to be because he had not used the verb in his sentence. At this moment it was very apparent to us that we were strangers, using strange language.

Mrs. B. then said how helpful the first session had been, how carefully we had listened to them, how we had made them feel we could help. This seemed genuinely grateful and yet one could not escape the feeling that we were being given good marks for our performance. Soon after this, Becky leaned across to her mother and said, "You have something on your face." It was a bit of fluff and mother dutifully brushed it away.

This small and seemingly insignificant extract does, I think, convey an atmosphere in which everything that was not familiar was potentially fearful.

Later in the same session we heard that Mrs. B.'s mother had died in a dreadful accident at sea, when on holiday her parents car had rolled from a ferry into the water. Mrs. B.'s father had survived but had been unable to rescue his wife. The pain of this tragedy seventeen years ago was still raw in her mind as she said to us, in great emotional pain, "You see Barbara's illness was not the first but the second great loss in my life." As she spoke, her husband put his arm around her and we too were visibly moved and very much in touch with the sense of the absolute helplessness of the human condition — the helplessness of the infant self when containment is inadequate or absent.

The family went on to talk about Mrs. B.'s state of anxiety if any family member did not come home at the time they were expected, how she continually anticipated another accident, although she realized what a burden this was to them. Jorge asked Becky how she coped with this and she said, "Well I just know that if I've told Mum I'll be back at two, then I must be back, whereas some of my friends would say to hell with that." "But it's all right," she added, "my friends understand." Later in the session all these three members of the family shared a feeling that the Barbara they had known had died, and the Barbara that they now knew who stayed with them at weekends was a frightening stranger. In a more recent session, after I had pointed out that Mr. B. seemed to be relating to me in a very tentative, protective manner, he talked about his very anxious mother whom he constantly and hopelessly tried to reassure, and both parents said, "Our children brought us their nightmares and now we bring you ours."

In fact we have been able to help them to contain some of the anxiety. Barbara did leave the hospital, spent some time in an aftercare hostel, and now has her own flat in a supportive home. She has a boyfriend and the parents visit her regularly. Becky has been able to work for her A levels and has plans for university, although at times she fears that she too may become ill during this period of her life when separation from her family is anticipated.

These families, as you will have appreciated, were in a great deal of mental pain, the pain of a lost mind, a family member who was felt to be temporarily dead to family life, an exile to a mad world.

They often asked the question, "Why did this happen to us?" "What is it about us?" and understandably they both desired and feared the answer. We were naturally wary of an omnipotent diagnosis but tried to set up a discussion in these families about the intensity of their interactions and relative absences of close relationships outside the family. The answer was often that they didn't know any differently. "This," they said, "was what family life was like." With Mr. and Mrs. A. in particular it was as if the parents' families of origin and the subsequent family they created were merged into one so that they experienced having been in the same institution all their life.

Let us look at some of the common features of the families I described.

1. They were families of higher than average intelligence. The parents were functioning successfully in the world of work. They had comparatively high levels of expectation of the children.

2. The parents, having experienced emotionally unresolved difficulties in the family of origin, wished to create a new family that would "get things right" and were determined to do so.

3. There was an atmosphere of correctness and perfectionism that veered dangerously on the side of a preference for the expression of literal fact rather than the expression of a more personal imaginative reality.

4. There was an emotional intensity that had consciously to do with supporting the family ethos, but was unconsciously felt as a demand to conform at any personal cost. Resistance led to exhausting battles of willpower between mother and daughter in both cases.

Any one of these aspects may be recognizable in any family but the combination of all four seemed to create a situation in which the phase of necessary skepticism, the phase that I am suggesting is essential for healthy individuation, is absent.

If an adolescent does not have the opportunity to experience the phase of necessary skepticism inside the family, he or she feels unconsciously compelled to exercise some form of violence to break free or to contemplate staying forever. In most cases this conflict does not take the form of a psychotic breakdown. An adolescent may develop a psychosomatic illness as an attempt to remain a child in the family. Anorexia would be a good example of this. Delinquency might serve another unconscious purpose, which would be to alienate the parents and to set in train a process that might lead to violent ejection from the family.

The intensity of the difficulties around separation seem to me to depend on three important variables: (1) the grandparental influence, (2) the extent to which the parents project into their children, and (3) the sensitivity of any particular child.

I will consider each of these briefly:

The grandparental influence: As a family therapist I see very few families in which the grandparents are alive, and/or in touch with them. In this case the children's phantasies about the grandparents are usually important and are often indicative of the family belief system.

In family A the consciously shared belief was that there was a close loving family in which liberal attitudes, particularly tolerance, played a major part. They were shattered by Alice's breakdown when in her psychotic parody of a tyrannical despot, the unconscious influence of her autocratic grandfather was brought vividly and horrifically to life. As John Byng-Hall (1988) suggests, a family myth is a consensus of what home truths are not to be told.

As I have suggested, it is not unusual for a family's self deception to be challenged by the skeptical truth-telling, hypocrisy-exposing impulses of adolescence. However if unconscious myths and secretiveness prevail, the black sheep of the family may be reenacted in desperate fashion with tragic consequences.

The secretiveness in the family may or may not be deliberate. It is more likely to be linked with the parents' unconscious denial of some undigested and unbearable historical pain.

In family B the "blue whale" story helped us to connect Barbara's adolescent breakdown with her mother's unresolved mourning of her own mother's horrific death.

As the therapists, we often found ourselves in some kind of grandparental role with the family. Mr. A. seemed to be acknowledging this when he said, "A member of our family founded your clinic." In a more direct way Mr. B. said, "We bring you our nightmares." These nightmares are very often the forgotten nightmares of the parents' childhood.

This links with my second variable, the extent to which the parents project into the children. Ordinary projections of the "I think you are going to be like me. I was never very good at spelling" variety are common enough and can be easily accepted or refuted with good humor. Projective identification, in which a role is unconsciously assigned to a child and unconsciously accepted by that child, is a potentially lethal blow to the child's capacity to emerge with his or her own unique identity, an identity that in due course permits a separate life outside the family. What I have termed the phase of necessary skepticism is the phase in which the adolescent begins to throw off the mantle of various assumed identities. In a family culture that is sufficiently open to external influence and tolerant of differences this does not need to be particularly violent exercise, although inevitably at this time the adolescent is likely to be particularly pedantic about what is the truth and what is a lie. It seemed to me that when Alice and Barbara approached this phase they did not know who they were. For so long the participants in a family organization that merged into, and even colonized the minds of each other, the new world held nothing but terror. You will remember that Alice, in her psychotic "police state" mentality wrote, "We are stuck together and I'll always be a part of you even if you put me on a rocket and send me to Mars."

As I write this, I am aware of the danger of being seen to blame parents for driving children crazy, a kind of post-Laingian position. There are, of course, destructive, psychotic parents. We can hardly be unaware of that in our current climate of sexual abuse and satanic cults. Many children run away or are taken away from these families long before adolescence; others tragically become permanent victims. In the cases I am describing, the parents wanted to provide their children with the best that they could offer. The tragedy seemed to be that the intensity of their well-intentioned wishes was incompatible with a particular child's capacity to receive them and make discriminate use of them.

In 1919, T. S. Eliot wrote a critique of Shakespeare's play *Hamlet*. Of course the dilemma of Hamlet the character is the dilemma of the Outsider writ large but unfortunately both time and context do not permit an exploration of that here. Eliot was unhappy with the play because he felt that there was an imbalance between the emotionality of the main character and the external events of the plot, which in Eliot's view did not match or justify the extent of Hamlet's anxiety and emotional intensity.

> The only way of expressing emotion in the form of art is by finding an "objective correlative"; in other words, a set of objects, a situation, a chain of events which shall be the formula of that particular emotion; such that when the external facts . . . are given, the emotion is immediately evoked. [Eliot 1919, p. 48]

I think Eliot's idea of an objective correlative has much in common with Bion's notion of a container. As the mother's mind and thinking capacity hold and process the infant's anxiety, so the structure of the plot holds and makes sense of the events of the play. What interested me particularly, about Eliot's essay was that it also conveyed something of the artist's need to make art, the urgency to outwardly realize an internal intensity of feeling and to find a suitable object for it. In his concluding remarks Eliot himself says,

> The intense feeling, ecstatic or terrible, without an object or exceeding its object, is something which every person of sensibility has known; it is doubtless a subject of study for pathologists. It often occurs in adolescence: the ordinary person puts these feelings to sleep, or trims down his feelings to fit the business world; the artist keeps them alive by his ability to intensify the world to his emotions. [p. 49]

It is possible that some people look to their children as both the culmination and container of all their intensity and almost therefore the purpose of their life. It does seem to be the case that the majority of families in which children are psychologically intruded on are those in which the parents need the children to *be* something *for* them but this is expressed unconsciously in that the parents are not usually aware of these needs in themselves, or of their projections.

At a later stage in the therapies of both family A and family B, it became evident that both Alice and Barbara, who were highly intelligent children, had each been conceived of as a potential genius. But all this had taken place long ago in the shared imaginative life of parents and children.

This leads to my third variable, the sensitivity of any particular child. I am thinking here of a particularly heightened sensitivity to atmosphere, to detail, and to the authenticity of the environment. By authenticity I mean that the child is, perhaps from an early age, unusually aware that something doesn't make sense or something doesn't "smell" or "feel" right. This kind of awareness is often attributed to high intelligence. This may be so but I think it is more specifically linked to a heightened imaginative capacity. This is evident in the extract that I quoted earlier from Kafka's autobiographical writings in which he remembers the misery and confusion of his multiple perceptions, what he thought, what he thought his father thought, and even what he thought his father thought he thought. As I noted earlier, the misery seemed to have to do with the knowledge that he could not speak about it. To rebel and be himself, he risked losing the love of the father that he both feared and admired. His salvation perhaps was to write, which he did from childhood to his early death. In his novel *Metamorphosis*, Kafka wrote about a family member who woke up to find himself transformed into a beetle whose fate was to be at first ostracized and then annihilated by his family.

In my list of sensitivities I am implicity including that of emotional sensitivity. Of course all children are emotionally sensitive because they are dependent on their parents' love and thoughtfulness. However if one agrees as I do with Melanie Klein's notion of innate disposition in children, then we can observe that some children even from infancy can tolerate a greater degree of frustration than others, and can also hold on for longer periods to a good internal object or some notion of a better future in the face of a present despair.

In the work with families A and B we heard many times about the tantrums of both Alice and Barbara in early childhood. This is a highly speculative area here because tantrums in themselves are often the child's way of objecting appropriately to some unwelcome intrusion, a baby sister being a very good example. However the reported frequency of the tantrums introduces the possibility that these children were particularly intolerant of the absence of a continuously good external object.

In conclusion I believe that if we are fortunate, we have some ability throughout our lives to be in some state of outsidership when occasion demands. In childhood we could hardly call it skepticism, although I have certainly seen such a look on a baby's face.

In a climate of temporary despair, whatever its nature, it is something to do with holding on to realistic hope and trying to think one's own thoughts, whether those thoughts are that the good understanding parent will return, or that one will make one's own mark in the adult world, or that one will be released from captivity in some oppressor's jail, or that the work that one does will lead sometime, somewhere, to someone else's hope or creativity.

SECTION III
Psychotherapy with Families

8

Working with the Dynamics of the Session

SALLY BOX

> A lot of people come to philosophy wanting to be told how to live — or wanting to be given an explanation of the world, and with it an explanation of life — but it seems to me that to have at least the former desire is to want to abnegate personal responsibility. One shouldn't want to be told how to live . . . And therefore one shouldn't come to philosophy looking for definitive answers. It's an entirely different thing to seek clarification of one's life, or clarification of the issues involved in particular problems which confront one, so that one can more effectively take responsibility for oneself and make decisions with a fuller, clearer understanding of what is at stake.

This comment was made by the philosopher Bryan Magee, in an impressive series of television conversations called "Men of Ideas" (1978). It has helped to highlight for me an important aspect of the approach to family therapy that is the subject of this book, and that may differentiate it from many others.

I would like to explore here some of the technical implications of this way of thinking as it relates to working with the families who come asking for help. How do we deal with their wish "to be told how to live" and their subsequent bewilderment at the lack of advice and suggestions that we offer? For even when the conscious wish in coming to the clinic is to "seek clarification of the issues involved" they may find themselves immersed in the very opposite of the rational processes anticipated. One of the most difficult but inescapable realizations emerging, especially from psycho-analysis, is that such issues are not necessarily susceptible to meaningful clarification on a purely rational basis. Problems based on unconscious, long-established emotional conflicts require a shift of emotional stance if there is really to be a fuller, clearer understanding. Moreover, the question for us has been what sort of method can provide the opportunity for such a shift to take place. Is it possible for these unconscious conflicts to surface and be enacted in such a way that they can be better understood and experienced differently in the light of a new response? It is the issues involved in providing such a method, suitable in the context of family work, that constitutes the main theme of this chapter and with the help of material from two rather different sorts of families, I would like to focus particularly on the way that the problems of handling the implicit anxieties are highlighted at the critical times of beginnings and breaks.

THE METHOD

If a major aspect of the therapeutic task is to promote the chances for genuine choices to increase then the methodological task becomes one of engaging with the compulsive qualities, patterns, and reactions that constantly qualify or impede those possibilities. It becomes one of pro-viding a space in which the obstacles to independent thought can emerge in the interaction of the session and can be met anew.

It is possible to think of the session as such a space in which a kind of microcosm of one patient family's world can exist and in which they can experience, in relation to each other and to us, some of the crucial conflicts that concern them. The family can use the boundaries that we provide for the members to demonstrate their particular patterns and preoccupations through the way they are with us. We, as therapists, may then draw upon our experiences with them in the sessions to help us understand these patterns and to interpret the underlying conflicts to which they relate.

In this sense, it is a setting that provides for significant internal dramas to be relived here, with the therapists not taking a history or reconstructing a picture of the early lives of the patient, but trying to create a situation in which the history is recalled spontaneously when the living internal relationships associated with it are experienced in the present.

The reader may understand that behind this lies a particular view of therapeutic interaction, such that if the therapist can be available for the powerful feelings invoked and can help to articulate the internal dramas that have the family in their grip and that interfere with their capacity to move freely in their lives, it may be possible for feelings previously unmanageable and extruded to find some means of expression and some possibility of being reowned. There is a chance that whatever the immediate reaction, the overall experience will be one of relief and a little step toward integration of each one's world, a living, learning experience as it were, with the therapists and the session serving as container, or, in other words, as a medium for working on unmanageable aspects and a mediator of family projections. The implication is that the increased scope implied in such integration carries with it the capacity to own aspects of the self hitherto split off and disowned, although the awareness of limitations and conflicts which this involves may at times seem a high price to pay for the enrichment it enables. Those who are familiar with it will recognize in the description of this process the debt it owes to Dr. Bion's (1962a) concept of *container/contained*.

Briefly, in terms of the treatment situation, the notion of containment refers to the way the impact of an experience—one's own or another's—can be registered and dwelt upon sufficiently for it to take some shape in the mind and be put in words that can help the patient to manage it.

In "A Theory of Thinking" (1962b), Bion suggests as a model the idea of the mother or her breast, as the container for the infant's intolerable feelings:

> If the infant feels it is dying, it can rouse fears that it is dying in the mother. A well-balanced mother can accept these and respond therapeutically; that is to say, in a manner that makes the infant feel it is receiving its personality back again but in a form that it can tolerate— the fears are manageable by the infant personality. If the mother cannot tolerate these projections the infant is reduced to continued projective identification carried out with increasing force and frequency. [1962b, 1967, p. 114]

> The infant projects part of its psyche, namely its bad feelings, into a good breast. . . . During their sojourn in the good breast they are felt to have been modified in such a way that the object that is reintrojected has become tolerable for the infant psyche. [1962a, p. 90]

Put in these terms, the issue would be what kind of containment or container is available for the painful, conflictual, or other undigested feelings and what happens to the family member or therapist who is the repository for them. The difference between a mother who can bear and somehow "metabolize" her baby's fear and pain, and one who, for example, is herself terrified of them, is a crucial element in the child's development and in his own subsequent capacity to bear and digest such feelings for himself. Similarly, perhaps, for the patient family.

What do these principles mean in practice? How are they observed in action and what is the process of transformation implicit in the idea of the therapist as the prime object for projections?

TECHNICAL ISSUES RELATED TO THE EARLY MEETINGS

It must be said that in many of the families that we see, no one has come acknowledging a wish for help for themselves as an individual and there is great uncertainty as to whether they dare engage in the kind of exploration together that is on offer. Many, as in the first case to be discussed, are actually coming more or less explicitly because of difficulties in living together or because a delicate and hard-won balance in the family is collapsing. A death in the family or the onset of adolescence is often enough to topple it. In practice, it may seem to be the referral itself or the experience of coming to the Clinic that is felt to represent the final tip of the scales: the extremely precarious tolerance of anxiety in these families tends to lead to its being converted immediately into action, or short-circuited altogether. In this way, all, including the therapists, may feel extremely inhibited about voicing uncomfortable perceptions for fear of provoking impulsive or violent reactions and destroying the possibility of treatment before it has begun.

It is not surprising then that the initial meeting is filled with anxiety—for therapists as well as patients. The very virtues of the setting and of a reflective, rather than a directive stance seem also to present its greatest problems and make the most exacting demands on the worker. To reflect on, rather than react to, is a hard transition to make at the best of times for therapist as well as family. It is a major task to recognize the pressures to enact the family's projections and the resulting tendency is to start behaving like a stage director, or a judge, or some other significant figure from their inner world, especially if it finds a corresponding figure in our own.

In practice, the problem is not only to recognize when and how this is happening and what is the particular constellation of which one finds oneself a part, but then to recover sufficient space in one's mind to discover a way of formulating the experience for the family so as to provide them also with a corresponding sense of space.

Particular problems arise from the fact that it is often in the most troubled families that the dynamics are most naked, and it may be easy for a therapist to observe a pattern in the family and then voice it to them in the hope that they will be able to learn from it and change accordingly. But many patients, because of their great emotional fragility, have developed defenses so pervasive that they are not able to use an observation put to them in this way.

As therapists we often find ourselves with these sorts of families caught between being persecutors driving them away on the one hand, or in some comfortable collusion that fails really to engage with the ill or problematic part of them on the other. This is a major reason for the value set upon the discipline of working in the transference, where the dynamic patterns are taken as they occur in the relationship to the therapist.

Contributions from psychoanalytic work with psychotic and border-line individual patients have spoken very precisely to both aspects of this dilemma and have helped toward understanding and responding to the projections involved in ways that I have found most relevant to our work with families. See for instance papers by Steiner on borderline patients (1977, 1979). In relation to excessive feelings of persecution they highlight, for instance, the importance of the therapist being prepared to experience himself or herself and be experienced, as the "bad" object or to represent some unwanted aspect of the self that the patient himself cannot as yet entertain.

So in families, while it is clearly a crucial part of the therapist's work to identify what he may be carrying for the patients, it may be necessary for him to be identified himself with it first and let himself be the focus for its examination, if he is not simply going to persecute the patient and drive him away. The efforts to struggle with these issues may be discernible in our interaction with the families to be described.

BEGINNING WORK WITH THE DUN FAMILY

In the Dun family, the fear of dependency and the taboo on neediness, or feelings otherwise considered childish, did not exclude concern and sympathy between the members but made it very difficult for them to be at all tolerant of their own pain or available in practice for that of each other. This family consisted of five members. The father, a lawyer, had recently died, leaving an older son, no longer at home, and two teenage daughters, Jane and Patricia, who lived at home with their mother. It was the younger of these two girls who was the referred patient though her family had agreed to come together with her, after a number of previously unsuccessful attempts at individual treatment. In fact, "unsuccessful" was the operative word for Patricia. She felt unable to work and enjoy life—

unable to get out of bed much of the time—and a hopeless failure compared to her sister, who was viewed as active, happy, and successful, and only later revealed her own worries about herself in terms of "drugging" and, as she herself put it, "running away" from all depressing things.

The therapists were a man and a woman who planned to see the family once a week. (It may be worth adding that the time for beginnings and ends of sessions, as well as the consistent arrangement of the room is adhered to as precisely as possible by the therapists and represents the physical boundaries of the setting within which other variables can then be more clearly identified and observed.)

The family members were intelligent and articulate and could tell us a great deal about themselves. So it was not too difficult to gain a vivid picture of them as a group and of the polarization and fights between the two girls, with mother in the middle. Mother was frustrated and hurt at their rejection of the meals she provided for them but saw it as her job to be brave and keep her spirits up, even if, as it emerged, she had to turn to the spirits in the bottle to do so.

But besides the more obvious picture the family conveyed with their words, our interest as therapists was to observe and experience the ways in which such a picture might get enacted in the sessions. This enabled us to understand some of the very painful aspects of the family's relationship together that had crystallized since Mr. Dun's death, and what patterns they had developed to deal with them. As with other families, the enactment sometimes came before the words, sometimes afterwards. But always the problem was to engage with the feelings entailed. For instance, it was from their difficulty in coming all together to the session that we experienced the intensity of the struggle in living together at home. In an early session, before a regular time had been settled, the older sister, Jane, had not appeared, and while the other children blamed mother for this, it seemed that her absence served a purpose for them all. When we spoke of the difficulty for them of coming here together, especially in view of the rivalry they had reported, we not only heard in a more immediate way about the fights, but it actually emerged that Jane had been given the wrong time for the session, not by her mother as Patricia had suggested, but by Patricia herself. Right at the end of the hour, she acknowledged in an almost inaudible whisper that it was she who had told her sister the wrong time!

In terms of the family dynamics, one might almost depict the two girls as representing opposite sides of a manic-depressive coin, one virtually immobilized by depression, the other extremely active, excitable, and physically taking flight, both from home and from the sessions. The session itself at times took on an atmosphere of drama and excitement in stark contrast to the frustrated and difficult air it often assumed when the therapists attempted to get more in touch with avoided feelings. The work was to stay with those feelings without being ourselves immobilized by them. In this way, the meaning of the defensive behavior was able to make itself known.

It soon emerged that the younger members of the family were extremely worried about their mother's unhappiness and the drinking associated with it. In fact, Patricia's depression seemed very much to reflect that of her mother and we began to be powerfully aware of the kind of despair that lay behind the fights and the drinking. We soon got a very clear idea of Mrs. Dun's hatred of those feelings of despair because of her way of reacting in relation to them with us. She was able to give us a fluent, though detached account of her husband's illness and death, of how this had upset the balance between the girls, and led to the increasing divergence between them, which culminated in extreme depression. When we felt the impact of this and recognized aloud how sad and unhappy they might all be feeling, trying to tune into it with them, Mother's reaction was most marked. First she could not hear; then when our words were repeated, she looked absolutely blank and uncomprehending. She pushed the therapists right away and was quite contemptuous. Shortly afterwards, she talked about a boring neighbor of hers and his boring girlfriend. She told us that the one time the family could be at peace and have a quiet evening together was when there were outsiders like that whom they could unite about. It seemed the boring couple stood for the boring therapists, and in terms of countertransference feelings, one actually did feel a bore and very crass and unstylish to be talking in such an unaffected or unscintillating way about sad or unhappy feelings. Perhaps, we suggested, they were feeling they might at least have a quiet evening together this evening, that we were like the neighbor and his boring girlfriend, and, if nothing else, we might serve the purpose of the outsiders they could unite against.

More important to recognize, however, was the way that it was really the depression that was being termed boring and then located immediately outside in the neighbor/therapist couple. It seemed that we were felt not only to represent the unwanted feelings called "boring" but also to be boring in the sense of pushing back to the family the sad feelings that were seen as so contemptible to Mrs. Dun and had usually to be rationalized or drowned in drink.

I think this illustrates the kind of unconscious processes of projection involved when unwanted feelings find a refuge elsewhere than in their owner's mind. It also serves to highlight the importance of the therapists' attention to the distinction between the family's readiness to talk about their unhappy experiences on the one hand, and their readiness really to get in touch with the feelings of sadness and grief associated with them on the other.

Betty Joseph, in a particularly useful paper, "The Patient who is Difficult to Reach" (1975), has examined the problem of getting into what looks like a therapeutic alliance, which is actually inimical to a therapeutic alliance because it is with a pseudo-adult part of the patient:

> The patient talks in an adult way, but relates to the analyst only as an equal, or a near-equal disciple. Sometimes he relates more as a slightly superior ally who tries to help the analyst in his work, with suggestions or minor corrections or references to personal history. If one observes carefully one begins to feel that one is talking to this ally about a patient—but never talking to the patient. The "patient" part of the patient seems to remain split off and it is this part which seems more immediately to need help, to be more infant-like, more dependent and vulnerable. One can talk about this part but the problem is to reach it. I believe that in some of our analyses, which appear repetitive and interminable, we have to examine whether we are not being drawn into colluding with the pseudoadult or pseudo-cooperative part of the patient. [p. 206]

I think this process is often very clear in families and Joseph's emphasis on the patient's method of communication rather than simply on the content is of course correspondingly relevant. In this case, it alerted us again to our family's extreme sensitivity and proud defense against their vulnerability.

The question for the sessions was: could they bear to get in touch with such feelings here and stay with them? Moreover, could the therapist help the process by being available as a temporary refuge for the hatred and contempt stirred up in the process—a place where the presence and management of such feelings could be observed and possibly learned from, at a little distance, so to speak.

Perhaps some further examples will serve to clarify. An important theme, for instance, was that of feeding—both in terms of what the family was telling us about themselves and the way they were behaving with us. In the lengthy discussion about why the children insisted on making their own meals, Mrs. Dun spoke of having to pull the food out of the deep freezer. It reflected the sense of there being insufficient ready nourishment to go around. It seemed that all of them felt in desperate need of comfort and not able to bear each other's distress. We saw Mother, for instance, dismiss with instant words of advice and reassurance her daughters' tentative efforts to convey their difficulties. We felt very strongly the shared anxiety that we, like them, would be unable properly to register their distress as a family and would misunderstand or misinterpret their communication to us. We perceived what it was like to be trying to communicate with such an object that was felt to be so thick and dense.

At the same time we could experience the despair and helplessness of being like that and, of Mother especially, at being found wanting and unable to meet the hungry demands. What food or what help was offered never seemed to be quite right. We were grumbled and griped at for the kinds of interpretations that we made, lectured at and reasoned with about not being more social and more like human beings with them, and while Mrs. Dun talked of her own depression when she had no one to feed, she showed us very clearly what it was like to have our interpretative food rejected and spat out.

But the family did make it possible to work with this, and when we interpreted that we, as therapists, were being given an idea of what it was like to have one's offers rejected in this way, Mrs. Dun, with the children's encouragement, spontaneously began to recall her own experience as a mother and the awful time she had had feeding both children as babies. This seemed to be the direct response to the emergence and identification of such feelings in the session in relation to the therapists. It is an example of the process in which the space provided can enable the obstacles to independent thought to emerge in the interaction of the session and be engaged with in the transference to the therapist.

Taking the experience from the other side of the relationship in this same sort of interaction, the therapists could take up the fear that the point would be missed and the connection to the family need not be made. The pervasive image of an impermeable object or unsatisfactory relationship was terribly distressing for all concerned, but especially for Mrs. Dun who would get into the most awful kind of impasse with one or the other of the therapists. However again, when I suggested on one occasion, that the current dissatisfaction was with me, as the dense one who misses the point, Mrs. Dun came back the next week saying that she thought some of the difficulty in the relationship with her husband was because she had not properly listened to him but rather had always had an answer for everything he tried to say to her. In fact, rather movingly, she seemed to have registered how she herself could behave in this unreceptive way. It was an example of the very sort of behavior that they kept accusing us of, as if the possibility of the therapist owning such attributes and acknowledging them could render them much less insufferable and overwhelming.

But such moments of linking are not always so easy to observe. They often continue to be interspersed with periods of intense frustration for everyone. In this case, there were times when the girls were anxious that their mother would want to stop the contact with us, instead of coming to an agreement to make a commitment to therapy as they increasingly seemed to wish. In the second session, for example (a week after they started) there was a reference to a row between Patricia and her mother the evening before. It was about abortion and the family got quite worked up as they talked about the value of human life and babies, of a week-old baby, in fact, compared to a plant. It seemed to Patricia that Mrs. Dun would be prepared to kill a week-old baby in the same way as she would be prepared to chop off a plant or cut a flower. The question seemed to be whether this week-old interaction between us could produce something new or was it to be aborted before it could develop. Could we really bear the struggle to take care of such a baby and all the mess and the pain and the difficulties involved in that? The interpretation of this led Patricia to say that she knew it was silly but that when we talked earlier about their skirting around things, she had felt, "Oh dear, if we go on doing that, they will decide not to see us." This enabled us to discuss thoughts about starting in therapy and to agree upon the practical arrangements for this.

In such a way the family shows us the fears and hopes they have in relation to the possibility of this new undertaking. We can then try to recognize and voice them as part of the process involved in their choosing whether to engage in it or not. The members of this family were clearly painfully aware of the conflicts in their relationships with each other and, fight it though they often did, they were evidently interested and able to grasp the meaning of the interactions at an emotional as well as intellectual level.

In some families, however, it may seem well-nigh impossible to get in touch with the meaning to the family as a whole of the presented problem and with the fears and phantasies that underlie it, or to know if anything at all is being achieved. The material on which I am drawing next is from a family in which there is again polarization between the parts. This time the family is more value laden and absolute as well as being accompanied by a striking lack of space for entertaining the conflicts implicit in bringing the two parts together. It may be interesting for the reader to consider the differences between the two families and to identify the kind of criteria that are relevant for evaluating their functioning from a dynamic point of view.

I will describe some interactions from early sessions before going on to try to look at the processes being discussed here in the light of the effect of changes and breaks in the treatment.

THE O'BRIEN FAMILY

This was a family of seven, referred because of the behavior of the two oldest children. Father was a semi-skilled laborer who had been absent from home a great deal. An illness of the mother's had necessitated these two boys, David and Martin, being placed in foster care when small. The family had recently become reunited and stabilized amid great hopes of a new beginning. But the main complaint, that of bedwetting, was one in a long list of items about the boys; they were presented as dirty, lazy, and in every way intractable. Besides Martin's bedwetting there were hints of stealing. Mrs. O'Brien was declaring herself in despair.

The three little girls, born after the mother's illness, seemed absolutely the opposite of their brothers: clean, rather grown-up, well behaved and beautifully dressed. Father was eager to cooperate and conveyed feelings of great anxiety and inadequacy while mother presented as competent, determined, and clearly seeking allies in her battle with all this incompetence and mess.

The remarkable polarity between the two groups, which was even expressed in the seating — male and female — was clear and one might expect to find that each group was carrying some features and characteristics for the other. It was equally clear that the boys had been brought by the parents, particularly mother, in order for the therapists to alter their behavior and especially to stop the younger boy, Martin (aged 16) from bedwetting.

The family's view of the therapists (again a male/female couple) seemed to come with them, so that even before they saw us in action at all, they clearly looked to the female therapist to take the lead in the sessions, just as the female partner dominated the situation at home. It is difficult to convey the extraordinary passivity of those boys in contrast to Mrs. O'Brien's bewildered impatience and unquestioning assumption that they would want the same of themselves as she did. It was not, for example, a matter of Martin wanting to stop his bedwetting because he was distressed about it. It was as if neither he nor anyone else would worry about it much if it was not for Mother's great expectations and her unremitting pressure on the boys to change. Even then it seemed that it was only the discomfort of this pressure that he minded rather than the bedwetting itself. When he eventually came asking if he could have help with it, the reasons he gave were to do with the nuisance of changing and washing his sheets himself.

In the first session both boys sat listening to their mother itemizing a catalogue of their faults, their stupidity, dirtiness, laziness yet showed absolutely no reaction to it. There was no sign of resentment, anger, or offense — nothing. In fact, the boys said practically nothing at all except that when the therapists tried to explore their feelings about coming here together, the older one, David, managed to say that they had not known they were coming until the day before. He was quick to add, though, that if his mother wanted him to come, then he was prepared to.

It was the beginning of a repeated demonstration of how Mrs.

O'Brien saw herself as thinking and planning for these boys and how they simply let her do that. Now here they were, obediently coming along and sitting impassively, almost as if deaf and dumb or subnormal.

Meanwhile the little girls sat listening intently until the youngest one started to play with the toys we had put on the table. Mr. O'Brien, solid, anxious, good-humored, appeared to be in general agreement with what his wife was saying, if a little embarrassed by it. The inescapable impression was that the two boys were damaged in ways that felt quite irreparable. In view of their histories this would not be surprising. But striking though the picture was, the question for the therapists was how could one start usefully to work with it? How, also, could one avoid getting caught in the pressure to take sides in what increasingly came to feel like a very intense tug-of-war between Mrs. O'Brien and her two sons, whose most difficult quality was the fact that even when their resentment was voiced, their major expression of it was at a passively unaware, unconscious level. Plied as we were with historical accounts of the series of traumatic events they had all experienced, it seemed clear to us that no amount of verbal engagement with that history could in itself hope to reach the sense of despair and futility that it had engendered. Furthermore, the relentless pressure to reform from one side of the family seemed only to entrench the resigned and intransigent behavior patterns of the other.

The therapists seemed to be expected to operate like auxiliary parents, in rather the same way as the grandparents apparently had. They were to reinforce the parents' own constant efforts to impress upon the boys the behavior that they were certain was right for them. We were expected to behave in an authoritarian way through the medium of criticism, advice, and prescription as did Mr. and Mrs. O'Brien themselves.

As it was, we could only comment on the boys' lack of response and suggest what might lie behind it. For something suggested to me, perhaps the intense searching look I was getting as I started talking, especially from the older boy David, that he was more alert and more in touch than he had seemed. We eventually suggested that to allow themselves to have feelings, or even thoughts, about what was happening, might seem to them too dangerous, too potentially explosive. It was David again who nodded and said, very timidly and warily, looking from his father to his mother and back, that "it might upset people." It seemed there might be currency in this family for the assumption that uncontrolled behavior would be preferable to outspoken disagreement or criticism.

As long as the boys were so apparently unconcerned about their own behavior and not at all convinced why they should change it unless through some external, almost magical, medium for which they need take no major responsibility, then all current efforts directed toward changing specific bits of behavior such as the bedwetting would fail, just as previous efforts in which pills, mechanical devices, and so forth had failed for lack of proper use. Also it seemed that the parents had some investment themselves in maintaining the status quo. By firmly attributing all the problems to the boys and locating them in their pigsty bedroom, the marriage could be kept relatively problem free in the way that both parents so desperately wanted.

The following example from an early session may give some idea of this process and of the pressures that the family put on the therapists to join in their way of operating.

After expressing eagerness to start where they had left off the week before, the family soon dropped that idea and reverted to the subject of Martin's bedwetting. He had been dry for a few nights and Mrs. O'Brien informed us, in a very secretive way, that he was having a "tonic" that the doctor had given him. She was very clearly implying that it was actually some drug he was getting. Then looking directly at the doctor here, she said in French, "Comprenez-vous?"

My partner was completely taken aback. It was as if he was meant to be the father having a private discussion with mother about little 3- or 4-year-old children, incapable of understanding, and the boys again behaved as if they were quite oblivious. But it was an opportunity to point out all this and to show how Mrs. O'Brien was wanting the doctor to join in a secret about what she was giving this boy of 16 for his health. She implied that her son was far too infantile to know or take any responsibility for himself. At the same time, it was also very clear how the boys invited everyone to speak for them, act for them, and think for them. As we suggested, Martin, in particular, was like a child whose extreme slowness made it easier to do up his shoelaces for him than to help him to do them up himself. The discussion of this led David also to take his courage into his hands and relate it to a similar situation he was in with Father and Mother. They deemed him incapable of managing the money that he had earned in his job, and after he had clearly demonstrated his practice of spending it all, they now insisted on keeping it for him, giving him pocket money from it and putting the rest into a savings account for him. It was another example of how readily he complied with an invitation to infantilism.

The problem for the therapists was not to get drawn into one or the other side of this struggle. Indeed, it was interesting to see how easy it was to fall into a similar kind of dependency mode of behaving as the family itself had—preaching or lecturing to them much as these parents did to their children, or joining with one part to discuss the other so that neither was actually engaged in being the patient or the problem. Technically this would be an example of the kind of enactment spoken of at the beginning — an "acting in the countertransference."

There was a great deal of pressure on us as therapists to direct them, instruct them, and judge them in the manner of specialists who could provide the formula for cure without them having to do the work or face the conflicts and pain involved in undergoing change themselves. For it became increasingly clear that all the arguments about the stupidity and dirtiness of the boys served to avoid the extent of the depressed and rejected feelings they were suffering. With all the emphasis in the sessions on the closeness between the parents, it took quite a while to bring into the open, first, how pathetically pushed out and forlorn the boys felt and, second, how really tense and loaded the fight for space, possessions, and attention could become when they gave up their servile positions, and when the atmosphere of rather hopeless resignation gave way to one that included a hope of something different.

The combination of a dependency culture such as this, on the one hand, and the difficulty of acknowledging the dependence or any of its implications, on the other, provides a set of conditions that are bound to highlight the problems associated with changes, separations, and breaks in the therapy. Later material from sessions with this family may help to illustrate some of the technical issues for the therapist in managing such changes.

Attempts to contain reactions to change and the implications of rejection

The first major change in the work with the O'Brien family was the necessity, on the part of the therapists, to change the session time. It is the family's reaction to this, linked to the events of the ensuing Christmas break, that I will describe.

The significant thing about our proposal to change the time was that although it was clearly inconvenient for them in terms of all their other evening engagements and activities, they took the attitude that it was up to them to fit in with us, Mrs. O'Brien with angry resignation and Mr. O'Brien saying in a comforting tone that their need was such that they must expect to make sacrifices. In fact, we had left a number of sessions to negotiate the change of time and we commented on their unquestioning acceptance of our proposal with no explicit objections. At some point Mrs. O'Brien actually said, "Are we allowed to criticize?" We tried to show them how their feelings of dependence on us, and need to comply really made them squash and restrict their complaints, criticisms, and disappointments out of all awareness in much the same way as they expected the children, especially Martin and David, to do at home.

The work that we did on this heralded a phase of much more interaction and participation on the part of all the family, both with each other and with us. Mrs. O'Brien, in particular, questioned the whole value of the therapy and they all made their ambivalence to it very clear. But the power of the attack and apparent rejection of our help also seemed to represent their way of dealing with the feelings they had of being pushed about and rejected by us. Notwithstanding some easing up, the emerging degree of hostility, and the continuing difficulties of tackling us directly with their dissatisfaction led to various forms of representation in action such as absences or, latenesses — accompanied by verbal material about strikes and go-slows. The more direct way of complaining could not be sustained by the family as a whole any more than by the boys, and was again denied and enacted instead.

But the theme of being unwanted was poignantly presented in some interaction around the older boy, David, in the sessions before the Christmas break. David had been talking about leaving home and going to America but he had actually done very little about it. He longed for people in the family — especially, perhaps, his father — to explore this idea with him, perhaps to ask him why he wanted to leave home or to show some regret or concern about it. Instead of this, however, Mrs. O'Brien attacked him scornfully for dithering about so much and not going ahead with his idea. It seemed that it was she and Mr. O'Brien who were most keen on his leaving home. If David had wanted reassurance that he was after all wanted at home, in fact he received the opposite.

When we took this up it led to Mrs. O'Brien saying that there was no point in talking about your feelings, for instance, the depression she felt herself, because no one would understand. That seemed to be the crux of the matter for all of them. There was very little idea of an object who could really pay attention, with the wish to understand and take in and help their particular problem. The dynamic pattern being demonstrated by David was one of dealing with the terrible sense of not being wanted by threatening to leave. In doing this he maintained the hope that people would then show a wish for him to stay, thus demonstrating his fear to be unfounded. It was this pattern that the whole family unconsciously seemed to reenact in relation to the therapists and the break.

On the day of our first appointment after the Christmas break, we received a letter from Mrs. O'Brien essentially saying that they would not be coming to their therapy anymore. It had not resolved Martin's difficulties and we had not offered him any kind of answer to his individual problems.

It was not possible to contact the family in time for that evening session but we did respond with great care, acknowledging their sense of frustration, but also stressing the importance before finishing the therapy of discussing together in terms both of this and of any alternative that might seem appropriate. We said we would expect them the following week. It did seem that they might be dealing with their feelings of rejection by rejecting us, much as the older boy, David, had done in talking of going to America. But if, as a family, they were functioning like him, we might expect them also at some level, to be testing our readiness to give them up and let them go away, just as he had been testing theirs.

Even with this possibility in mind, however, we were surprised at the alacrity and apparent enthusiasm with which they responded to our letter. Mrs. O'Brien telephoned immediately to say that they would be coming for their appointment. The ensuing sessions were spent discussing their doubts and resentments and considering their wish to terminate. But, in some way, this episode did seem to present a milestone in the treatment and it was clear by the third session after Christmas, not only that they wished to continue, but that there was actually a very different atmosphere and feel about the interaction with us. They began to show much more explicitly their interest in us. Do we see other families and what do we think of them in relation to these other families? It seemed, somehow, more possible to work in the transference. The elder boy presented a dilemma about changing his job and the notions of change did seem to be in the air. There was a sense of them standing on the threshold, debating whether to go over it. As if to emphasize the more positive feeling, one of the little girls gave to each of us a drawing she had made during the session. Altogether the general despair, despondency, and discouragement that usually prevailed did seem now to be a little tinged with hope from time to time and with occasional surprising moments of genuine concern in the family. Of course every sign of hope or movement like this is subject to being undermined. Each break seems to put the treatment in jeopardy again and face us with the question, what are we really doing, attempting to work with such a situation in this way?

It is notoriously difficult for individuals as well as families in treatment to be in touch with the significance of interruptions and changes in the sessions and, of course, it is often those most in need who find it hardest to know about or think about separation. For this reason, efforts to prepare for impending breaks tend to feel forced or futile, just as attempts to make links between other experiences and the feelings they evoke seem often to be falling on barren ground. We can begin to identify a constellation of associated features that characterize a family like this and give substance to questions about the appropriateness for them of engaging in this form of treatment.

The concreteness of thinking, constant pressure to action, and extreme dissociation from any awareness of the real sources of behavior can all be seen as expressions of the difficulty for each individual — as well as the family as a whole — to suffer their own and each other's feelings.

This mode of response in the family to the need for their feelings to be entertained and suffered is reflected in the difficulties for the therapists to provide such containment in the treatment. It does seem possible to provide some sort of containing experience, if only through finding contact with the relevant feelings by their evocation in the therapists themselves. It is clearly when this sense of containment fails that the increased tendency to act out ensues. But the question of feasibility remains and the possibility of providing adequate containment for a family such as this depends partly on our skills in managing their experiences of loss and change in the treatment. There is a tendency for us to underestimate the effect of breaks on all families who are engaged in ongoing therapy, but especially those who may seem to care least about them. I have been trying to indicate the significance of these breaks in highlighting the family's way of functioning. Concretely I think it is evidenced by the number of families who drop out, or whose therapy seems to stagnate at such times. While in individual therapy, we seem to be more tuned in to the subtleties of reactions that are provoked by these interruptions and more skilled at working with them as an important part of the therapeutic process, yet the corresponding need for such attention in work with families is obvious.

Most, if not all, of the families we see have quite severe problems related to mourning — often crystallized through an actual death in the family, but usually dating much further back and representing a major aspect of their functioning in general. If we can be alert to it, the breaks can provide an important opportunity to work on this with the family, instead of simply being the occasion for more drastic actions, as so often happens.

9

Making a Space for Parents

ANNA DARTINGTON AND JEANNE MAGAGNA

In this chapter we will be concentrating specifically on work with parents. This will include observations and thoughts in relation to the parents' experience of bringing their child to a clinic for an assessment for psychotherapeutic treatment and the dilemma that they face when the child is accepted for treatment. In the latter part of the chapter there is an account of psychotherapeutic work with one couple whose children were in individual treatment.

Since a major part of this book is concerned with aspects of work with whole families, either in assessment or longer-term treatment, perhaps we should explain why we have chosen to focus exclusively on one part of the family system. The reasons are twofold. First, given that we draw on an underlying family point of view, in which the family relationships and problems are carefully taken into account, there is always a certain flexibility in our thinking about the best way to approach any given family. It is not always the case that they are seen together as a group, because it is not always appropriate, advisable or desirable as far as the particular family is concerned. Secondly, when a decision is made, for whatever reason, to offer individual treatment to a child, it is our experience that the impact on the parents is not always given the recognition it deserves.

In 1932, Melanie Klein, speaking from the position of a child analyst, wrote of the parents' dilemma:

> The child is dependent on them and so they are included in the field
> of the analysis; yet it is not they who are being analysed and they can

> therefore only be influenced by ordinary psychological means. The relationship of the parents to their child's analyst entails difficulties of a peculiar kind, since it touches closely upon their own complexes. Their child's neurosis weighs very heavily upon the parents' sense of guilt, and at the same time as they turn to analysis for help, they regard the necessity of it as proof of their guilt with regard to their child's illness. It is, moreover, very trying for them to have the details of their family life revealed to the analyst. To this must be added, particularly in the case of the mother, jealousy of the confidence which is established between the child and its analyst. [p. 75]

In this chapter we hope to throw some light on these issues of guilt, ambivalence and jealousy and to illustrate ways in which parents might be helped with their own difficulties.

INITIAL EXPLORATION AND ASSESSMENT

A child, identified as troubled in some way, is referred usually by the general practitioner, sometimes by the school or social service agency, and sometimes by the parents themselves. The parents will have been involved to a greater or lesser extent in this referral process, and they are likely to expect the child to be the focus of our attention. They bring him along, sometimes reluctantly, expecting to tell us about their worries about him, or to give us information or simply to wait quietly in the waiting room while we make our diagnosis. Whether or not it is immediately apparent, the parents are usually in some distress, having anxiously anticipated their meeting with us.

Society places a high value on child care and "proper parenting" and while the child remains a child he is usually thought of as the innocent or wronged party if he gets himself into difficulties. It is likely, therefore, that the parents approach us expecting to be blamed or criticized. It is even more likely if their own internal worlds are peopled by blaming and blamed figures. We have in mind those who have internalized their own parents as highly critical (Klein 1932). We, as the authority figures, "the people at the clinic," will be expected to behave in the same way as the internal figures.

During the assessment we are concerned to listen, to observe, to receive the impact of the family disturbance, and hopefully to provide an experience in which their anxieties will be shared and attended to carefully and considerately. The issue of "who is to blame" is likely to be a central concern of the family at this stage and we would like to consider some of its manifestations in more detail. Of course, the very word "assessment" is problematic in that it carries all sorts of connotations of being judged and scrutinized. It would probably be better to describe this phase of the work as a mutual exploration.

Adolescents, like Suzy in the following example, often prefer the opportunity to be seen individually.

> Mrs. Allen, divorced mother of Suzy, aged 16, saw a psychiatrist for two interviews during the assessment phase while Suzy was seen twice by a social worker. One of the presenting problems was the fraught relationship between mother and daughter, and the workers decided to offer a joint appointment to both. Mrs. Allen was an intelligent and capable woman who ran a successful secretarial agency. Arriving for the third appointment with her daughter she carried a shorthand notebook, which she proceeded to open. Pen in hand, she looked expectantly at the social worker, inquiring politely as to her diagnosis of Suzy's problems. This surprised the workers because during her individual sessions with the psychiatrist, the mother had been able to talk fairly freely about her worries in relation to herself and to Suzy. It was suggested to Mrs. Allen that she might be very frightened of her first meeting with the social worker and that she might feel the social worker was party to all Suzy's accusations against her, and would then be wishing to put her on the spot having taken careful note of all her misdemeanors as a mother. This seemed to free Mrs. Allen to close her book and join in. Later in the session she was able to talk about some of her guilty feelings about putting her job interests before her children. She also spoke of her feelings of rivalry towards the social worker who she had assumed was some sort of "perfect mother figure" rather like her own mother who made her feel she could never do anything right. It did not surprise the workers when Mrs. Allen said that her only really happy times in childhood were when she had her father all to herself.

In that example Mrs. Allen was all set to put the social worker on trial in the same way that she anticipated being put on trial herself. Sometimes parents may deal with their discomfort in other ways. For example, Mr. Y. said of his son, "I just don't know what's the matter with him. We've always done our best, he's had everything he wanted from us" or Mr. and Mrs. X., speaking of their daughter, "It seems as if she's never liked us. Even when she was a baby it seemed we could never do anything right for her." Such statements help the workers to understand the extent and nature of the distress felt by the parents because they convey a sense of grievance and a feeling that all this suffering is the fault of the child. The worker may even experience pressure from the parents to make an alliance with them against the child, as if to say "we adults try to help and look at what the child does to us." We might see this pressure as arising from anxieties in the parents that the worker may join with the child in some accusation against them. If so, we would share these thoughts with the parents in the session — as the social worker did with Mrs. Allen — in the hope that we would be able to alleviate some of the anxiety by acknowledging it.

Perhaps it would be useful here to differentiate this sort of approach that addresses itself to the underlying anxieties from another in which we might allow ourselves to be seen as helpful by making reassuring comments. The parents of a referred child are likely to be feeling not only guilt about real or imaginary harm done to the child but also a sense of shame in relation to the exposure of this. The wish to be reassuring is in some ways a natural response to someone greatly troubled by feelings of guilt.

> Mrs. Bond came to the Clinic because of the referral of her daughter, Rachel, aged 8, who had been suffering from night terrors for several years. Mrs. Bond was seen on her own and was quite distraught in the interview and said she could hardly remember when she had last experienced a peaceful night's sleep. She was alone, her husband having left her soon after the birth of Rachel, her only child and they lived in inadequate cramped accommodations. She cried profusely as she recalled violent feelings toward Rachel. Mrs. Bond's therapist was extremely sensitive and receptive to her distress, so much so that she felt quite overwhelmed and was prompted to tell Mrs. Bond not to worry so much. The therapist had said she felt sure that Rachel's fear of being murdered in the dark would soon be overcome. Then, in response to an urgent question from Mrs. B., the therapist offered some advice regarding the management of Rachel's bedtime. To the therapist's consternation Mrs. Bond simply became more distraught. The reason emerged when she said that she had been telling Rachel every night for almost two years, that there was nothing to worry about, and that there wasn't really anybody trying to murder her.

The point of this example is to demonstrate that the therapist's efforts to reassure were interpreted by Mrs. B. to be due to the same inability in the therapist to bear the anxiety that had led her to make similar comments to her daughter. It had also led her to seek the advice that flowed naturally from family and friends, but it had brought the mother little relief from the anxiety about her child's terror and her own violence. Instead the reassurance and the advice tended to increase her despair.

If we, as therapists, hurry in with reassurance, it is likely to be in response to our own discomfort as if to say "please don't feel so awful because it makes me feel so awful." Our need to offer advice may arise from similar motives, although the parents, in their anxiety, may urgently request it from us. It is the anxiety underlying their request, rather than the request itself, that is crying out for attention.

There is also the problem of truth, or putting it another way, of our own ignorance in the face of a new situation. We actually don't know who did what to whom, when and why. We don't know who is to blame, if indeed anybody is. We don't know to what extent the guilt or the regret or the worry is based on fact or fantasy. Reassurance can be experienced by the client as our not wanting to hear or to know.

Transition from assessment into treatment

During the assessment phase the task of the therapist is to help the family members to locate and identify the areas of pain and stress. When some mutual understanding has been reached, it is then possible to think with them about what form of help would be most appropriate, whether, for example, the child should be offered individual therapy or whether the family as a unit should be the focus of treatment. These decisions obviously depend on the experience of the assessment work, the family's own preference, and degrees of disturbance and motivation in individual family members. (These points are referred to by Beta Copley in Chapter 4.) There are also other factors such as the prevailing attitude of the clinic team toward particular methods of work, as well as individual preferences and staff availability.

Often when individual treatment for one child is indicated, parents are offered an opportunity to continue to explore their own difficulties in relation to the child. They may feel ambivalent about their own involvement in treatment for a number of reasons. Since the role of the referred patient in the family is very often one of holding and representing disowned conflicts and anxieties for other members, parents often feel quite exposed and unprotected when seen on their own in the absence of the referred child who would normally be the focus of attention, concern, or attack. We have found this especially to be the case when the assessment phase is completed too quickly and there has not been sufficient attention given to the exploration and understanding of the parents' own distress. Those of us who work in child-centred agencies are probably familiar with the situation in which the psychiatrist or child psychotherapist sees the child and the social worker sees the parents. While this may be a rational and appropriate division of tasks it can, and sometimes does, develop into a sort of two-tier system of intervention in which the child's therapy is regarded as of prime importance and the work with the parents is some sort of back-up resource where information is gained from and advice given to the couple. Sometimes the father is not given sufficient encouragement to attend the clinic and therefore by implication his role in relation to both mother and children is often overlooked.

This two-tiered system may have to do with issues of role and status within the agency. The social worker may be regarded as someone whose primary task it is to protect the therapy of the child from parental intrusion or sabotage. The implicit message would be that the social worker is also responsible for protecting the psychotherapist's work. This might involve the social worker in various activities such as contacting the child's school to exchange information, arranging therapy times and transport. In this case the actual work with the parents could develop along similar lines — reminding them about therapy times, asking for historical details and for accounts of the child's behavior at home. It is possible that the parents will then experience themselves as united into a cooperative management role with the social worker, forming a sort of subsystem supporting and supplying the therapist–child couple. In one sense this may fulfill a need in the parents to feel useful and helpful in the situation but it may also in the longer term undermine their own parenting capacities in a less obvious way. This emphasis on their management role leaves very little space for exploring their own feelings, for example any resentments about the clinic workers appearing to have taken over responsibility for the child, jealousy of the relationship between child and therapist, feelings of envy towards the child for all the personal attention he is receiving. The worker too may have to deny similar feelings in herself about working in this auxiliary role with the inevitable limitations it places on the use of her own professional capacities. The following example illustrates the way in which a child's treatment was nearly sabotaged when parental feelings of jealousy and redundancy were not recognized.

A social worker was seeing Mr. and Mrs. Davies during the therapy of their daughter Tracy, aged 5. They came in the fifth week full of news of the marvellous improvement in Tracy's behavior at home. The social worker knew the child's therapist had made good contact with the child and felt optimistic about alleviating some of Tracy's anxieties. The social worker was therefore extremely pleased to be able to share the parents' expressed feelings of relief and gratitude. Mr. and Mrs. Davies, who had met the therapist briefly on one occasion, went on to express their great faith in the child's therapist, extolling her experience, wisdom, patience, and other virtues. They seemed quite unable to talk about anything else; in fact the social worker found it difficult to get a word in edgewise.

When she discussed this in the workshop later she remembered a sensation during the interview, that her jaw had begun to ache from smiling. She also remembered that she had felt quite depressed following the interview, although she had, at the time, attributed this to other factors. She had felt sure that the parents had little further need to come but in discussion she was able to see that they had, in fact, idealized the child's therapist and caused her, the social worker, to feel quite redundant.

Mr. and Mrs. Davies cancelled their own and Tracy's appointments for the next week. The following week Mr. Davies brought Tracy to the Clinic, telling the social worker that his wife had the flu and was still unable to come. The social worker, remembering her own feelings after the last interview, enquired further as to Mrs. Davies' state of mind. Mr. Davies said that she had been crying a lot which was "natural after flu" but she had been further upset by Tracy who talked of nothing but "the nice lady at the Clinic who gave her toys to play with." When Mrs. Davies had cancelled Tracy's appointment Tracy had told her that "she didn't love her Mummy any more."

The social worker recognized the feelings of depression and redundancy in the parents and was able to help Mr. Davies to bring his wife to the next session, where their feelings were discussed and shared. They later admitted to a considerable jealousy of Tracy's therapist, but had felt unable to express this as it seemed so "ungrateful when everybody was doing their best to help."

This example highlights the way that the workers' countertransference experience served as a useful signpost to the underlying feelings that were opposing the parents' conscious wish to cooperate. If the child himself is reluctant to come, or hostile to the therapy, then of course it is even more difficult for the parents to maintain their conscious cooperation in the face of their underlying reservations.

It would seem appropriate here to share some thoughts about the parents' experience of handing over a child to a therapist and how this situation might be managed. In our experience it has been helpful for the parents to meet with the child's therapist before treatment starts, even when another team member has seen them and plans to work with them. Such a meeting allows the parents to see and talk to the person about whom they are likely to have many anxieties and phantasies. It is also an opportunity for them to perceive the therapist more realistically. In addition, it reinforces a respect for the parents' responsible and decisive role and the necessity of their cooperation. It gives the therapist an opportunity to discuss therapy times and arrangements for bringing the child to the clinic. It is a chance for the parents to ask questions, to give factual information, and to prepare themselves for some of the difficulties that they may encounter in the handling of the child at home as therapy progresses.

Sometimes it is appropriate for the child's therapist and the parents to meet during treatment to discuss a change in the child's therapy times or to share some important information concerning the child. This possibility of direct communication does have the advantage of maintaining space for the work with the parents, a space freed from the interference of message-carrying functions.

However, it is always important first to explore the meaning of such a meeting for both parents and child and for the therapists to clarify their own respective positions. It is not uncommon for therapists who are treating different members of one family to become caught up in the family dynamics in such a way that they begin to act from their own countertransference experiences. They may find themselves in relationships characterized by rivalry or intrusiveness, which mirror the family members' current difficulties with each other. It is often helpful to have one member of the team who is not involved in direct contact with family members and who, in discussion, contributes a more objective and overall perspective that represents and supports the integrity of the whole team. (See Chapter 6.)

ASPECTS OF ONGOING THERAPY WITH PARENTS

So far we have concentrated on the problems of beginning, of initial exploration, assessment, and transition. Now we would like to describe aspects of work with parents in various stages of treatment. To illustrate this, we will refer to the therapy sessions of one parental couple, Mr. and Mrs. Garcia, who were in joint treatment with two therapists for several years. They were parents of two children referred for individual therapy.

Mr. Garcia was a highly successful Spanish middle-class businessman, and Mrs. Garcia, also Spanish, an active, talented, and articulate woman. They appeared socially confident and capable people with a wide circle of friends and a variety of interests. They were extremely concerned about the behavior of their two children (a boy aged 11 and a girl aged 9) who were underachieving at school and who had become increasingly clinging, demanding, and generally unhappy at home. The parents readily agreed to therapeutic help for the children and also responded favorably to a suggestion that they should be provided with an opportunity to discuss their difficulties on a regular weekly basis.

Immediately following their decision to have treatment for themselves and the children, but before treatment began, there was a short holiday break. During this time, the couple made a brief and rare visit to Spain. While there, Mr. Garcia had an acute and near fatal illness. This seemed highly significant in that Spain, while being their country of origin, was also the country in which their own families had been severely persecuted by the government during the Spanish Civil War. The fathers of both parents had been killed and Mr. Garcia's mother had been badly beaten. Mr. and Mrs. Garcia had both escaped to England as teenagers and had met in London in their early twenties.

The treatment began after Mr. Garcia partially recovered. There was a marked contrast between the still confident and capable appearance of this couple and the shared knowledge that, when faced with a concrete reminder (Spain) of their parents' immense torture, they had almost collapsed through the near death of the husband. Hearing about the couple's holiday, the therapists found themselves experiencing a fear of helping them look at their difficulties. The fear was that something painful, even a painful reminder of the past, could result in a catastrophe of some sort. The therapists were acutely aware of the connection between father's anxiety-provoking illness and the finalization of arrangements for treatment. They wondered if the illness was a kind of communication in advance, demonstrating anxiety and guilt about having things brought into the open in therapy.

The unfolding of shared anxieties in the transference

It would seem useful here to describe what we mean by working in the transference before going on to illustrate this with clinical material.

The therapist's aim is to focus on the emotions that are most immediate and pressing in the experience of the therapy session, the idea being that internal change can best be facilitated through interpretations that meet anxiety at the moment at which it is being experienced. So the material that the couple brings is scrutinized by the therapists with a view to the clues it offers to what is actually happening in the session. The therapists avoid introducing topics or making judgments about the rightness or wrongness of the parents' actions or attitudes. Instead, they aim to provide a situation in which the couple can talk about whatever is on their mind, however insignificant it may seem to them, or however controversial they fear it will be (Strachey 1934).

The focus of the work is the transference relationship between the couple and the therapists. In facilitating the unfolding of the transference the therapists are concerned with matters of (a) place—relating to the experience as it emerges inside the therapy room, and the way in which it links with other relationships outside, (b) time—relating to what is experienced at the moment rather than yesterday or in the last session and (c) receptivity—a capacity to accept and bear the presenting anxieties, however uncomfortable or painful for the therapists. Within these parameters there are also more specific considerations. It is not so much the content of the communication but more its meaning and significance that are of concern to the therapists (Meltzer 1967). It is important to focus on the method of communication, the way the patient actually speaks and the way in which the patient reacts to the therapists' communications, in order to provide an understanding of the immediate experience (Joseph 1975).

Once it has become evident that a particular anxiety exists, its true nature may only become apparent in a careful observation of not only what is going on between the therapist and patient but also on what is going on inside the therapist, what it is that is being transferred and what exactly it feels like. It is through the therapists' ability to discriminate among the different emotions evoked in themselves that a clearer picture of the internal world of the patients emerges. The figures of the internal world and the relationships of these objects, one to another, are projected onto the therapists who receive them and provide an opportunity for them to be reexperienced and retested against the reality of a new and more favorable relationship. The parents' eventual capacity to face and bear their own emotions, respond to each other's needs, and help their children depends on the internalization of the experience of being helped to bear their emotions with the therapist couple.

During their first few meetings with Mr. and Mrs. Garcia, the therapists experienced powerfully and dramatically the impact of the fear and the anxiety that the couple themselves could not tolerate. At that time, it seemed, they could only evacuate it into others or express it in the form of stress-induced physical illness. So the anxieties that were denied by the couple were experienced by the therapists, who found themselves feeling fragile and tentative in the face of Mr. and Mrs. Garcia's lively and excitable accounts of their daily life.

The therapists also experienced a merging of identities.

Mr. and Mrs. Garcia would often arrive late and come straight to the room without informing the receptionist of their arrival. On entering the room they frequently inquired as to the therapists' health and state of mind, and generally behaved as if they were at a dinner party telling amusing anecdotes and paying exaggerated compliments to the therapists, referring to them as "charming young ladies" in a patronizing way. They talked almost continuously and often simultaneously.

The therapists found themselves feeling bombarded and unable to think. When one of the therapists managed to interrupt to make a comment, the other therapist noted that she had been just about to make the same comment.

After the sessions the therapists tried to make sense of their countertransference experience. They felt undifferentiated one from another, having the same thoughts and experiences, closely identified as if clinging together for survival, like babes in the woods. It seemed as if all boundaries were being disregarded. The therapists found it difficult to comment on the Garcias' late arrival to the sessions, feeling that the couple would feel humiliated and treated like children. It was also difficult to end the sessions on time and the therapists, although relatively experienced, were somehow made to feel like fumbling and nervous students. The parental couple's anxieties about the exposure of any vulnerability in themselves was being experienced by the therapists by means of projective identification (Klein 1946). If all boundaries were merged and confused, then it was impossible to see or think clearly, and seeing and thinking seemed to imply the revelation of something quite terrible. The therapists had to acknowledge and work with Mr. and Mrs. Garcia's intense feeling of humiliation in relation to coming to therapy and also their dread of what therapy might involve. Gradually the couple felt safe enough to begin to talk about some aspects of their family life and in particular their worries about the children.

In the initial stage of therapy parents naturally tend to talk about their children, since they have usually been a focus of anxiety and the ostensible reason for their approaching us. As they discuss their children the therapists try to provide them with the experience of containment for their distress. The therapists listen and try to understand rather than give advice or provide good solutions. (See Chapter 8 for further elaboration of the concept of containment.) Often the description of the child will include many references to what has been split off and denied in the couple's own personalities. We could see this as "the child in the parent" representing some sort of unresolved pain from their own past experience of being parented, which remains alive in their current relationships and gradually becomes apparent in their relationship with the therapist. It is important that the parents are given enough space initially to air their grievances about their children and each other, in order that the specific nature of their own unmet needs may be understood.

After discussing their shared worries about their children for several weeks, Mr. and Mrs. Garcia started to express their impatience with each other. Their attacks on each other did not provide any relief of anxiety; instead they appeared to become more guilty and more distant from the therapists who seemed to be increasingly perceived as judges. It was as if their disagreements had become a way of avoiding contact with the therapists, who were so feared by them.

Early in a session Mrs. Garcia spoke of how futile it was to come to the session and speak to her husband. Then she said he felt it was very difficult for him to talk to her because she always said he was angry. Mr. Garcia said he doesn't like talking to her because she always says she knows how he feels. She said she read in a magazine that it is reassuring to say "I know." The therapists interpreted the couple's fear of the therapists' criticisms and the feeling that they might apply psychoanalytic knowledge from books in a dogmatic or purely judgmental way.

When the therapists, rather than the other partner, receive the complaints about such things as coldness and unresponsiveness and do not respond in a revengeful or hurt manner, the parents discover that it is all right to complain and then may begin to explore the way in which they experience the therapists as meeting or not meeting their needs.

Mr. Garcia described how his wife felt that coming to therapy was like a prison sentence and Mrs. Garcia said that she felt there should be a point in their lives when they could stop looking at themselves and asking where they had gone wrong.

Now that the couple's transference feelings were becoming more explicit in their relationship with the therapists, it became clear that the Garcias viewed the therapy as a punishment for the damage that they felt they had inflicted on the children. These intense feelings of persecutory guilt were extremely distressing and as yet they could only bear to locate the distress in each other, rather than speaking for themselves, which seemed to feel too direct and too much of an exposure.

Mrs. Garcia described how her husband had been unable to cope with the pressures of family life. He had cut himself off from emotional things because he had been through so much as a child.

Mr. Garcia described his wife's near breakdown when she heard some upsetting news. Later he described the current relationship between his wife and her mother saying, "You can feel the tension when they are both in the same room. It's hard to describe because the actual behavior can't be faulted. Her mother is dogmatic, sterile, and narrow-minded and my wife dare not criticize her in any way."

This image of a severe mother who is at the same time too fragile to be criticized, appeared again and again in their material. It seemed to match the therapists' countertransference experience, which was a feeling of having to be gentle and careful so as not to confront the couple with powerful interpretations, but at the same time feeling incompetent and rather hopeless about being able to help, rather like a mother who could hurt but who could not hold the child. Much later in the therapy, after these feelings had been further explored in the transference, it became evident that this was how Mr. and Mrs. Garcia had both experienced their own mothers as children.

The other way in which the Garcias avoided a direct confrontation with their own distress was to locate it in their referred children.

At times they said that they were only coming to therapy "for the children's sake" with Mr. Garcia adding "for the children I would do anything". Mrs. Garcia cried profusely after a discussion with one of the children's therapists who had said that the treatment would last three or four years. She was worried about having to tell the new school about the child's treatment, feeling that he would be ostracized, stigmatized by friends and treated like a "nut case" by the teachers. Mr. Garcia wondered if the difficulty in talking with others about the children's treatment had to do with his wife's own difficulty in acknowledging that the children needed treatment. These were understandable and genuine concerns in their own right, but they also reflected the couple's fear for themselves and their worries about what the therapists would see and discover in them. Mr. Garcia expressed this anxiety.

To summarize, this first phase of therapy was characterized by intense feelings of persecution that were defended against in the following ways: by a merging and confusing of boundaries, by a massive projection of feelings of inadequacy and neediness into the therapists, and by attempts to locate distress elsewhere — into the other partner and the referred children. We have shown how projection into the therapists rather than each other enabled the parents' therapy to progress.

The use of manic defense

As the therapists became more aware of the couple's difficulties, they came up against a mutual defense of a very manic kind. We have already alluded to the fact that both Mr. and Mrs. Garcia had suffered considerable deprivation as children with experiences of parental separation and loss. Although they did not speak of early childhood memories, they conveyed an experience of parental figures who were preoccupied with intense anxieties for their own safety in an actual situation of political persecution. As we have shown, the therapists experienced in the countertransference something of the anxiety that the Garcias sought to avoid. Mr. and Mrs. Garcia, meeting and marrying in England, but with a shared traumatic past in Spain, had clung together as survivors, determined to make a new and better life. (We have already described how the therapists experienced the "clinging together" in the countertransference.) For thirty years this couple had been developing a psychic structure for surviving together. The structure that had evolved seemed to be heavily reliant on the notion of a "super parent/spouse," a father/mother or husband/wife who was highly idealized as successful, capable, impervious to criticism or self-doubt, able to tolerate and administer to the needs of the whole family. As we will show, at different times, they both strongly identified with this omnipotent super parent/spouse and continuously reinforced each other in this iden-tification. For example, they were both engaged in fund-raising and various philanthropic activities on behalf of refugee children while at the same time their own feelings of childlike vulnerability were denied and thus cruelly neglected. This was directly related to the actual difficulties they experienced in parenting the children. They encouraged the children to grow up and be "strong and capable" long before they were ready. It was also likely that this had been Mr. and Mrs. Garcia's own experience as children. They had both, at an early age, assumed parental responsibilities in their families of origin as a consequence of the premature death of a parent.

This kind of projective identification with a super parent/spouse with omnipotent powers to obliterate painful experiences could be likened to what Winnicott (1965) has described as the *false self* or Helene Deutsch (1942) as the *as if* personality. In Mr. and Mrs. Garcia's case, this identification with a super/parent was a way of coping with helplessness, neediness, and rage. Because of their difficulty in holding and bearing these painful states of mind, which were exacerbated by the external traumatic events of their childhood, they became identified with a parent who is a model of tough self-sufficiency, one who could bear anything. This identification was a way of avoiding, however temporarily, the pain of mourning the lost parents.

> The therapists' task was to try to help the couple to differentiate between what was real and actual in the experience of being marital partners and parents as opposed to what was merely being inside this omnipotent super parent/spouse and therefore quite out of touch with their own dependent needs and those of their family. If the therapists explored the necessity for this super-parent structure prematurely, before the parents had sufficient inner resources to face these anxieties, the parents felt more persecuted and retreated even further inside this defensive structure. For example, Mrs. Garcia, in response to an interpretation, would sometimes "become" one of the therapists to look at her husband's difficulties — to, as it were, get inside the therapists' skin both for protection and as a way of staying in control. This was an example of the use of projective identification. When a therapist drew attention to this, Mrs. Garcia temporarily relinquished her reliance on the defensive structure and experienced panic. She gave a vivid example of how she felt at that moment in the session: She described sitting in a car at the traffic lights, with the window open. A group of youths was walking down the street in her direction. They did not look tough but as they got near her, her heart beat rapidly; she panicked and immediately shut the window. She was worried that they would beat her up.

> This example demonstrates the panic that Mr. and Mrs. Garcia experienced whenever there was felt to be even a slight crack in their super-parent armor. When Mrs. Garcia experiences a space in which the youths, containing her own projections of an enraged, deprived, young self, can touch her she feels threatened. Being in contact with the therapists' helping capacities involves letting in this rage about

previously unmet needs. It is humiliating and she wants to "roll up the window," stay inside the car/therapist identity and keep unbearable parts of herself out. In this primitive state, the excluded part of herself is concretely felt to be a "tough enraged youth." She fears that getting in touch with her needs would mean actually becoming a violent youth. She told the therapists that incidents like that often happened. Mr. Garcia quickly intervened to say that he knew all about his wife's anxieties and added "the point is can anything be done, can anyone help?" He went on to describe an American president's lack of understanding of the needs of the Cambodian people and the cutting off of American aid and supplies to these people.

When Mr. Garcia starts to wonder if someone can help, he is immediately confronted with fears that his needs (placed in the Cambodian people) will not be met and that a catastrophe (his protest) will follow. It is worth mentioning here that one of the therapists was American and this particular session was shortly before a holiday break, so support was actually being withdrawn from the couple at that time.

The above examples clearly show the important characteristics of the object relations that the couple shared in their respective internal worlds: a highly idealized, super-capable, all-knowing, totally self-sufficient parent and a desperately needy, enraged child, unattended to and unheard. Being in touch with the needy child inside themselves threatened an explosive overthrow of their coping, adult selves. For this reason, dependency was to be avoided at all costs or treated with contempt. When one parent expressed painful feelings, the other would deny the problem, or trivialize it by making a joke or behaving in a generally manic, excited way. The therapists too were experienced by the couple as either "up" (trying to expose the couple's weakness in a cruel way in order to be superior and triumphant) or "down" (naive, young, inadequate and inexperienced people).

In discussion after sessions when the therapists explored their countertransference feelings, often one of them would feel pleased, almost excited about having done some useful work in a session and the other would feel hopeless about the prospect of any change. The therapists themselves seemed to find it difficult to stay in touch with their capacity to offer something helpful in an ordinary way because it so easily became converted into a kind of naive optimism or deep pessimism. The therapists became more critical of each other and at times felt quite competitive.

They no longer felt merged or united but were more aware of their differences and disagreements. This seemed to reflect the process of differentiation that was taking place in the parental couple.

The following example illustrates the cruelty to the self and to the other that is implicit in the omnipotent manic denial of vulnerability.

> Mr. Garcia came to a session feeling depressed. He said that he had "come down with a bang," that he felt "near to tears" and "redundant." His wife, finding this intolerable, quickly interrupted, saying that they had to get on with life, it was no good filling themselves with doubts. She spoke briskly and in a matter-of-fact-way, indicating by her manner and expression that it was simply a matter of putting on a brave smiling face. Mr. Garcia attempted to join her in this mood, saying that he could not wallow in these feelings; he thought he would go back to work full-time the following week.

Mr. Garcia had, in fact, been strongly advised by his doctor to work part-time. Since his serious illness in Spain the previous year, he remained at some risk and needed to rest and take care of himself. His wish to rush back into full-time work, at this moment encouraged by his wife, represented a denial of both internal and external reality. They again take refuge in the omnipotent idea that through some exciting activity, feelings of depression and humiliation, experiences of damage and dependency can be obliterated. The concern about the cruel neglect of the self and, in this case, an actual risk to life was not acknowledged by them but projected into the therapists, who found themselves extremely concerned and anxious about Mr. Garcia's health.

It is important to mention that due to limited availability of male staff at the time of referral, both therapists were women, and in some ways, this made it more difficult for Mr. Garcia to stay with his depressed feelings at the times when his wife was disowning hers. It was felt as humiliating for him to be seen as a man in a "weak state," particularly in the presence of three women and it was necessary for this to be openly acknowledged. Two women therapists tended to reinforce the phantasy that one parent could "do it all", as if the therapists were actually demonstrating that the male role in the parental functioning was a redundant one. Of course, as is usual in co-therapy, the actual experience was that aspects of "maternal" and/or "paternal" functions were fulfilled by both therapists. Nevertheless, it was extremely important to discuss with the couple the meaning they attached to the absence of a male therapist.

We have described the therapeutic work with the couple's shared psychic structure, which we have called "super parent/spouse." We have suggested that this structure was based on denial and projection of intolerable, painful feelings and was characterized by manic and omnipotent behavior. This phase of therapy was characterized by an increasing sense of differentiation and some acknowledgement of vulnerability.

Emergence of the "child in the parent"

With a lessening of the need to maintain the defensive structure of the "super parent," and with an increased capacity to bear deeper, more painful feelings, Mr. and Mrs. Garcia became ready to reexperience childhood anxieties under the more favorable conditions provided by the therapist couple. Now that they were more able to experience the therapists as having something good and useful to offer them, they were confronted with their anxieties about sharing. These included jealousy of each other's relation to the therapists, jealousy of the therapists' relation to each other, and anxiety about there not being "enough" for both of them. They were later able to link their anxieties with the behavior of their own children in early infancy. Mr. and Mrs. Garcia would often demonstrate jealousy by a withdrawal of interest.

For instance, when Mr. Garcia described his difficulty about being a father, getting close to his children, and his flight to helping charities and long hours of work, Mrs. Garcia sat immersed in her own thoughts, sealed off in a world of her own. Similarly, when Mrs. Garcia dramatically described some of the difficulties she experienced in managing the home without help, Mr. Garcia appeared inattentive and uninterested.

Progress in the therapy could almost be measured by the closeness or distance that one partner felt toward the other when one of them was voicing a worry. The therapists focused their interpretations on the mutuality of the problem, the effect of one partner's difficulties on the other in their shared life together.

Mr. and Mrs. Garcia's jealousy of the therapists' "togetherness" was sometimes expressed by their talking simultaneously, both urgently addressing themselves to the therapist sitting nearest to them. The therapist couple sometimes felt divided in a quite radical way and experienced this as the couples's attempt to separate them.

After a session, one therapist felt that she had been "soaking up" the intensity of the couple's distress in such a way that she had felt quite unable to think or to comment on what was happening. The other therapist felt that she had been reeling off "textbook" interpretations, responding to the discomfort of being out of touch with feelings by intense intellectual activity.

Bion (1959) has demonstrated the nature and function of attacks on linking and the detrimental effect they have on the therapist's helping capacities, particularly in relation to the therapist's ability to think creatively. In the previous example, the therapist couple was experiencing not only an attack on each one's individual ability to think, but also an attack on the link between them, their cooperative effort as it were. In fact, the parents' unconscious jealous attacks seemed to be directed against three different creative links — the link between the mind of one therapist and the mind of the other, the link between thought and feeling, and the link between activity and receptivity.

Another difficulty in sharing occurred when Mr. and Mrs. Garcia, having felt helpful by the therapists, were then faced with the anxiety that there would not be enough to meet their overwhelming needs. They were worried that the therapists were not strong enough, capable enough, or caring enough.

> During one session they talked rapidly about their anxieties about themselves. They frequently broke into each other's conversations. At one point Mrs. Garcia remarked that her husband was "greedy as a pig," ostensibly referring to his attitude to food. They later had difficulty leaving the session, still talking while putting on their coats, saying "we've got buckets more" and finally, as they walked out of the door, "we hope we haven't bored you to death."

Although they were so preoccupied by their worry about "there not being enough," they were now more in touch with their anxieties and able to talk about them, rather than simply projecting them into the therapists.

At other times, the difficulty of sharing their good relations with the therapists as well as the pain of the damage and loss was masked by an eroticization of their positive feelings toward the therapists.

Mr. and Mrs. Garcia would come to the sessions in yet more elegant and colorful clothes, Mrs. Garcia beautifully made up and Mr. Garcia transmitting the piquant aroma of some expensive male cologne. They would comment on each other's appearance and generally appear to be excitedly competing to be "the best" at winning the attention of the therapists.

At one stage in the therapy when this excited behavior was a recurrent feature, there were again somewhat unexpected repercussions in the countertransference. In discussion after a particularly difficult session, one therapist remarked that she could not understand why the couple ignored a seemingly important comment that she had made. The other replied in irritation that it was possibly due to the fact that she was wearing a rather tight-fitting dress and therefore could not expect to be taken seriously.

This kind of sexual rivalry between the therapists who usually worked cooperatively and easily together, related to the phantasies apparently aroused in Mr. and Mrs. Garcia whenever they experienced the therapists paying more attention to one of them than the other. In Mrs. Garcia's case she behaved as if she were having to bear the humiliation of her husband flirting with two other women before her very eyes. In Mr. Garcia's case he seemed to anticipate the humiliation of three women "ganging up" against him and threatening his masculinity. So the good contact between the therapists and "the child in the parents" could easily become spoiled by rivalry, possessiveness, and greed, masked by adult sexual seductiveness. It was necessary for the couple to understand that the frustrations of the "needy child" and the intense competition that this aroused was experienced as so unbearable that it was converted by them into a more exciting sexual relationship with the therapists, which was felt as more bearable.

It was noticeable that in the later phase of therapy when the good contact with the therapists was more easily maintained, it sometimes led to a resurgence of jealousy. It was only through the couple's repeated experience of the therapists' capacities to tolerate and understand the jealous attacks that they were able to face the nature of the rage inside them about previously unmet needs and to understand the way in which this rage and jealousy threatened to sabotage the helping process.

Gradually they became more in touch with their feelings of loss and unhappiness and were able to express a genuine and increased concern for themselves and each other. The following example is from a session near the end of the second year of therapy.

> Mr. Garcia said that a friend's father had recently died and he had offered to paint a portrait of the father as he remembered him in his prime. He said it would be an epitaph. When the portrait was completed he saw that he had portrayed the friend's father as an old man dying. Since then he had been unable to paint anything. Mrs. Garcia spoke of her husband's paintings, describing how beautiful some of them were. She had never been able to talk to him about why he had stopped painting.

> Later, and in subsequent sessions, Mr. and Mrs. Garcia were able to relive some of the acute pain about the premature death of both their fathers and Mrs. Garcia talked freely about her concern for her husband's health and her fears that he too would die. This also led to an increased awareness and concern about similar fears in their own children.

This is not, and cannot be, a complete account of the Garcias' therapy. In fact, this last example indicates the beginning of a more fruitful phase of the work. Mr. Garcia's health did improve gradually and the couple made considerable use of their therapy, as did the children. The developmental relationship between the parents' and the children's therapy was, of course, a significant feature. If the parents' difficulties had not been attended to, the children's treatment could not have progressed.

CONCLUSION

The purpose of this chapter has been to examine some aspects of assessment and psychoanalytically based therapy with parents. The necessity of reaching an agreement with parents for treatment as patients in their own right has been noted. The possible detrimental effects of superficial reassurance and advice have been illustrated and attention has been drawn to the fact that work with parents may suffer from the interference of having to carry messages and make practical arrangements on behalf of the child's therapist.

The method of work described here includes delineating the child and adult parts of the parents' personalities and noting how each parent encourages the other to function as a part of his/her own personality in relation to the therapists. The parents' shared internal objects are shown through their response to the therapists' interpretations and examined in the light of the therapists' countertransference experiences. Obstacles to growth such as jealousy, guilt, the use of the manic defense and projective identification are illustrated. Interpretations based on an awareness of the "child-in-the-parent's" shared experience with the therapists in the sessions are considered as the basis for growth in the parents' relationship to each other and their children.

10

Psychic Pain and Psychic Damage

GIANNA WILLIAMS

This chapter describes in some detail a short period of co-therapy that a male colleague and I conducted with a family residing briefly in England. Concepts that we had both found useful in analytic work with individuals were used as a frame of reference in the therapy. At the end of this chapter, I discuss the usefulness of transferring a model from one setting to another. In particular, I try to differentiate depressive anxiety from depression and to focus on a particular type of psychic damage that is the crippling consequences of defenses against psychic pain.

From the beginning of our contact with the Johnsons the sense of "ending" was a salient feature, and what emerged as one of the most relevant problems in the dynamics of this family was separation, loss, and endings, and the difficulties associated with them. The fact that my colleague and I knew from the outset that our work would be short-term probably enhanced our opportunity to explore this area.

THE INITIAL CONTACT

Father wrote to the clinic asking for help because of his own and his wife's concern for their 17-year-old daughter Paula. In his letter he described Paula as depressed. A week later Mr. Johnson telephoned asking with some urgency if an appointment would be forthcoming and conveying the feeling that the situation had deteriorated since he first wrote. My colleague and I offered an appointment for Paula and her parents with a view to possible family therapy.

No other members of the family had been mentioned prior to the first session. But to the second session the parents also brought their 9-year-old son Simon. We knew that Father was Australian and Mother was Scottish. The referral had been received at the beginning of March, and the family was to remain in England until the end of December.

I will give a detailed account of the first session in order to share the experience of getting to know this family.

The predominant feeling during this first meeting was one of tremendous urgency. Father made himself the spokesman for it. As soon as we sat down, he began speaking in a slow but very insistent voice about Paula's symptoms and his anxiety about them. Paula did not enjoy her present school, she had lost all interest in studying, she hardly ever went out, and she didn't seem interested in sightseeing. Mother nodded in agreement, but remained silent during most of this session. At first, Paula seemed to conform to her role as designated patient. A tall, rather obese girl, her face totally masked by a hood of dark hair, she was observing us unseen and seemed not to want to be involved in any way. When my colleague remarked on this, Paula slightly opened the curtain of hair and in a soft, but very angry voice, said very explicitly that she herself had no wish to come and see us, but that father had been "adamant." She could see no point in it. She hated being pressured, she was pressured enough at school; at home they pressured her about sitting with the family at meal time while she was on a diet and didn't want to sit with them at the dinner table. Father intervened, saying that there was a point in coming, and that we had to find a way to engender some *"joie de vivre"* in Paula as she took pleasure in nothing. "Adolescence will be over before you know it," he said.

Father's words had an urgent ring to them and their impact was very strong. I felt that the pressure to engender instant hope was weighing very heavily on us and that a strong feeling of hopelessness was being evoked. I thought that this projection might be a significant communication in terms of the countertransference. Perhaps we could come to know the feelings this family could not tolerate only by having them engendered in ourselves. I acknowledged the urgency of father's request, but said that we were bound to fall short of the family's expectations in terms of "instant hope.

Paula said it was absurd anyhow to feel hopeful about anything when the world was going from bad to worse. She spoke with great feeling about ecology and pollution and seemed much more angry than depressed. Mother intervened then and somewhat dismissed what Paula was saying.

Mother expressed her concern about the imminent arrival of Sonia, a friend of Paula's, who was going to stay with them. Sonia's outlook on life was, if possible, gloomier than Paula's. "We should bring her here too; Sonia and Paula together will really get into the doldrums." Mother's intolerance of Paula's gloomy communications suggested her own fear of "getting into the doldrums."

It was becoming increasingly clear that a mandate was being given to the therapeutic couple: very quickly exorcising this dreaded feeling of depression, engendering *joie de vivre* in Paula, and taking care of the somber Sonia. As we voiced the perception of being given a mandate by the family, Father said in a detached tone of voice, as if he wished for the information to go on record, that he himself knew about being "in the doldrums," because he had gone through a bad spell of depression three years ago; he had received some help, and "it was now completely over." By the end of this first session, Paula still looked very sullen, but now we could see her face, because she had emerged from her hood of hair.

During the first meeting and the subsequent two sessions, it became evident to all the family that although we acknowledged the pressure, we were not going to provide an instant cure nor yield to their urgency. We defined the boundaries of our initial contact by saying that we were willing to continue exploring the family's problem together with them to see if it might be useful to embark on a prolonged period of treatment.

All their voices remained very soft throughout, but resentment and disappointment made themselves heard in other ways. We were told of another absent–present member of the family who could profit by coming to us for help, a maternal uncle. He was very prone to violent tempers, but whenever he got angry and felt like yelling he lost his voice completely. He had been given many physical examinations but no organic causes could be found for his symptoms. We were probably being told—through the suggestion that someone else "should join the session," like Sonia in the "doldrums"—about a significant problem in the family, which was difficulty in dealing with hostility and aggression. We had been struck, for instance, by Paula's particularly soft tone of voice when at the height of her anger.

The fourth member of the family, 9-year-old Simon, was probably the one who least lost his voice when it came to expressing negative feelings. In the third session, he told us about a teacher he hated and put a great deal of feeling into saying so. This teacher, he said, cannot control his temper and shouts at the children all the time, or else "he just puts you outside the door for no reason at all." Mother confirmed that his teacher was indeed very high strung and suggested, with a laugh, that he too might benefit from our sessions. We were getting used to this type of message, and Mother may have laughed, I think, because she too was beginning to notice the recurrent suggestion: "someone else should join us."

Although the maternal uncle and the teacher seemed chiefly to represent split-off aspects of family feelings, Simon's complaint about the unpredictable man who "just puts you outside the door" might have had something to do with the family's uncertainty during this period, when they were "put outside the door" at the end of each session.

At our third meeting we offered regular weekly sessions for the remainder of the family's stay in England. We realized that despite our falling short of their expectations, they all experienced considerable relief when we agreed on a longer-term contract. It was then that Mother said our work must have been of help already, because Paula appeared to have come out of her shell a little. She was going out more and had enrolled in an art class. Mother was pleased, but she regretted that the art class met only once a week.

Once we had decided to offer a treatment contract, we felt freer to work in the transference and to connect Mother's "only once a week" to our offer of weekly sessions. Before we had decided on a longer period of treatment, we were more cautious in interpreting infantile feelings.

THE TREATMENT

Reaction to the first holiday break

As I have already mentioned, the brief duration of our contact loomed large from the beginning of our work. Mother was the one in the family most in touch with feelings about the brevity of the treatment.

The Easter holiday came shortly after we agreed on regular weekly sessions. Mother was very aware of the two-week break and said it was a pity to have an interruption so soon after we had started. Father seemed to ignore our mention of the holiday, and Paula and Simon did not take much notice.

The first time we saw the family after the Easter holiday, it was Simon who spoke with great feeling about not liking his parents to go out and leave him at home with a baby-sitter. Paula would baby-sit sometimes, but she sounded much less disposed than Simon to being in the lonely corner of the oedipal triangle. Her friend Sonia was now staying with the family and Paula was not left alone when the parents went out; she had a friend of her own age. It did not sound as if Sonia and Paula were at all getting "into the doldrums"; they seemed to be getting on very well, going out often and having a good time. Paula's attitude seemed to highlight

Simon's much less privileged position. I described how, in the third session, Simon had spoken for the family in expressing resentment at being left outside the door, which had probably reflected his predicament as the youngest member of the family. Now he was voicing, perhaps on behalf of the others as well, how it feels when parents go out with some reference to the break in the treatment and to the therapists as a couple that had gone away and not been available.

In reply to our interpretation about the holiday, Mother said that during the break they had a very frantic time. She spoke of a very hectic period of sightseeing and complained that Father had to do everything fast, "as if life was slipping away." She also mentioned his concern that they would not have seen everything by the time they return to Australia. She said that she didn't mind for herself. She enjoys what she does while she is doing it. There seemed to be a link between this communication and the fact that, indeed, we would not be able to look at everything that needed looking at and working through during our brief period together, but the sense of urgency seemed to have been shifted onto sightseeing.

At one of the subsequent sessions it became apparent that the family equated the therapeutic relationship with sightseeing, for defensive purposes. Here, in some detail, is the material that led to our discussion of this crucial issue.

At the beginning of a May session, Father told us in a rather offhand way that the family had been visiting a number of museums, and the tone of the communication suggested that we might be one of the sights they were visiting. While talking about the British Museum, I was struck by the word "mummy," and I tried to figure out what connection there was between the museum material (and these particularly dead exhibits) and my feelings at that moment of the session. I felt particularly inhibited and had difficulty in talking during the first part of the session. Could there be a link between the mummies Paula was talking about and my sense of being somehow deadened at that point? Was the Tavistock being turned into a tourist sight and I into a museum piece, some sort of mummified mother-mummy? In subsequent conversation with my colleague, who had felt much freer to interpret during the first fifteen minutes of the session, we concluded that the dead feeling had been lodged chiefly in me during that part of the session.

The family's perception of the Tavistock as a museum to be visited served many defensive purposes. The uniqueness of specific museums seemed to be obliterated—the message appeared to be that there are museums in every town, and they could go on with their sightseeing even after they had left England. It was also significant that this devitalizing transformation of therapists into museum pieces occurred immediately after the holiday. Our deciding to have a 2-week interruption and behaving like a live therapeutic couple who can come and go had been resented, not only by Simon, but by all the family members. By deadening an object before it died on them, that is, before separation occurred, feelings of loss and mourning were bypassed and avoided. When we had interpreted this deadening process to them as a particular defensive maneuver, Mother said, quite sadly, that there actually was very little time before treatment came to an end. She had counted the weeks that remained. She did not know how many weeks we intended to take off during the summer, but she knew that they had to leave England by the end of the year.

It was only when the mood of the session shifted in this direction that the family could examine with us some of their more frequent defenses for avoiding psychic pain. A certain capacity to hold depressive anxiety was required if one were to examine defenses rather than employ them. The frenetic element implicit in moving from sight to sight had also been present in the family's relationship with us. At times we were given a wealth of material and were kept on our toes if we were to distinguish significant content from significant process in the interpretive work. As the atmosphere became less frenetic, after some therapeutic work had taken place, we could begin to talk more about the frenzy.

It was important to clear Mr. Johnson of the charge made by the rest of the family that he was the only "compulsive sightseer" who needed to speed from one sight to another. Indeed, they had all willingly joined him during those holiday activities. In this context we spoke of the joint defenses that was implicit in treating us as one of the sights to be rushed through. My colleague and I felt that this was the point at which Father really became involved in the treatment. It is interesting that on this occasion he spoke for the first time about his own parents and family. It was the first time, too, that he appeared in the role of someone's child. Mr. Johnson had much more difficulty than the others in acting like someone who had had a childhood himself. One might give some thought to the significance in family therapy of the point at which either of the parents or both are able to cross this threshold and talk about their relationship to their own parents.

Father spoke of his mother, who had been dead for three years, and said that his depression had followed her death. He said that he could not forgive himself for having avoided contact with his mother during her long illness. He lived in a different part of the country and very seldom visited her, less often than he might have. He was sure that his mother's ill health had gotten worse when his sister left home, never to return, because her marriage had not been approved of. He implied that his absence and his neglect had contributed to the deterioration of his mother's health. He had been away when she died, and still had not put a tombstone on her grave. Father spoke with much feeling and sincerity about his difficulties in sustaining pain, mourning, and loss. Simon was sitting next to him and drew very close to his father. This was one of the sessions in which the whole family could sustain feelings of sadness, loss, and regret, depressive rather than pathologically depressed feelings.

It was a good opportunity for us to link their difficulty in dealing with feelings of loss and mourning with the way they were attempting to negotiate the ending of their relationship with us. When we spoke about deadening the relationship, Mother had a very spontaneous response to the interpretation. She said that she very seldom forgets people's names, and she was surprised that none of the family could remember my colleague's name when they got home. All they could say was "Doctor . . . what?" The whole family seemed to agree that this was another defense against the risk of losing somebody valuable. It might be described as "out-of-mind before out-of-sight."

In this and subsequent sessions we worked steadily on the themes of both sadness and anger. Father showed concern about his tendency to lose his temper, especially with Simon. He wanted his son to be perfect and probably set very unrealistic standards. As Father climbed down from his usual position of rigid authority, there was the risk that the family might take this as a moment of weakness and gang up on him. Mother said she found it extremely difficult to be angry when her husband was present, but when he wasn't there, she could be very angry to the extent of occasionally doing mental, if not physical, violence to the children. Mother had never presented an excessively idealized picture of herself, and this acknowledgment did not evoke the same kind of attack that the pricking of Father's bubble had. Father merely said that he found it easier to tolerate his wife showing anger than painful emotions. When visiting relatives had left for Australia she cried at the airport. Father could not bear her open tears. Both my co-therapist and I felt that this remark contained an implicit accusation against us, as if we were seen as wanting to put the whole family in touch with tears that had not been shed.

Persecutory feelings

I should now like to focus on the emergence of persecutory feelings, which seemed to indicate a shift from depressive anxiety back to a much more schizo-paranoid dimension. These shifts occurred at different times during the treatment. Two specific examples seem particularly significant, although they did not emerge in close sequence.

The first very persecutory image we encountered was in the extremely vivid description of a female cousin of Father's who was coming to visit the family. We were struck by the possible link between this overpowering relative and the therapeutic couple, because the woman was described as "always full of good advice" about rearing children and sorting out family problems. She always acted like an expert, and her expertise seemed to extend to many fields. They found it very unpleasant to go to museums with her because she always knew so much more than anyone else. They also remarked on her accent. She always affected a very pure English accent in Australia, so they could well imagine how hard she would try to speak perfect English on her visit. It was not clear whether this particular remark was aimed at me and my foreign accent, or at my colleague, the only one in the room who spoke with an English accent. What did seem clear, however, was that the links between the cousin and the therapists suggested that we were perceived as overpowering people who flaunted their expertise and knowledge of families. Something was perceived as very persecutory, probably not in our accents but in the content of our communications. A significant reference to the cousin seemed to coincide with what was happening in the session: Father told us that when his cousin phoned recently from Australia, he so much disliked the sound of her voice that he held the phone away from his ear and didn't really listen to what she was saying. During the same session, twice when my colleague tried to speak, Father drowned his voice with his own. Father seemed unable to listen, even before he knew the content of the message.

It proved harder to deal with the summer holidays than with the Easter holiday, because the family had been looking more closely at some of the defenses they used to shield themselves from missing someone. Their defenses, then, were less operative and they were more exposed to painful feelings. After the summer break another relevant person was mentioned, someone who had never been mentioned before. This was the maternal grandmother, who had moved from Scotland to Australia and was described by each member of the family in turn as somebody they did not look forward to seeing when they returned; indeed the feeling of persecution seemed to be shared by them all. She was described as a domineering person; she had helped them financially and therefore felt entitled to organize their lives. They feared her proximity when they returned to Australia. The family saw her as someone who was willing to offer a great deal, but for a high price, the price of their freedom. What seemed to emerge in terms of the family's relationship with us was anxiety about the strings that might be attached to whatever we gave to them, and fear of becoming dependent on us. The holiday break had been difficult to tolerate and heightened the feeling that we might be imposing a rather high price on them.

Dependency and independence seemed to be in the air in this session. We learned from Mrs. Johnson that Simon had taken the subway alone for the first time. The whole family seemed extremely happy and proud of this achievement. They also mentioned a maternal aunt who had difficulty going any distance from her home and entering unfamiliar surroundings. She had planned to visit the family in England but was afraid to leave her home environment. The adventurous Simon and the almost house-bound aunt seemed to represent the two poles of independence and extreme dependency. The main anxiety apparent in this session was fear of being enslaved in a relationship of utter dependency.

Conclusion

During the last weeks of treatment, feelings of persecution lessened considerably as we interpreted them in the transference. The parents — more than the children — were particularly able to sustain feelings of loss and to prize what was going to be missed with the end of our contact. Father had often spoken of resuming family therapy when they returned to Australia. Although we agreed that further help might be desirable at some point, we thought it might not be helpful to replace us immediately with another therapeutic relationship, because of the family's specific problems of working through their feelings of mourning.

Some months after the family went back home, we learned that they "were giving themselves time" before seeking further help. The home-coming had been fraught with difficulties, but they seemed to have coped without serious crises.

It is hard enough to interpret a communication in the immediacy of a session, so my hypothesis about the written communication, "we are giving ourselves time" is very tentative. We had certainly not offered this family answers or solutions. We had tried to give them a taste of allowing and valuing a 'space for thinking' rather than resorting to fast action or other painkillers. This internal space is also the essential prerequisite for keeping experience alive. I think there are grounds for hope that we have been granted a space in their mind and that we are not totally out of sight, out of mind.

DISCUSSION

I have described the dynamics of this family as if I were speaking of an individual struggling with a problem. Indeed, this was a hypothesis we were testing out in our work; we were trying to apply an individual model in a family setting. To clarify this frame of reference, I shall continue to discuss the Johnson family in terms of dynamics that could apply to work with individual patients. Whether this transposition is feasible or not, our working hypothesis gave us much food for thought.

At the first session we were presented with a designated patient whose father had described her as "depressed." Our first perception of Paula seemed partially to confirm this. Perhaps this was a problem of pathological depression, but whose depression was it? The feelings of great hopelessness engendered in both therapists in the countertransference shed some light on this and it might be helpful, at this point, to refer to Meltzer's (1978) distinction between hopelessness and despair. One may be hopeless, without hope, but still painfully yearn for hope. Or one may despair, give up hope and no longer feel pain. If we call the former hopelessness and the latter despair, hopelessness seems closer to feelings of depressive anxiety, while despair, often accompanied by anger and grief, seems more typical of pathological depression. In this context pathological depression can be seen as a defeat in the struggle with depressive anxiety. "Depressive illness arises as the result of the inability to face or adequately deal with the conflict aroused in the depressive position" (Rosenbluth 1965, p. 20).

At the outset Paula was probably so weighed down by the family projections that she had given up struggling and "grasping after hope." Our sense of hopelessness was engendered chiefly by Father's urgency in delegating the struggle to us. Father asked for an injection of "joie de vivre," he was afraid that "adolescence would be over before Paula knew it"; and Mother wanted us to keep Paula and Sonia "out of the doldrums." The whole family seemed to be making meaningful communications and suggesting that the problem was one they all shared. The countertransference message seemed very clear: the co-therapists were being asked to keep hope alive, because the family could no longer sustain the psychic pain involved in the struggle to save hope.

The urgency of the request was probably proportional to the weight of the intolerable anxiety. We must act quickly and provide a fast remedy. A specific psychic pain had to be held and be given meaning, so that it could be borne instead of massively projected into one member of the family. It sounded as if Paula had given up the struggle and was "in despair" when she said that it was absurd to feel hopeful when the world was going from bad to worse. But there were also signs that the projection was not too firmly lodged in her. For instance, when Father alluded to his own "bad spell of depression," although he needed to add that it was now a thing of the past and it was completely over, Paula seemed only too willing to shed the role of designated patient. Her initial appearance, with her hair masking her face, suggested a "character in search of an author," a frequent feature of family therapy, but she soon emerged as a character "in fear of an author," an unwilling receptacle of projection. There was no need to engender "joie de vivre," for she found her own liveliness once the role assignment was lifted.

It was technically very important that the therapists open themselves in the countertransference to the projections that were present, thus discovering what the pain was about, rather than redistributing the pain at a distance, as if checkmating the different family members in turn. The projection of deadening in one of the sessions served many defensive purposes, but at the same time it made us concretely aware of the anxious feelings and sense of paralysis involved in identifying with a lifeless object. This, of course, is a significant feature of pathological depression.

There was abundant evidence that depression was accompanied by massive persecutory anxiety. This is another feature that differentiates pathological depression from depressive feelings. There was a shared nightmare in this family. The individual members felt the anxiety to different degrees, but there seemed to be a shared internal object that took different guises; the image of a damaged, and potentially vengeful mother appeared in the very first session, when Paula spoke at length about ecology. The polluted earth, like a neglected mother, might turn vengeful and starve humanity. Paula's communication seemed to be a nutshell version of a problem we were to hear about later: Father's own mother had not been looked after during her long illness. She had been neglected during her life and had not been mourned after her death; no tombstone had been put on her grave. This unmourned persecutory object appeared to be at the core of father's "bad spell of depression" and to have put him into the doldrums.

Until very near the end of treatment, the transference could shift to very persecutory feelings in the family's perception of their relationship with us; the therapeutic couple might become the persecutory object. My colleague's voice became as threatening as that of the formidable cousin. There was indeed a risk of becoming persecutory and acting in the countertransference unless we were vigilant. We must avoid marching ruthlessly over the family defenses, prescribing compulsory mourning and compulsory psychic pain. Instead we tried to contain the anxieties underlying the defenses and thus make the latter less necessary.

This family employed several defenses. There were attempts at quick solutions and a search for analgesics as a defense against psychic pain. Manic defenses were abundant, such as the frenetic sightseeing. It was important that these be seen as a family pattern and not delegated to Father. The casual transformation of a valuable object into a dusty museum piece might recur when the Johnsons went home, were they to embark at once on a new contract of family therapy. Every member of the family employed projective identification, engendering the sense of hopelessness in the therapeutic couple during the first session also and through their communication about Egyptian mummies. There were cross-projections within the family: Simon was made to bear all the oedipal pain; he was the one "left outside the door" or left at home when the parents went out. It was important that these aspects be picked up in the transference, so that the family could see them as a shared predicament that recurred in their relationship with us. It was equally important not to collude in making Mother the spokesperson for all the depressive feelings the family could allow itself. She seemed to have assumed that function. She was the only member of the family who openly commented on the Easter break. She counted the remaining weeks of therapy and she expressed gratitude for Paula's improvement.

Father resented her because she could afford to cry when a relative left. This frequently happens when a desirable aspect of internal structures is lodged in one member of a group, because that person might easily become the five-star patient, the one who is "really making use of treatment." I find this kind of projective identification, the opposite of scapegoating, extremely frequent in group processes, especially in family work. It might elicit a very undesirable preferential attitude in the therapist.

Given the brevity of our work, we could not expect to help our patients replace a persecutory or idealized object by a good object. But we could guard against taking a judgmental stance, which would be persecutory, and we could refuse to collude in idealizations of the kind represented by requests for instant solutions. To grasp the urgency of the request to fulfill an idealized role (a frequent demand when persecutory anxieties are present) it might be useful to consider the specific element of persecutory anxiety in the process of mourning.

In "Mourning and its Relations to Manic Depressive States" (1940) Melanie Klein says:

> The poignancy of the actual loss of a loved person is in my view greatly increased by the mourner's unconscious phantasies of having lost his internal good objects as well. He then feels that his internal bad objects predominate and his inner world is in danger of disruption. [p. 353]

I think this helps clarify the predominance of persecutory feeling in pathological depression. The link between an impaired capacity to mourn and sustain feelings of loss and depression was a predominant feature in the Johnson family's psychopathology.

Severe states of depression might lead to such deadlines that no attempt is made to restore "joie de vivre" and there is a total abandonment to "joie de mourir." No such gross pathology was present in our patients. Consider for instance, Father's urgency in grasping all the good things in life, "because life is slipping away." The manic edge is evident, but there is also a recognition that life offers good things that are worth grasping. Persecutory anxiety led to the request that we become an idealized object that could counteract the dread of deadlines. We could not meet this mandate, which would imply collusion at a schizo-paranoid level where persecutory and idealized objects remain split, but it was important that we understand the anxiety that exerted such pressure on us to fulfill that role.

In the last weeks of our work, depressive feelings increasingly emerged and pathological depression diminished. It is natural that depressive feelings fluctuate, and we tried to draw the family's attention to the problem of holding psychic pain. Our hypothesis, derived from work with individuals, was that there is a close relationship between psychic pain and psychic damage, and that impoverishment of the enjoyment of life and relationships can derive from an intolerance of psychic pain. As Kahlil Gibran (1926) said, "the deeper that sorrow carves into your being the more joy it can contain" (p. 36). We feel that we gave some help to this family to increase their capacity to bear psychic pain without feeling too persecuted. Moreover, it is possible that the psychic damage resulting from intolerance of psychic pain may also have been lessened.

11

The Micro-Environment

ARTHUR HYATT WILLIAMS

During ten years of therapeutic work with families, it has become increasingly impressed upon me that the family is the link between the individual and the wider social and cultural milieu. It is the prototype of all small groups. How does it impinge upon the young person who is developing as an individual? It becomes clear practically, as well as making therapeutical sense, that the impact of family upon the developing individual young person both facilitates and restricts. It is a push–pull system and there are other functions too. If we regard the family as the basic ecosystem of human beings, ideas about such phenomena as pollution, stasis, change, and self-cleansing arise. When the family interactive ecosystem is working satisfactorily, we, in the caring services, are unlikely to be given a chance to observe it. Instead, we are called in when something goes wrong and the family functioning becomes impaired, distorted, or comes to a full stop.

Like other relatively safe situations that facilitate development by being to some extent cordoned off from the wider environmental milieu, the sanctuary aspect of the family may, and often does, slip from its facilitating function, first into stasis and then into an increasing restrictiveness, so that what was a sanctuary becomes a prison.

Only after a considerable time did my co-therapist and I realize that the family about which I am now writing had slipped into a closed prison-like restrictiveness. One cause of the situation that prevailed when we were called upon to give family therapy to the Stone family was the way in which both parents, but especially the mother, needed to treat the adolescent members of the family as if they were babies, even though they were almost grown up. This attitude, of course, was unconsciously determined.

The reasons for the referral of the Stone family were that the 18-year-old son was said to be violent and unmanageable. Also, the family doctor said that the whole family reverberated with turbulence allegedly set into motion by the disturbed young man in such a way that the doctor was given no peace. Previously, psychotherapy had been given to this young man but though there had been some temporary lulls in his behavior, the benefits of the treatment had not withstood the effects of breaks in the sequence of his once-weekly sessions. At the time of referral to us, the situation had reached a crisis point.

The Stone family consisted of Father and Mother in their early forties, Stuart, aged 18 and Carole, aged 16. The father was a highly verbal, intelligent businessman who nearly always started off speaking in the sessions by recording a catalogue of the depredations of Stuart, complaining how Stuart arrogantly made impossible demands and then became verbally abusive when the demands could not be met. After the words came the violence, which was expressed by physically aggressive assaults upon Father, Mother or Sister or upon any article of property that was immediately accessible.

In the session, Stuart would sit listening to all this with rapt attention, nodding his head in affirmation or shaking it in disagreement. It was clear from his facial expression that Stuart enjoyed being the object of attention. However, if something was said that touched him at any depth, he would explode into verbal abuse and follow up the violent words with deeds. Stuart customarily tried to set one person against another, and by seductive eye movements would try to gain an ally. He would set his mother against his father or onto one or the other of the therapists. In general he was softer and more ingratiating to the males and harsher, nastier and more denigrating to the females. Retreat on the part of his mother or sister participating in early stages of therapy seemed to evoke further nastiness, often including scorn and mockery of a sadistic and insulting kind. Counterattack on the part of Mother or Sister resulted in violence, often in the form of crude physical attacks aimed at inflicting pain.

For example, on one occasion Stuart verbally attacked his sister Carole, who shouted back at him, whereupon he got up from his chair to hit her, saying, "That'll teach you not to speak like that to me." Carole was thus reduced to tears of pain and humiliation. Stuart attacked his mother violently on one occasion. He did not initiate an attack upon his father but

during his father's attempts to restrain him, when my co-therapist designated the toddler part of him as being in a tantrum and unable to bear any
"adult" advice from a more grown-up part of himself or from either of us
or from any other family member, he was particularly enraged. Father
then intervened at a moment when I was feeling anxious about the threat
of actual violence to my co-therapist. Stuart mocked me and also imitated
me without mocking but never threatened me with violence.

CO-THERAPY

Before going on to recount the history and vicissitudes of the therapy, I
would like to discuss the effect of the fact that the two co-therapists were
related to each other as man and wife.

On previous occasions when my wife and I have worked together as
co-therapists with families, it has become clear that there are special
features about our relationship. In most kinds of co-therapy, families tend
to try and incorporate both therapists as family members. Sometimes they
polarize the co-workers, designating one of them as good and rejecting the
other as bad. The situation usually fluctuates. Family members almost
invariably have fantasies and suppositions about the relationship that exists
between the two co-therapists: that they are involved in sexual orgies, or
are quarrelling and fighting. When the two therapists are actually married,
there are even more efforts to set one of them against the other but there
is also a tremendous feeling that they are in fact inseparable. The link
between the therapists in this case did provide a firm holding framework
within which the family could be contained. But as well as the family's
feeling of confidence that the therapists who are married to each other are
able to withstand any attacks consciously or unconsciously designed to split
them apart, there was in this case the shared feeling of being confronted
with a powerful therapist gang-up against them. The family often felt that
power, and sometimes omnipotence and/or omniscience, resided in the two
therapists together. The supposed use to which these persons would be put
depended upon how the family viewed them, and if the family members
felt persecuted by the situation, they saw it as being precipitated solely by
the therapists. On the contrary, if the therapeutic couple (viewed as one)
was experienced as a helpful combination, they tended to be idealized. It
is not intended to suggest that the attacks by family members upon the
formal linkage between the co-therapists had no effect. Alternatively, it
was clear that at least two things happened to us: (1) we each experienced
the family member or members differently and, (2) what was actually
projected into either or both of us, if insufficiently worked through by us

after the sessions with the family, made our work less effective. On the other hand, when we were able to work through both our similar and our different experiences in relationship to the Stone family, something like a stereoscopic view became possible. It may be that two co-therapists who are actually married can find greater opportunities to reach a more digested and therefore more integrated view of the family in therapy than the unrelated couple, where their only meeting time may be the therapeutic session with the family. It is to be emphasized that in family therapy the co-therapists should arrange to meet at least once between one session and the next one to discuss and review what went on in the last one, referring back to previous sessions in order to keep in touch with the trend of therapy. With family therapy carried out by co-therapists who are married to each other, however, many meetings occur between sessions and often issues are brought up and discussed as they occur to one or the other of the therapists.

FAMILY ECOLOGY AND THE MICRO-ENVIRONMENT

While thinking of a way of looking at the Stone family and the violent member who was regarded as their prevailing problem, I was impressed again by the need to look at individual psychology and group pathology in order to see what kept the family together within a micro-environment.

Ecologically speaking, the family consists of a small unit. It starts off with the marriage of two people and begins to crystallize some identity when the couple set up home together. Further development takes place with the advent of each child. Contact with the extended family and with various other ecological systems in the wider environment is established. The situation that develops is far from a static one.

Looking at the family as a micro-psycho-social and economic environment brought to mind the memory of seeing a micro-environment in the English countryside. Many years ago I saw a large excavation made in the course of extracting gravel. After the end of the marketable gravel had been reached and the workmen had departed, leaving a large, wide cavity, changes began to take place. After each rainy period a pond was formed. At first, it dried up between storms but then ceased to do so as an impervious layer of diatom and other skeletons of microscopic creatures accumulated. Thereafter a very impressive micro-environment slowly developed, eventually reaching an ecological balance. There were trees, not only around the edge, an array of plants, and a wide variety of fresh water creatures from water voles to frogs, fish, and dragonfly larvae. There had been formed an oasis, which facilitated the settlement and breeding of diverse forms of life, under conditions that favored growth and development. It was less exposed than the world around it. It was comfortable, though eventually to some creatures it must have been restrictive. I began to think of the similarity between this micro-environment and that of the family. There is often the same protection from the outside world, interactiveness, ecological balance, and, ultimately, restrictiveness. When the balance has been disturbed by forces acting within the micro-environment or impinging from the world outside the environment, homeostatic processes are set into motion to restore it. In the case of the family where this effort has failed, there comes a point at which they need therapeutic help.

The difference between the natural history of the two ecosystems, the pond and the nuclear family, is demonstrated by the way in which they break up. In the course of time, the deep-rooted sallow bushes will pierce the impervious bed of the pond and the water will leak out, leaving only an area of damp land. The nuclear family ends when the growth to independence of the children results in their leaving home at an appropriate time so that only the two middle-aged parents are left to reconstitute themselves in the two-person relations with which they began their married life together. It must be emphasized that the development of the children from infancy, toddler stage, latency period to adolescence, and finally adult status poses problems for the family ecosystem. These problems affect the parents differently at each crisis of growth and development. This applies whether the crisis is about physical growth or educational achievement. Transformations destabilize the family ecosystem. In some families the main efforts of the family members are directed to the task of negotiating the destabilized periods. In other families, and particularly in the Stone family, the energies of the parents are concentrated on the restoration of stability. These efforts are often successful in reducing strain. This can, however, be at the expense of the more desirable growth through difficulties toward independence and separateness within the overall framework of continued interrelatedness.

In this family Carole remained childish and Stuart rebelled against retribution but they colluded with each other and often even demanded total service and subsidy. When the children leave home, fresh adaptive efforts are required on their part, each in turn, of course, and on the part of the parents, whose role has changed and become more limited.

The Stone family was in the course of such a period of change, with Stuart having reached the age of 18 and Carole, 16. There was a resistance to the process of growth toward independence in both the adolescents, and a resistance to change in and reduction of the established ecology of the nuclear family which was shown in the behavior and attitude of the parents. Thus there was a collusive effort on the part of the whole family to perpetuate the status quo, and to prevent what was regarded as the prospect of the death of the family.

There was a collusive idea in the family that keeping in was safer than letting out because letting out might be tantamount to letting die. Fear of persecution coming from outside was exemplified by the fact that both mother and Carole always locked all the car doors when they were driving anywhere. In line with this attitude was the way in which they treated my wife and me during the early part of the therapy. They reacted as if to say "We will complain. That is why we came but you must not say or do anything to any one of us even if it only *seems* to be critical." The point of this seemed to be that they could put into us any disturbing state of mind of an individual member of the family as a whole, but once this was done we must not hand anything back to them. If we did, one or all of the family members experienced what we said either as a persecution or as a rejection or both. Having felt incorporated into the family "pond," we were being used as therapeutic lavatories or dustbins and only after considerable work did this situation become modified.

ASPECTS OF ONGOING TREATMENT

It is difficult to describe the atmosphere that began to develop, but both my wife and I became aware of an atmosphere of brooding threat. I had known this atmosphere before when dealing with people who were in a murderous state of mind. The murderousness of which we became aware was not in direct form but was associated with a complete lack of care about life—care about the lives of other people—and we were left filled with anxiety about what might happen during the period between sessions. My wife made our anxieties explicit in one particular session but there was then no time to open up the subject before it ended. The brief mention of possible attack on life did not mitigate the anxiety of the two therapists. I would like to stress a point of technique, namely that brief mention may do more harm than good, and that working through a difficult state of mind, individual or shared, takes time and work.

At the next session there was an atmosphere of gloom and fear. The story emerged that Stuart had parked his car, opened the door to get out, and a drunken cyclist had struck the door, skidded and fallen heavily on the road, struck his head upon the hard road surface and died in minutes of an intracranial hemorrhage. Stuart was prosecuted and found it impossible at that time to feel sorry for the dead man. He was beset only with concern about being found guilty. To us this indicated that Stuart and the Stone family were in a state of mind in which there was no thought for others, no real regret over irremediable harm done, but only a shared wish to avoid blame or punishment. The implication was that there could be no learning from the experience of this awful incident and without such learning the catastrophe might be repeated. Stuart was not feeling guilt or remorse. He was not feeling sorry for the man who had lost his life but, on the contrary, was angry with the victim for causing him so much trouble. He felt aggrieved and wronged. This state of mind is characteristic of that of the very young infant, and in a young man of 18 is indicative of a severe degree of emotional immaturity.

The family, only marginally more concerned, was mainly protective toward Stuart. My wife and I were shocked and sad. Also, we wondered how much this was an overdetermined situation, and how much it was an entirely fortuitous disaster to which the Stone family and Stuart were responding in a characteristic way. The sadness we felt may have been that which Stuart and the rest of the Stone family could not face in themselves. The state of mind that eluded them at this stage was that of feeling depressive anxiety in which sadness and regret are tolerated and from which arise attempts to make amends for harm done.

When the court case was over the family relaxed, and there was a good deal of rather macabre jokiness. It was at this point that we were able to point out the shared attitudes of the Stone family. Other people did not really matter at all except insofar as they were useful to them. When family interpretations were made there was an immediate scurry to load that which was experienced as blame or accusation onto Stuart. It was constantly made clear that Stuart was repeatedly set up as the executive agent of all the family violence and aggressiveness. The elements of family interaction in the session consisted of accusations used as missiles, mockery and devaluation with the aim of deskilling a family member or either therapist. Softsoaping, placation, and threats were all elements used in dealing with the therapists, but self-accusations were experienced as if they were coming at one or another family member from either or both of the therapists.

COUNTERTRANSFERENCE EXPERIENCES

Quite early in the family therapy as we observed the undercurrent of incestuous sexuality between the two young people, we drew attention to it but it was denied. We, the co-therapists, designated as grandparents, were nearly always set up as critics, but not in a straightforward way. My wife, who is about the same age as Mrs. Stone, was loaded with anger and disapproval, the anger and disapproval that Mrs. Stone would normally have felt, while I experienced a mixed response. On the one hand, I could see what dreadful things Stuart said and did, but at the same time I responded to a certain comic quality in his behavior. The response would have been appropriate had I been watching a comic play but to Stuart's burlesquing there was a more serious and ominous side. I used to feel embarrassed when I found myself smiling or even laughing at what was going on, especially when I looked across at my wife and saw that she was angry with me. I later realized that I was being conned by the shocking amusing aspect of infantile behavior that was a result of Stuart's switching on to one of his joke-selves — a practiced parade of the naughty little boy. My wife, however, was filled with disapproval of the manic current that had taken over with its mockery and cruelty — another aspect of Stuart's behavior.

In the discussions we had after the session, we reached the conclusion that we were being "programmed" differently, probably by means of projective identification, so that we became possessed by different feelings. We had not experienced the different responses to specific family issues in this way before. Since treating the Stone family, however, we have had further co-therapy experiences with other families that suggest that what we thought was happening to us really belonged more to the Stone family than our own individual psychopathology.

There is a likelihood that adolescents project differently into parents and other authorities and as a result often do see them at loggerheads with each other. Our different responses to a family may have been related to the different feelings experienced by different family members at a given moment in time, with the implied taunt being added in the form of the question "How do you cope with this?" The projection into another person of a state of mind belonging to the projector was first described by Klein (1946) and named *projective identification*. The object or projectee experiences what has been put into him, and the projector, the subject, is freed, at least to some extent, from a state of mind that is unbearable in one way or another. The equation can be and often is reversed, so that what has been put into someone is returned, and this is what Stuart appeared to do — return what had been put into him as well as much of his own violence which was added to it. I must emphasize that projective identification is not the same as projection. In projection a state of mind of the self is ascribed to someone else, not actually evoked in him.

We realized after some period of time that the Stone family sometimes communicated as a whole and sometimes as individuals. When they did so as individuals by means of projective identification, it followed logically that we as therapists were likely to be "taken possession" of by states of mind that were quite different from each other. The different feelings that had been evoked in us had the effect of driving us apart so that we had the problem of attempting to bring together and to understand the differences. It will be evident that those differences really belonged to members of the Stone family and were the ones they had been unable to harmonize. How we, the two co-therapists, coped with this situation was to try and work upon our own states of mind. This was particularly important in the intervals between the family therapy sessions in which we differed. When we had been able to do this and to respond to what was happening in the following sessions, we noticed that the family members were able to work better with us and also with each other to some effect between the family therapy sessions. This exemplifies the need for co-therapists to work over together, after sessions, the often painful experiences, so as to provide a basis for further work with the family.

STEREOTYPING TO AVOID INTRAPSYCHIC CONFLICT

Nevertheless each family member behaved in his or her individual and characteristic way and the pattern was fairly fixed and constant. Stuart listened to everything but was more prone than the other family members to externalize what he had learned from the therapeutic session, and to apply it to the others rather than to himself. To some extent the other family members also behaved in a similar way, but less exclusively so. Father intellectualized everything; Mother felt accused of being a failure and wept copiously. Carole, when she felt accused, accused somebody else, usually Stuart, but at times she quarreled with her mother or her father or with either of the two therapists. She had a high-pitched voice and a babyish expression. These individualized roles that the family members took meant that there was no individual feeling of responsibility for any aggression. What was the most troublesome was a serious quantum of noncontained violence that floated about, and for the convenience of the rest of the family it continued in the main to be settled upon Stuart. He in turn was susceptible to this loading upon him of all the awfulness, and his response was complicated. He was angry and outraged but also excited and exhibitionistic like the actor in a melodrama who plays the part of the "baddie." Being the recipient of what the other family members put into him gave a sense of importance as in the well-known children's game "It." By "it" I mean that he was singled out by the family to act upon their behalf as a receptacle for, and perpetrator of, all the family violence. But as well as being pleased at being "it," Stuart was persecuted and aggrieved by having that role thrust upon him. The enjoyment of being "it" is a more serious feature as it is perverse and is alienated still further from normal healthy functioning.

At this stage we began to interpret the way in which the family violence and antidevelopmental aggressiveness were put into or upon Stuart and how, despite all protestations to the contrary, in many respects it suited the rest of the family for this to happen. It relieved them of guilt, externalized the responsibility, and gave them all a cherished grievance together with a comfortable sense of their own virtue. It also fitted in with the vain and exhibitionistic aspects of Stuart as he basked triumphantly in the notoriety of every tense and reproachful family situation. This was a perverse aspect of his character. At other times he was able, with some justification, to feel persecuted at being set up as a scapegoat by both his parents and his sister. This attitude, it must be stressed, was an indication of the more healthy aspect of him that developed further during therapy, albeit slowly.

One of the features that we noted in all members of the family, but especially in the two adolescents, was that introjection, involving the taking into the self of experiences, communications, or interpretations of either or both the therapists, seemed to constitute a psychically indigestible meal. This in Stuart usually resulted in an action or a series of actions by means of which he unburdened himself of what had gotten into him. It also meant that nothing received in the way of an interpretation—or any kind of experience, say at work—was ever retained in his mind long enough for it to mature in cask, so to speak, and thus lead to some development and personal integration.

There was another aspect of not learning from experience shown mainly by Stuart but also by his sister and to some extent his parents. This was the addictive nature of the relationships affecting not only the nuclear family but markedly manifest in the relationship with both therapists. By addictive I mean a need and a dependency but without a growth toward freedom, ultimate independence, and personal sovereignty.

MUTUAL EXPLOITIVENESS

Among the situations that we thought were important was the sibling rivalry between the two young people, characterized by a tyrannical, controlling attitude on the part of Stuart toward his sister and a more subtle manipulation stemming from her. Both young people seemed to have an infinite expectation of service and devotion from their mother, but Carole did not attack Mother with the same fury as Stuart did. Remarkable also was the greedy and demanding love Stuart expressed in relationship to his father. He had successfully pushed Carole out of the relationship with his father. He was also peremptory and arrogant. Need and greed displayed in this way without care and responsibility in relationships is why we thought of him as a parasite. He extracted all the goodness that he could and appeared to be unable to benefit from it. When the hosts upon whom he was parasitic rebelled or refused him he became violent and destructive. Mr. Stone appeared secretly to share his son's view of women as slaves to be exploited and ill-treated, though his view was expressed in a more muted way and in more diplomatic terms by him than by Stuart.

Whenever some concern for family members or either therapist, girlfriend, or person at work began to be felt by Stuart, the pain aroused by the dawn of insight into the way in which he behaved toward them immediately became intolerable and designated as persecutory. Depressive anxiety based upon guilt and remorse thus was rapidly replaced by persecutory anxiety based upon a sense of aggrievedness. Stuart then acted upon his feeling that he had been wronged and tried to punish the object of his concern, thus compounding the attacks upon other people. This aspect of his relationships with other people was very important in the early stages of the family therapy and it was characterized by exploitativeness and an absence of regard for the individuality or personal sovereignty of any other person with whom he was in close contact.

One feature of Stuart's arrogance was his expectation of enormous success at his work in business. He managed to arouse expectancy of great things from him in his employers and usually began to do a new job with application and initiative, which brought a degree of initial success. This did not last long. Trouble started when he became discontented and bored because his rise was not meteoric. He began to treat the people who worked with him very badly, so that sometimes a spirited secretary would refuse to do what he told her to do. At other times he would be reported for rudeness or arrogance. Eventually he would be asked to leave, and then, having saved no money, he would again become a total charge upon his father. Gradually it dawned upon us that Stuart's identification with his father included an imitation of his father's attitude toward other people, especially his subordinates at work. What Stuart did, however, was to caricature and distort his father's attitudes and behavior. In this there was an attempt to "be" his father, but also at the same time an attempt to mock him. In the therapy he did not do this to my wife, but he certainly did it to me, and to give him his due, he put up a very creditable comic impressionist act. But the caricaturing and guying was part of a defense against really experiencing being dependent, lonely, and envious, and what was unproductive was the way in which the caricaturing stultified any real learning from that particular facet of experience. In order to learn from an experience it has to be borne for some considerable time and this was very difficult for Stuart to tolerate. In contrast, when Stuart became angry and destructive, paranoid processes predominated with escalating intensity. When he was in a manic psychic current he was mildly grandiose, condescending, and quietly mocking. It was an "I'm all right, Jack" attitude.

Both of these states of mind defended him against psychic pain. He could not sustain the approaches to the depressive position because of the pain associated with that, and any brief reparative activities consisted of manic reparation, which is associated with the avoidance of painful personal feelings despite glib protestations of regret or good intentions. There was for some time little ability to learn from what was going on in the therapy until he gradually developed the capacity to own some of his parasitic and destructive aspects and painful state of mind without immediately rushing into action. The first steps toward this improvement followed from our being able to relieve Stuart of some of the projections and projective identification put onto and into him by other family members.

SHIFTING OF VIOLENCE

The course of family therapy seldom does run smoothly and if it does so one should suspect that nothing is happening. Usually it goes from crisis to crisis with scattered intervals of comparative calm. At one point there was a misunderstanding between Father, who was unwell, his daughter, and wife. Mrs. Stone indulged in a bit of mischief-making, contradicting what Mr. Stone had said to Carole. Suddenly Mr. Stone flew into a violent rage and threw his plate of food at his wife's favorite picture. Then he proceeded to throw everything everywhere, wrecking the room. This episode of violent and destructive behavior was recounted in detail in the next session by Mrs. Stone, while her culprit of a husband listened sheepishly and looked like a small boy in the headmaster's study at school. On this occasion Stuart, very much alerted by the smell of trouble, quickly made a takeover bid for my therapeutic role and interpreted, with less caricature than usual, Father's regression and childish anger.

My wife drew attention to the way in which the mantle of violence had now fallen upon Mr. Stone and wondered what would happen next. She speculated about how long it would be before violence was forced back into Stuart. We had not long to wait, and it did not really surprise us when the next session began in the old familiar way.

Stuart had lost his job and broke up the drawing room at home. A contributing factor had been intolerable jealousy that was roused when

Carole announced that she was going to marry her boyfriend. It appeared that the marriage was to be many years in the future, but Stuart had felt upstaged by it. He had had a succession of girlfriends. The relationships had not lasted because each girl, after a brief infatuation, had found him to be quite intolerable. The clear statement of disapproval of Stuart's unacceptable behavior, instead of acting as a guide and helping him to moderate it, goaded him to further nastiness, even amounting to violence and that finalized his rejection by the particular young woman of the moment.

The next shift to violence was to Mother. Carole spoke rudely to me and her mother remonstrated with her, but was then answered even more rudely by Carole. Mrs. Stone, with no warning, stood up at this point, quickly crossed in front of me, and hit her daughter hard four times. Again my wife drew attention to the way in which the violence had settled upon Mrs. Stone who, for that moment, carried all the family violence on behalf of everyone in the family.

One of the problems that confronted the therapists was the way in which the work done in a family therapy session was undone during the time gap between two sessions. It was like Penelope's tapestry, woven by day and then dismantled by night. At times the violence floated round in a very unstable state, waiting until it settled upon some family member. There was always something of a relapse during our periods of holidays, or when Mr. and Mrs. Stone went on vacation leaving the children to cope for themselves on their own in the family home. Against the backdrop of improvement and relapse changes of a more ongoing nature eventually did begin to show themselves.

ASPECTS OF MANIC DEFENSE

Before recounting the last phase of therapy with the Stone family, it is important to discuss some of the ways in which mockery and guying were used during the course of the therapy. At first, we thought that the mockery was one feature of a pervasive and shared manic defense. Later, we were able to see in more detail that although mockery was part of a manic defense against experiencing pain, it was also against being the recipient of all interpretations that struck home. There were two separate uses of it: it was used as a defense against acknowledging their destructive impulses and if that defense failed the aggressive impulses were acted out concretely; it was also used as a defense against good experiences such as developmental impulses and good identifications and against the two therapists when they were at their most helpful. This use was under the sway of envy. It was in this state of mind under the influence of envy that the sudden relapse occurred so that the two therapists felt hopeless and were anxious lest their endeavors had been for naught.

Caricaturing was a specialized kind of mockery. Stuart used it a great deal but so also did Father. As we stated earlier, Mr. Stone deskilled and patronized females. My wife suffered from these attacks more than I did from Mr. Stone who would repeat her words incredulously, and then smile as if to imply: "You are madder than I thought you were." Caricaturing also had an element of less destructive identification about it, and especially in the case of Stuart consisted of quickly seizing the identity of the other person without any discrimination or working through. It resembled the imitation of words by a parrot rather than the learning of a language by a person. (Melanie Klein has described this process in her paper, "On Identification," 1955.)

THE LAST PHASE OF FAMILY TREATMENT

Stuart had settled into a new and better job. Things seemed to be a lot better. Then we were told that Mr. and Mrs. Stone were going away on vacation together, leaving the young people to look after the house and after themselves. But at the next family meeting it was clear that there had been disturbances. Stuart had become very keen on a young woman and according to Carole had hardly been in the house. He had given her no help during the absence of the parents. She said that he had been a parasite upon her and that she had done her best to do all her own work and also act as "mother" in the home. Stuart said that Carole had been diligent and excessively fussy, demanding of his time and attention. It was said that Carole got into a "state" when Stuart brought home his girlfriend late at night, though he had not taken her to his bed.

On the return of the parents Carole had complained bitterly and they had scolded Stuart, who then became destructive in the old pattern of behavior. They said that he must leave home and find a place for himself. Stuart left home at once, not for the first time but for the third. On this occasion, however, he went out and found his own place, while previously his father had found a place for him. Meanwhile he had broken up the furniture at home and had ended up in a disturbing and upsetting fight with his father. It was all very alarming. We wondered whether relapse was total, but through it all we were aware of a plea implicit in Stuart's destructiveness. It ran as follows: "As long as I remain embedded in this family I will never be able to behave responsibly and control the destructive little-boy part of myself." We interpreted this and the parents and Carole were outraged, but Stuart agreed seriously and sadly, looking very relieved. During the interval between sessions Stuart had shown regret for his behavior. He apologized and had attempted to make amends as best as he could. These seemed to be reparative activities that did not have the manic quality of former times. We both felt that something different was happening in him.

At the next session Carole began by saying that she had decided not to come to any further sessions because there was nothing wrong with her and she only came to do Stuart good. Stuart retaliated by treating her as if she were the little child, calling her piggy, which infuriated her, and patronizing her in his former outrageous way. Toward the end of the session, when both therapists were wondering if there was a way of interpreting an undercurrent of tempting but frightening incestuous sexuality that might have determined or at least worsened the troubles when the parents were away on holiday, the next event took place.

Carole, goaded beyond endurance, suddenly got up from her chair, rushed across the consulting room, and bashed Stuart several times about the head and shoulders. As she did this I thought that she looked more like an outraged wife or fiancée whose spouse or lover had been unfaithful to her, than an angry sister. To our surprise Stuart was not violent in retaliation but instead tried to control his sister as gently as possible. He looked awkward and embarrassed and finally picked up his sister and half pushed her onto the consulting room couch. Before letting her go he lingered over her in what looked more like an embrace than an attack. I thought of Romeo and Juliet.

We interpreted along these lines, linking what had just happened in the session with the difficulty that had arisen during the parents' vacation. We pointed out that they had been left together to play the well-known game of "mummies and daddies." This was very exciting and very frightening, particularly to Stuart who had made many sexual advances toward his sister when they were both young children. We also pointed out how, at the beginning of family therapy, all of them had refuted our interpretation about the incestuous undercurrent that was going on between Stuart and Carole.

Carole did not come again, but events moved rapidly with Stuart, who stated that he wanted to get married soon. He told his girlfriend about his difficulties and he asked whether the therapists would be willing to see him with her for one interview and then to find him someone who would help him with his own problems. He was very worried lest he should wreck what was felt by him to be a very good relationship. We did see them together and also saw Mr. and Mrs. Stone as a marital couple at a later date. Stuart was referred to a colleague for individual help.

SUMMARY

In looking back and considering what happened during four years of fortnightly psychotherapy, there was first the phase of the embroilment of the two co-therapists in the confusing cut and thrust of life in the Stone family. The experience of being drawn into an interactive situation that was verbally and sometimes physically violent made it possible to see how convenient it was for the most disturbed member of the family, Stuart, to become the scapegoat target for all the family projections. These included violence, arrogance, and dependency in its infantile sense.

When this phase had been understood, though not brought under control for very long at a time, the violence began to move round the family from Stuart to Father to Mother and then to Carole. Violent feelings were aroused in the two co-therapists who were thus enabled to see and feel what life in the Stone family was like. There were glimpses of the shared parental need to keep the baby adolescents at home, in the family pond, and the collusive aspects of the exploitative young people.

In our particular method of working, the family was treated as a unit and family interpretations were made. As well as this, however, individual interpretations were made and these were intended to illuminate the behavior of a family member who was acting on behalf of the family or rebelling against the pressure to act on their behalf. Transference interpretations were made and countertransference issues discussed fully by the therapists between sessions.

During the first stage of treatment the emphasis was on containing some of the explosiveness in the family. Then substantial progress was made through a loosening and sorting out of the projections, the uncovering of the incestuous undercurrents, and finally the freeing of the index patient, Stuart, to ask for individual therapy. It was clear that by the end of family therapy, the family was able to countenance the end of the nuclear family phase and the young people were ready to move out of the enclosed, restrictive home into the wider social milieu.

Transference with a Single Therapist

BETA COPLEY

REFERRAL, EXPLORATION, AND SETTING-UP OF THERAPY

A mother wrote to the clinic saying that her son Sean had various problems at school; she thought his future was uncertain there and asked for advice on what kind of school might be best for him and whether treatment would be appropriate. She described him as an intelligent, creative, and likeable 14-year-old, but with an unusual personality. The school supported the referral. An initial family exploration was thought to be a good starting point on the basis of the mother's apparent involvement with, and estimate of her son, although more formal methods of assessment might be called for later if a change of school was indicated. At that time the composition of the family was not known and I wrote offering to meet mother and son together, adding that it would be useful, in my opinion, if other members of the family living at home could come too. The decision for me to see them alone was taken because a co-therapist was not available at the time.

Three members duly came. They were an Irish family: Mother, a singer, and called by her first name, Mary, by the children; Sean, a tall, gangling, frail young-looking 14-year-old, and his older sister Dawn, 17, also tall and thin, made up the family living at home. The parents had been divorced for several years and their two older children were married and lived in Ireland. Father, a musician, also lived in Ireland and rarely saw or corresponded with Sean and Dawn. I clarified my approach to them and offered up to four exploratory family sessions, explaining that it would be up to all of us to think about if and how to continue.

> As the session proceeds, Sean complains about Dawn's presence, Dawn encourages him pseudo-maternally to tell his problems, Mother asks if Dawn should go and Dawn volunteers to do so. I recognize their objection to how I have set up the initial contact and that there are feelings about who should be here/and maybe also about what sort of place the clinic is felt to be. I also point out that they have all come, and I stand by my view that it is potentially useful to start in this way. They seem to accept this. Sean now talks about school and being punished for such things as yawning. Mother talks of the school's high standards and Sean's work having improved in some subjects. Sean contradicts her at some length. Mother explains that he has transferred from a less academic school. She says he wants to go to boarding school and makes the first, subdued reference to some kind of difficulty at home. I look questioningly; Sean finally volunteers in a fairly robot-like voice that it is because he is totally disobedient. Again I look questioningly and Sean says he is quoting, saying exactly what Mother wants. Mother disagrees calmly. Dawn says one has to be calm and intelligent to get anything from Mother. Mother ignores this and talks of her two intelligent children, mentioning with pride Sean's possible "lateral thinking" and how as a child he told her his views on the universe. Dawn is bright, she says, but they are more lax at her school. I ask for Dawn's comments; she tells me she has struggled to overcome some bad habits and work harder. Mother says she will send Sean back to his previous school if he wants, then possibly to boarding school. She says she wants advice about this but actually gives her opinion on various schools as if the issue is decided and now sounds sympathetic to Sean's complaints about school. Sean says he doesn't want to go to boarding school; it's too late. I comment on the family's involved interaction and wonder aloud what, if anything, is now wanted of me and the clinic; to provide sanction to their sorting out the school question themselves? To look at their family interrelationships? This apparently gets lost and a family argument ensues in which Sean furiously complains of inappropriately early bedtimes and Mother says calmly that the children manipulate her. Sean starts to weep and wants to go. Dawn angrily and mockingly refers to the family's tiny television set kept locked in a cupboard by Mother. Both adolescents then expostulate on what they consider to be Mother's awfulness; she calmly disagrees.

I comment rather firmly that we now no longer seem to be hearing about school problems but rather something that sounds like the kind of complaint that could come from parents about a child, but in this case from Sean and Dawn about Mother. Sean tells me what I say is interesting. I point out that we are near the end of the session and try to draw things together. They have come with apparent urgency about the school situation but seem to be dealing with it without me. I am then told that negotiations are under way for Sean to go back to his previous school! So I wonder what they are coming for, if about family relationships there seem to be numerous voices to point out various "wrongs." There also seems to be some despair, indicated by Sean, that this contact could only be experienced as a repetition of past difficulties. They accept my reiterated offer of further exploratory sessions, Mother with pleasure, Sean graciously, and Dawn saying that any contact would be like touching the tip of an iceberg.

The second session was not until the beginning of the subsequent term because Sean was ill. Dawn was away on this occasion, taking exams. Meanwhile I had written to the school, with the knowledge of the family, clarifying matters.

Sean has a long scarf that he rolls and unrolls, seemingly endlessly. He says he is "impossible" and "disagreeable" and that Mother had told him to say this. He adds that they have an "agreement," the nature of which he will not divulge. Mother complains of his disobedience but speaks of difficulties from birth and no longer sounds as if she is complaining. She feels it was helpful to talk last time and encourages Sean to talk now. As Sean does so he suddenly asks if I mind if he lies on the floor; his back is sore. He seems to expect a decision from me, but in fact lies down apparently with great urgency, saying, "sorry, sorry"; meanwhile I am still trying to say something about what I am being asked and why I do not respond directly to his request. Mother says in a matter-of-fact way that his back wasn't sore before, but that he often sits on the floor. He says, "Mary, for God's sake, if I sit on the floor of your room looking at you, I might as well lie on the floor, yes?" He lies flat out. I take up the initial feeling of urgency, pain, and weakness and that the latter seems to change once the floor is reached. I also comment that we seem to be hearing about a close contact between mother and son and try to interest them in the observation of Sean's movements with the scarf as reminiscent of an umbilical contact between mother and baby. Mother responds, saying he was born with a caul round his neck, purple, strangled. He was left to cry on a slab; she couldn't move as she was having stitches and Father could not be firm with the midwife about picking Sean up. It was a bad start and she wanted to make it up to him. I contrast a close sensuous "making up" relationship with "lack of obedience," and also ponder the meaning to me of the "sorry, sorry."

Sean now volunteers to tell the secret "agreement" with Mother, namely that he would obey her, but had made her promise that she would not ask him to do something like putting his hand in the fire! On further exploration I learn of their liking for not only eye contact but also kissing and cuddling. Sean accuses Mother of not telling him before that the cord was around his neck. I talk about birth and separation being depicted as murderous and wonder about any possible link between obedience and closeness. I also comment that Father seems to be seen as ineffectual and Dawn out of it, as she is in this session. This leads to my questioning feelings about Dawn's return. Sean says he doesn't care; Mother says she will do what he wants. I comment on this potential obedience to Sean's wishes but hold out for more family exploration at this juncture. I incidentally learn that Sean is now back at his old school.

All three come to the third exploratory session in which Dawn whiningly criticizes Mother for not reminding her of the appointment. I attempt to link this with her absence last time and feelings about the close relationship between Mother and Sean talked about then, namely two close together and one left out. They also all come to the fourth session. I try to review with them and think about possible future plans, if any, this being the end of our designated exploratory period. Mother wants to come and look at what she expects of the children and they of her; Sean rejoins that she is too rigid and will not change. The session then disintegrates into a family row about Mother not doing the washing because Sean will not clean his room. Dawn is vaguely adjudicatory and Mother is called a liar. In the midst of all this Sean refuses to speak and reads a paper, though at some point attempts to take charge of the proceedings with the air of a superior father. I try to relate to my temporary exclusion from the session, wondering if this is in response to my request for us to try to think about our contact. I also take up the wish for change exemplified in the cleaning and washing, but apparently accompanied by the need for someone else to change first! Finally I try to gather together some of the issues we have talked about and offer to see them until the end of the term and then review again. All agree to come, Dawn speaking of feelings of desperation and Sean claiming he is coerced.

THOUGHTS ABOUT HOW TO PROCEED

I have tried in Chapter 4, to discuss initial explorations with families, so I will not dwell on this now but rather try to share my tentative formulation and reasoning in relation to this family. Sean, the indexed patient, clearly had considerable emotional and learning difficulties and could be said to be in need of therapy. Should I have offered him individual sessions? There did seem to be a number of contraindications at this stage, some of which led to my thinking that a family approach might be more suitable, at least for a time. For example: there was a strong, sensuous quasi-folie à deux with Mother; there was separation seen as murder at an infantile level; there was the probability that he carried a lot for the family, such as at times the part of a "superdad" or partner for Mother; there was his lack of motivation in that he saw himself coerced to come; and there was his apparent lack of stamina and backbone to sustain difficulties, such as a long journey. These probably interlocked with family dynamics of obedience, control, and underlying multiple projective identifications. Sean's acting against educational authority was not uncondoned by his mother although educational achievements were expected. He appeared to be a potential emanator of persecutory and confusional anxiety for the family as well as being liable to take flight on feeling despair. This would not bode well for individual therapy without strong motivation. Hope and potentially more depressive feelings appeared to be more lodged in his sister, and energy and motivation in both the females. The family presented as isolated, fatherless, husbandless, probably also largely motherless in practice, though with constant contenders for the vacant roles from infantile elements in all members. Real maternal functioning seemed, for example, to be replaced by sensuous contact between Mother and Sean, by Dawn at times acting in a pseudo-maternal role by projective identification, and also by Mother being cast as an absolute authoritarian without any real authority. The family had many elements of a matriarchal narcissistic gang formation as described by Meltzer and Harris (1986) and was also prone to act as a Flight-fight Basic Assumption Group (Bion 1961). In offering family therapy I made it clear that the possibility of individual therapy for any member of the family at a later date was not ruled out, although this would not be with me. I thought that if initial family work had any effect on the gang formation, multiple projective identifications, and separation difficulties, individual therapy, if wanted, might then be more feasible.

FAMILY THERAPY

In the first two sessions of the formally designated family therapy there was much nonverbal activity by Sean, which included making distracting faces, eating, and pulling his shoes off and examining his often smelly feet with interest and pleasure. Dawn was quite scathing to her mother; the latter remained calm or laughed. Sean's movements were described as "just restless" by his mother and "just a nuisance" by his sister, my interest in possible meaning being seen as absurd.

We learned that while feeding at the breast Sean used to drape himself all over Mother and kick any part of her that was handy. Any possible aggressive component voiced by me was decried, so that I thought inwardly that there was a collusion in allowing real maternality and paternality to be kicked away. We also heard how in an attempt to avoid jealousy Dawn was not told when the birth was taking place, but when she first saw Sean was told, "See what we have for you." Dawn was upset at Sean's behavior in the session and wanted him excluded. She complained that Sean and Mother laughed at serious issues and that she felt like a sour old woman when she became serious herself.

My problem, of course, was how to relate to all this. I took up different feelings about mothers and children; how the latter could be invited to be "mothers" or "fathers" or perhaps experience themselves as such. I also talked about exclusion, laughter, and joining together as being possible ways in the family of dealing with potentially painful issues, and wondered aloud if there were feelings about my possible response to what I had to say being ignored; in other words I tried to draw in the anxieties and defenses of members of the family as potential transference issues.

As the work continued so did the nonverbal activities from Sean. He would, for example, read the paper or move a box he had brought with such delicacy that the unrevealed contents seemed of the utmost fascination. Mother often appeared distanced from anxieties, though not always, as in the following session in the second term.

Mother comes in, distraught, saying Sean has thrown her key down the toilet. Both adolescents complain of Mother taking the television set away to make them do homework. Mother voices her anxiety that she might have to call in a male worker from the Social Services with whom she has been in touch to control Sean. Meanwhile, Sean juggles with an empty carton behind his back. I raise disjointedly such issues as to whether we can have any sort of key to our minds here to think about the problems away from the fascination of "visuals"; whether there can be any control that is not felt to be weak and useless or violent and disastrous. Mother relates how she, against Sean's wishes, has visited his school where he was reported to be unsettled and troublesome. Sean says he doesn't mind what she does as long as he is not sent away; he then kicks her. Mother appears not to notice at first. I ask if I am meant to be the one who is to stop him as a missing male. Dawn does in fact say stop. I question solemnly the nature of the kick and its not being noticed. Is it an attack, or a "control" against being "thrown away?" It certainly seems to have meaning. They all leave in tears.

In the next session we hear that Mother has hit Sean twice; he demands a double apology. Hitting twice is a double offense against the nonviolence agreement of the family! (I am aware that this account is much more coherent than what actually happened, because for much of the time the atmosphere of the session was one in which any space to think felt nonexistent and we were in an atmosphere of "white noise," laughter, and visual disturbance, some of it now openly directed at me.)

By the third session I have become a clear target for mockery. Mother talks about the possibility of sending Sean away for a time, as had actually happened to Dawn. I comment on the variation on the theme of two together and one away that had come up once before and, in trying to draw in some other material, make some allusion to three points of a triangle. The children tear my meaning to pieces, introducing isosceles, equilateral, and equiangular triangles, not seemingly just to concretize, but actually to confound thinking. I take up this attack, how I am in fact made pointless, and wonder aloud if I now have the status of some kind of family joke. Mother mildly rebukes the children: "Aren't you being just a little rude to Mrs. Copley?"

Many more examples could be given of the family's barrage of interactions between themselves and toward me, such as in this beginning of a session soon after: Dawn (to Mother), politely, "You begin"; Mother, "What shall I say?" Dawn, "That's a bloody silly way to begin." Accusations and recriminations abound, tending to be virtually unattended to by family members or to be the subject of further scathing abuse by the children.

Toward the end of term Mother recounts how when the children were little the whole family used to hold hands in a ring just to please Sean and say "We are a family," over and over again. Sean closes his eyes as if asleep and farts. Shortly after this Mother tells a dream of hers in which there is a bridge between the United States and Russia and a threat of atomic war. Sean, on the other side of the bridge from her, appears as her favorite younger brother; he shoots, but the gun doesn't go off. Sean is furious at Mother's telling the dream, seeing it as an invasion of his privacy and threatens not to come again. Dawn speaks of a nightmare in which she was joined to Father and Mother. Sean at some stage speaks of a dream of Mother and Father being reunited, with an implication of violence and the children consequently being well out of it. I try to relate to the argument as I see it about the ownership of the dreams, the violent and confused feelings in the room about togetherness and separation, and also the nightmare component in family dreams. There is the "making happy dream" of total togetherness, which is contemptuously attacked; there are nightmarish feelings of destruction associated with separation between favorites; also there is linking of couples who are felt to be potentially invasive and enmeshing of others. I do this, however, in a disjointed and incomplete manner, amid interruption, mutual argument, and not much interest. I feel separated from their favorite "warring" arguments and say so. (It does become possible to refer back to some of the issues in the dreams later on when talking about nighttime anxieties and fantasies.)

Soon after this Dawn asks Mother not to shop in an area where they might see a distant relation of their father's shopping with her apparently happy family. Mother sees this request as attempted control. I point out the different responses to the pain of seeing a happy, "together," but not dangerously "joined" family, and go on to suggest that they feel it would be painful for them to visualize me with a happy family, including a father and children, in the coming holidays.

I think that I had begun to be perceived as a potential container and thinker. The predominant feature of the term's work was, however, also the attack on this, development motivated both by grievances about an earlier absence of containment and thought, as well as from envy. This was carried out actively by the children on their own but also on Mother's behalf. But the family wanted to continue therapy. I offered till the end of the third semester, to be followed by a review and a further decision. There were complaints by Sean about not having individual therapy—he had not had it and therefore should have it so he could decide—buffet style!

METHOD OF WORK

I try to make the family my primary focus of attention. I endeavor to notice the interaction in the room, to gather in anxieties in the service of containment (Bion 1962a) and after some inner work try to convey something of this back to the family. My response may often be less of an interpretation as such than some form of observation and examination of what is being expressed. I do not aim to treat the family as a unit, but rather attempt to see the material from a family point of view. In the service of this, and also of potential individuation, I think it makes sense to talk with individuals and clarify what they may be feeling. But I would not want to make comments or interpretations that could in any way smack of what Bion called *psychoanalysis in public* (Bion 1961). I hope rather to try, again following Bion to make use of the current group dynamics to gain what understanding may be possible and re-convey it in a family context, if possible with some transference reference to myself, very likely drawing on countertransference experience. Thus, with regard to the above dream sequence, if I was in fact able to do it in the session, I would not want simply to single Sean as the prime "farter" on togetherness or highlight his particular relief at not being involved with a dangerous combined object, nor yet again to pick out the possibly incestuous phantasies expressed by Mother. I would instead want to try and get in touch with the family component of individual contributions, including apparent collusions and shared phantasies. But I think it is useful to disentangle what the individual is doing in relation to, and possibly for, the family without singling him or her out pejoratively. I could probably, for example, have made more of the fact that Sean was designated as the recipient of happiness in the family "holding hands" episode, and have linked this with his being the enacter of the attack on it—in other words trying to show a part he could be playing within and on behalf of the family.

By both holding and opening things up in this way I attempt to put the family in a position to grapple with some of their multiple projective identifications and shared phantasies so they have some opportunity to gain access to split-off parts of themselves. I try to work fairly actively, because I think not to do so in the face of multiple projections can only be experienced as non-containing.

Dare (1981) in a thoughtful paper writes how three British psychoanalysts, Bentovim (1979), Cooklin (1979) and Dare (1979) have shown a convergence of view on certain connections between the theories of family therapy and psychoanalysis. I too see some similarity in the kind of work I try to do but also a number of differences. Dare's article is illustrated diagramatically, and he speaks of the therapist making treatment interventions to the interaction lines of the family members, shown as drawn between individual member and individual member. In practice this probably does differ considerably from an approach in which I try to speak to "the family in the room" with the interaction of the members' inner worlds in mind. I thus see my approach as laying more emphasis on interaction with internal family figures of the present than with what Dare calls the internal world of family figures of the past, for example in trying to relate to the shared phantasies for all the family underlying the dream episodes I have quoted (followed by a reference to myself). When contrasting the family therapist with the analyst Dare (1981) writes: "Would-be therapeutic activities are directed at attempting to get the family members to interact with each other and then to change the sequence and patterns of their interactions" (p. 282).

The method I try to follow leans so much on the concept of containment that one cannot say there is an attempt to change, but rather to find space for potential change through the relationship with the therapist/s. I think that this is a real difference and not just a verbal one. In relation to transference, Dare writes that "transference interpretations are not part of effective family therapeutics" (p. 293). This view has much in common with that held in some parts of the Tavistock Clinic; for example de Carteret & Whiffin (1982) write that "the most fundamental transference is not to the therapists but to other members of the family" and hence that transference to therapists "does not have to be the primary route of change" (p. 9). I do not work in the transference as in individual work and imagine that it is the continued attentive containing function of the therapist/s, verbalized or unverbalized, and the introjection thereof, that play the major part in creating space for change. Maybe change in members' behavior, including possibly what they "transfer" to each other may follow. However, I do think that some perception of transference manifestations, including those at part-object level, has a part to play as I hope to show with further examples of work with this family. This may either be directly expressed to the family in the here and now or used inside the therapist to inform what he or she may say to the family in a different mode.

THE THERAPY CONTINUED

The next, third, term could be subtitled "the era of Sean's feet."

These are again exhibited, their display being accompanied in the first session by Mother's bringing beautiful brocade to sew and Dawn's being constantly active with her watch. I take up these family activities as support for their minimization of their experience of my vacation. Sean assures me that taking a vacation is the only good thing I do and verbalizes that in my remarks about "on behalf of the family" and "passing the parcel" I am alluding to a notion of "passing the awfulness". I agree, suggesting that this is what is happening at the moment with Sean acting as the passer on behalf of the family to me as the recipient. The atmosphere is heavier this term; the attacks on thinking are present but feel somehow more coherent. Sean comes late and spends much time in the toilet and is apparently to be missed by the rest of us. "Permission to go to the toilet?" he asks; this is in fact never withheld by the others. His feet and their smell are so present that after talking about it on one occasion I open the window. I try to clarify the toilet component of the "awfulness" for which he acts as agent for the others as well as on his own behalf. Sean now complains bitterly about my intrusiveness into the family and I suggest that I am felt to interfere with the notions of what is or is not "awful." Individual therapy would be good, Sean maintains, because it would not be with me. Dawn speaks of my constant references to pain as clichés. But they settle for renewal in the fourth term as an ongoing arrangement. On leaving the clinic the family is often to be seen waiting for Sean to lace his boots.

After the next break the children look well, though Mother less so. Dawn tells me the clinic is useless and they shouldn't come. Sean claims to be well because of not coming to such a useless place but also says it is good to let off steam. They proceed to put odd bits of rubbish they have brought with them into my wastepaper basket. I say that I do seem to be useful as part of a clinic into which feelings of uselessness can be put. Sean tells me I am not allowed an individual opinion as a therapist. Out of the blue he asks if my daughter got good grades in her exams and comments that I have a son at college, with an implication that they are doing well. He also inquires after my dog, all put so convincingly that I have to reexamine my own family in mind! I talk about a belief that I have different families in the clinic and at home that relate to me in different ways and that I have a different place in my mind for them. In the next session there are questions from Dawn about the purpose of family therapy. How do you train? Sean claims to know that the potential illness for which his mother is being investigated is psychosomatic and that she just has symptoms to make the children feel guilty. I postulate the notion that there are families connected to me with members who are therapeutic to each other, as opposed to blaming each other when a member is ill. Can such therapeutic family feelings be learned? Or are these things that are just known about?

In the next session Dawn is distressed, claiming she is tyrannized at being made to come and also mentions the long journey. It wouldn't be so bad if they had a car. With some trepidation I remind them that they have seen my car and I wonder if the family members wish they could have a lift. Dawn seems persecutedly enraged at the idea. "It would be no better; I have no interest in them," she says. But Mother alludes to Dawn having said that she thought I could be quite a loving kind of mother and could imagine me taking my children camping. Dawn rejoins that Mother had once said to her that I had reminded her of an eccentric spinster professor by whom Mother had once been taught. With projective identification between family members in mind, I point out that that was the kind of view of me usually voiced by Sean. Dawn says he isn't intelligent enough. Sean chants gently and repetitively my first name followed by that of my secretary, which rhymes with it, conveying a feeling of softness. It becomes possible to talk to them about the tyranny of being and feeling made to be, by each other, a family very different from a camping holiday family that I would willingly carry around in my car or in my mind. But there also seems to be some wish for a "softer" relationship with me. Dawn then speaks of being allowed to come to this nice room with plants, allowing me to talk about some perception of change in the session.

It appeared then that there was a kind of transference to me as someone not only in relation with other families but also as a maternal presence where families could relate to me and each other in a less tyrannical way. There was also the question as to whether change was possible. Maybe the reference by Dawn to being allowed to come to "this nice room with plants," linked with Sean's soft chanting, implied that there could be the possibility of a better relationship, and contact with a different, better part of me. This contrasts with fear of being entrapped in a sadomasochistic relationship with me and with each other (Meltzer 1973).

A session follows that come shortly after this one. It is relevant to say here that on a previous occasion Mother had spoken of the need for Sean to do homework, but that she would rate his doing a "voluntary" piece of work of his own devising, relating to something he has read in a popular daily paper, as being more appropriate than the homework set by the school. This is similar to the earlier observation of Mother's "support" of Sean in his difficulties with the first school. It is indicative of a "Gang Family" described by Meltzer and Harris (1986), in which educational progress may be expected, but family defiance, pride, and scorn inhibit the development of a trusting relationship to teachers.

In this session Mother and Dawn come together; Sean arrives a few minutes later. Dawn, openly designing, says "Let's talk about TV. We've been a year without it. Why, Mary? "Mother replies that it is because of all the unpleasantness; she won't have the issue of TV used to express rudeness or to avoid homework. But, she says, Dawn now takes responsibility for her homework, and Sean sometimes works too. Maybe some change might be possible. Mother says she will reconsider and set a time for homework. Sean comes in. Dawn tells him they are talking about TV, Mother will reconsider, and it's a question of time for their homework. Somewhere I say that this is being discussed here presumably in the hope that I will preside over some sort of family council. Sean says Mother will never reconsider, he won't grovel, and Mother will never tell her new laws. Attempting to gather together for the family, I point out the versions of a mother in the room: implacable or possibly flexible and/or presiding — perhaps with a father in mind, and that there are also different notions of change. Dawn persists in trying to get Mother's requirement made clear. Sean says he doesn't care, he can see TV at friends' homes. Dawn (still persistent) asks, how much homework? One hour? Sean (more cooperatively) asks, "an hour, hour and a half"; he indicates that homework is "okay," except for some aspects of two subjects and admits, unusually, to getting muddled as well as bored.

A discussion ensues; Dawn advises Sean to change one of the subjects to an easier, more enjoyable one with which she could help from experience — she did it when she was in school. The second subject is German and Sean refers to difficulties with two teachers. Mother says how she could help with his German homework by speaking German, even while busy or cooking; he could learn it without thinking. I take up what might be viewed (obviously not by me) as a kind of family helpfulness, and try to contrast an approach of possible thinking about a change of subject, where help might be available, to the suggestion about German where there would be an automatic "togetherness" form of learning, not needing thought. I remind them of how we have often spoken of "pass the parcel" of hatefulness; now it seems that the parcel would be of niceness, based on a belief that the family has to do it all, as if they were in some way joined. Dawn and Sean exclaim "umbilical cord!" quite mockingly (a reference originating in the early scarf episode with Sean). I speak of a risk that mocking me might be more pleasurable than pursuing the thinking about this difficult issue they have undertaken.

Mother says she does understand that Sean needs individual help. I ask if this is something the family can do. Sean looks as if he is about to throw the paperweight on my desk at me and says something I do not catch about the family all together. Dawn says they were doing so well about the television! Sean says how impossible I am; I never help. Mother points out that I am paying attention to him and that he has said the family doesn't. Sean says he's against me and enlarges on this. Dawn says Mrs. Copley does try though she's inarticulate. Sean shouts abuse, and leaves the room, saying it's better without him. I say the changed atmosphere may be felt to be my fault, on account of my introduction of what they think are intrusive attempts at thinking and the notion of separation. Mother says my concepts, though strange, are all right for her but too difficult for the children, but then maybe they should talk like that. Dawn says it's hopeless. They nearly got TV, perhaps it's her fault, she shouldn't try and gloss over homework difficulties, but the others are too inflexible. She feels sick before the sessions; nothing has changed. I wonder if my talking is felt to be too incomprehensible or too painful and say something about the painfulness of allowing change. Dawn says she does understand most of what I say; sometimes it takes time but most of it clicks and feels right. Sean comes back into the room. "Sorry," he says. "I had to be alone." Mother and Dawn have become rather intellectual and I comment that Sean is bringing back some of the emotion into the room for further work, but it is the end of the session.

Another theme began to build up around this time. It started with complaints by Dawn, herself sounding like a mother speaking of a thoughtless teenager, on the subject of her mother going out with a "boyfriend" and waking her and Sean by coming back late. We gradually got in touch with more infantile anxieties, especially those of Dawn, who was terrified of being left at night. We also heard of cruel, mocking attacks directed by both the adolescents toward Mother's boyfriends. Following this, it became possible to do some work around feelings of being left and attacks on coupling, touching on the earlier dream material.

In this fourth term and the following fifth one, a notion of a potentially more benign parental couple was followed up in various ways, as was the children's actual relationship with their father, with whom they had no contact ever since I had known them. In one session Dawn complained about the dilapidated state of the house, Mother of poverty and the need to pay for heating, and Sean about lack of curtains, which he tyrannically demanded. Jokingly, he said he didn't want people to see his genitals (as if they were to be deprived of this pleasure!). In the countertransference I felt myself concerned about the poverty and wanting to bring them curtains from my marital home! I took up what seemed to be a different sense of pain; a feeling of being "gotten at" by something missing that maybe my other families had. Mother undertook to provide net curtains (which do not give night cover). I thought there might be some embryonic wish, in Sean in particular, to curtain off areas of intrusive infantile sexuality allowing some adolescent development, and I spoke to this in everyday terms. But with these changes the situation felt in a way even more painfully unbearable. The next holiday, Christmas, seemed to underline their growing differentiation of what they felt to be my home and my other clinic families from their own.

> At the beginning of the fifth term, after Christmas, I hear that they have quarreled so much that they had not given each other their presents on Christmas day! Sean comes in late carrying some hard, icy snowballs, which I suppose were "no balls" attacking the notion of a fertile Father Christmas in relation to me, from the stance of being left out in the cold. I talk to them about being trapped in a frame of mind, the *Huis Clos* or "*In Camera*" (*No Exit*) of Sartre's play where Hell is experienced as being permanently locked in a room with two others (Sartre 1944/1982) in comparison with other families who have a possible "Father Christmas." Mother is resentful and more openly critical, advising me to read more optimistic family therapy writers (her negative feelings more directly voiced rather than through the children). I do talk about envious feelings about my holiday and the pleasures of others, but also raise the question of poverty in connection with the children's lack of relationship, at both emotional and financial levels, with their normally denigrated father.

Soon after this both children contacted their father and went to stay with him independently on several occasions. By now Mother thought the situation at home had improved considerably and Sean was much less troublesome. But the school remained concerned and in the session things became much tougher still. Sean took to arriving even later and would frequently sit menacingly handling a paperweight on my desk.

> On one occasion toward the end of term Sean arrives late, picks up the paperweight, carefully tears a little advertising label off it, and then appears to peel off some protective felt, making me feel as if a nipple is being torn out of a breast and the latter skinned. (After the session I see that he has carefully preserved the little label he led me to believe he was destroying.) He also attempts to poke into locked drawers in my room. He demands his "share" of talking when he is here, interrupting any attempts I may be making, in what is now the latter part of the session, to convey any understanding I have to the family. Sean tries self-righteously to claim this space and Mother points out that she would not be rude enough to stop him. Dawn tries at times to support space for me, saying "Let Mrs. Copley speak." I try to speak softly but firmly, leaving a choice as to who is listened to. I suggest that the conflict in the family is whether they perceive me as talking in relation to their needs or just rudely interested in hearing my own voice. Sean leaps to his feet and wrenches a flourishing plant of mine literally up by the roots. Mother does nothing; Dawn tells Mother in a supervisory tone that she should really restrain Sean; I leap to my feet to rescue my plant! Mother tells me aggrievedly that she thought it wasn't my policy that others should intervene and refers to Sean lying on the floor in the second session. I suggest that Sean's action and the inaction of the others combine to underline how painful my attempt to delineate a particular function for myself is felt to be for the family, because of the envious, excluded feelings it arouses.

ENDING

The end came somewhat precipitately as far as family work was concerned. The school was very worried about Sean and through them the chance of individual therapy with a male therapist became available. I thought he now might be able to use this, and it was acceptable to Sean, partly on the basis that it got him away from me. Mother was also to have some individual therapy in that setting, but she and Dawn continued with me for a sixth term to work on the ending, with Sean as a notional member of the group. During this time we were able to do some work on issues that arose between Mother and Dawn, including areas of difficulty that in earlier sessions were often felt to originate in Sean. Sean joined us for a final session after the end of the sixth term. He looked physically more solid, seemed calmer, and was living voluntarily away from home, with Mother's at least nominal consent. He was, however, still capable of expressing such views as, "I hope this session is going to be as delightful as all the others"! I had a session with Dawn after this to explore with her whether she wished to seek individual psychotherapy. She was able to own a number of problems including her bitter rivalry with her mother, and in fact started successful therapy with a colleague shortly after. Sean it seemed, became alienated from the family for a time, but some evidence emerged indicating that he then both received and used some genuine, as opposed to pseudo-maternal, help from his sister.

CONCLUDING THOUGHTS ABOUT THE THERAPY

The initial view that the indexed patient, Sean, was the prime emanator of confusional and persecutory anxiety, exercising negative functions within the family, seemed to be confirmed. He also appeared to be the chief protagonist for a "minus-K" kind of super ego (Bion 1962a) with "an envious assertion of moral superiority without any morals", (p. 97). This may be related to both a lack of meaningful containment and the presence of a sensuous response to his infantile emotionality. Negative identificatory processes and lack of containing capacity were apparent in the mother. This included, I think, a tendency to use the children for the expression of some of her own hostile feelings. Dawn, often in bitter rivalry with her mother, as well as enacting a superior mother, was also a holder of potential thinking and depressive pain for the family and fulfilled positive functions.

Did any change take place, and if so, what and how? There may have been some minimal introjection of the noticing, differentiating, and containing processes in the therapy. This could apply to anxieties concerning death and separation and also to the family's experience of someone who bore and was prepared to work on their attacks on thinking. Attention to the projective dynamics both within the family group and in relation to the therapist may have helped family members to be in a better position to approach the relocation of projections. They could sometimes move out of their gang state of mind and shared mental claustrum to allow themselves the possibility of experiencing other states of interrelating with each other and me. A little more freedom of mental movement may have occurred, varying among individuals in the family, for example in relation to thinking about problems of learning, albeit for brief periods. Massive areas of jealousy and particularly envy were untouched, though beginning to be recognized and defended against bitterly; envy seemed to come particularly to the fore after a little work had been done on the "joined" family.

As far as individuals are concerned, there were moments of relief for Sean from being the gang leader and some insight for Dawn about her pseudo-maternalism. A small crack may have developed in the mother–son sensuous relationship, as seen in Sean's expressed desire for some curtain to be placed around his infantile sexuality, and the later more amicable separation. Through transference experiences both children appear to have been in touch with less totally denigrated internal parents and thus more able to grasp an opportunity to find out for themselves what they actually felt about their father. Perhaps one could say that some of the pathological knots were at least loosened, allowing more scope for individual adolescent development and a more stable base for individual therapy. Some introjective identification with what were perceived as the containing, thinking, and even loving aspects of the therapist had made a difference to the functions that family members were able, even if only briefly, to convey (Meltzer and Harris 1986).

TRANSFERENCE MANIFESTATIONS AND THE SINGLE THERAPIST

Much of the family work of the kind described here by my colleagues and me is carried out by co-therapists, preferably a man and a woman, working together. Such a co-therapy pair probably invites a parental/grandparental transference in a general sense with a whole object oedipal component implied (though mostly spoken to in the sessions in relation to the therapists in the here and now). Briefly, such co-therapists have the advantage of being able to help and support each other in the work, and the family can benefit from the skills of both partners. In particular, the therapists may be seen and used differently by members of the family, and the various views of their mutual relationship that emerge can be a useful source of understanding as is discussed by Hyatt Williams in Chapter 11. To work in this way requires a time commitment from two therapists not only during but also in between the sessions when work needs to be done by the couple, particularly on the understanding of how they are being used by the family. The need for a couple with a common theoretical approach and family therapy method, as well as the ability to work together is also clearly indicated.

There are losses in working alone: for the therapist, the help of a partner; for the family, the possibility of their relationship to a couple in the transference. However, a therapist who works in a clinic where no suitable partner is available, or one who wishes to try to conserve resources may feel emboldened to try to work alone. If seeing a family alone, however, I would not want to give up the possibility of having some discussions with a colleague or colleagues, which is something I certainly needed and appreciated with this family. (This need not of course necessarily take place in one's own clinic.)

I also think there may be some aspects of the work that could actually be facilitated by working as a single therapist, at least in certain cases. A therapist can work more directly and actively on the relationship with a family than can often be done in couple therapy. I think this is particularly relevant to material with a part-object or psychotic feel to it like, for example, the attacks on my thinking that occurred with this family. With a single therapist, too, more preoedipal material is likely to emerge in a way that can be more directly experienced in the relationship with the therapist. With this family, preoedipal transference manifestations included notions of me as a primitive container, a representative of the body and mind of an internal mother, a mother with a father together at a primitive level, as well as the clearly apparent mother with home children. In the sessions where the attack on my plant occurred, the transference was probably at an oral level, relating to the differentiation of the breasts and their creativity in the infantile mind. The emergence of such material did not seem to preclude that which was more oedipal, for example phantasies relating to couples, including the therapist's imagined partner, nor make it impossible to be in touch with the children's relationship with their own father.

The nature, use, and understanding of transference in family therapy is clearly something very different from that in individual therapy and for that reason I have preferred to speak of transference manifestations. These are obviously difficult to follow and understand, but must bear some relationship to where the family is in its shared phantasies and its conflicts around them. Thinking about these may help us to get a feel of how we are being used, as well as by drawing on countertransference experience. Both can be used to inform our response in the here and now, and in further thinking about the family. Although not working directly "in the transference," as in individual therapy, I have tried to show how transference manifestations clearly played a telling part in the dynamics between family and therapist in this piece of work. It is possible that as a single therapist, there may be more chance of working both in greater depth and on a wider range of some families' experiences and relationships in the sessions.

13

The Aftermath of Murder

ROGER KENNEDY AND JEANNE MAGAGNA

INTRODUCTION

This paper describes the consequences of an act of murder and murderous phantasies in a family seen in weekly therapy by male and female co-therapists. We shall discuss details of sessions with the family in order to illustrate various themes, in particular, the way that a murder affected the object relations of the individual family members and thus the family dynamics, the difficulty the family experienced in coming to terms with the loss of the murdered mother, and the role that perverse sexuality seemed to have in preventing adequate mourning for the mother. The two main hypotheses suggested here are: (1) when there is a strong murderous phantasy, or an actual murder in the family, there may occur, during the phase of regret and remorse, a life-risking psychosomatic symptom that symbolizes an identification with the attacked or murdered person; (2) perverse sexuality may be used to fend off experience of damage and loss which has occurred either in phantasy or in actual life, because experience of the damage and loss presents such a new catastrophic shock to the psychic structure of the people involved. We think that these hypotheses have consequences for understanding family dynamics, individual pathology, and the predisposition to murder.

FAMILY BACKGROUND

The family consists of the presenting patient Roy, aged 14, his sister Jill, aged 18, and the uncle and aunt, who raised the children. The actual mother of the children was murdered several years before the referral. Their father has had only intermittent contact with them and he was not involved in the family therapy sessions.

Roy was referred by his school because of the concern that his preoccupation with sex could be a danger to the girls there. He was thought to be oversexed, obsessed by pornography, and involved in stealing incidents while truanting. He had a somewhat supercilious, smiling and "couldn't care less" attitude. He had no close friends, apart from his sister, preferring, as he described it, "to sail his boat alone." He was of average intelligence, had difficulty concentrating, and was poor at reading.

Jill gave the impression of being fiercely independent. She had educational problems and had a reputation at school for "precocious sexuality." The children had a close "conspiratorial" relationship, and both, but particularly Jill, were often hostile to their aunt and uncle, while idealizing their father. The father had no regular work and he appeared to have been involved in various small-time criminal activities. The uncle and aunt had been barely on speaking terms with him for several years. The uncle, a banker, was rather enigmatic. He came for only two sessions, said he disliked talking, indicating he was a stutterer as a young man, and also that he had a strict and intimidating father. His wife was strong, dominating, and somewhat obsessional and rigid. She was articulate, rather abrasive, and had a tough overconfident veneer. The dead mother was described by the aunt as sweet and gentle, but taken advantage of by the father, through his ventures with money and other women.

In the initial assessments, the aunt clearly showed strong ambivalent feelings toward the children. She conveyed, on the one hand, extreme bitterness and resentment about having to care for them since their early childhood and at times it seemed that she intensely wanted to be rid of them as soon as possible. On the other hand, it was evident that she was very concerned about Roy's predisposition to follow in his father's footsteps. The uncle seemed to have washed his hands of the children.

We have several versions of the murder of the mother. It seems that a waiter, the lover of the family's maid, robbed, strangled and then cut the throat of the mother while the father was away. Although Jill claimed she witnessed the murder, others reported that she found the body in a pool of blood after the murder and ran to a neighbor saying her mother was unwell. There was a suspicion, though not substantiated, that the father was somehow implicated. Pornographic material involving murder was found among his possessions.

ASSESSMENT AND TREATMENT

Roy was first seen for an individual assessment while his aunt and uncle were seen jointly by another worker. Because Roy had little motivation for getting help, individual therapy was felt to be unsuitable. It was also felt that he was in the middle of a profoundly difficult and perverse system of family relationships that required exploration before individual therapy for any of the family members would be feasible. When family therapy was suggested, the aunt and uncle reluctantly agreed to follow this recommendation.

We shall look at three phases of family therapy: an introductory phase in which there was a consolidation of the relationship between the aunt and Roy, the only family members present at this point; a second phase, abandonment and horror in which feelings of being abandoned and the horror about what might be revealed in the sessions predominated (the children came alone apart from a few sessions during this phase); a third phase of somatization and flight in which, although Roy's symptoms had improved, the family members had various physical illnesses including the aunt's near fatal complication following minor surgery. Subsequently, the family broke off therapy. The discussion of the various phases will be followed by a summary in which we shall bring together various themes in this unusual family history.

INTRODUCTORY PHASE

In the first session, the aunt did most of the talking, in her rather breathless way. She made excuses for her husband, saying that he was too busy. If nothing happened, he would not be able to stand it. Jill was unable to get time off work. It seemed that the aunt had brought Roy to be individually treated. She was incensed with our suggestion that, although recognizing Roy's difficulties, we felt the family shared some of them. Roy often smiled superciliously in a passively aggressive manner.

The aunt began by saying that things were not so bad, and that they could all really cope. She continued by talking about what she had to do for others, which took up so much of her time. For example, she had two "geriatrics" to look after, her mother and mother-in-law. She mentioned concern for her own capacity to mother: "Roy had the same bad upbringing as my children had." Roy did not volunteer anything. He had to be asked several times by both therapists before he would speak. He said that he was annoyed that when he was in his previous boarding school at the time his father was in an "open-air prison," he had not received his father's letters. His aunt pointed out that he had in fact read them, but Roy still could not remember. The aunt mentioned what a bad lot his father was, always in trouble, and having to be bailed out by her and her husband.

In the last part of the session, the aunt discussed Roy. She hated him when he lied or was lazy. The previous day she went to work hating him, but when she returned he had cooked dinner, and so she forgave him everything. She seemed easily swayed by his charm. Her anger, she said, was "all or nothing." We commented on how difficult it must have been for her, being and yet not being a mother to the children. She responded by saying that what she didn't like about Roy was that he did not bother. We commented on how the whole family was not bothering to come together to the sessions and we wondered whether Roy's attitude reflected something about the whole family's attitude. This made some sense to them. The aunt also said to Roy, "Why don't you attack me?" We pointed out that he seemed to be attacking her by not accepting what she gave him and through his passivity. Near the end of the session we were discussing Roy's educational problems. The aunt was angry with a teacher (who had the same last name as Roy). Her last words were, "I would like to . . . her." The unspoken word seemed to imply some kind of violence.

In the next session, the aunt complained about how much she had to organize and check up on Roy. We commented on how Roy seemed to be kept in this position like a much younger boy in relation to her. Roy described his own attitude. "I'm conceited . . . I love myself, I do. If I do something well, I think I'm the greatest." We discussed how this attitude might hide his pain about not being able to do everything he attempted successfully. We then talked more about the relationship between Roy and his aunt.

She found Roy's early physical maturity surprising saying how big he had become. She talked with some excitement about the difficulties in coping with such a large boy. We discussed how Roy might be a source of excitement for the family and how, by his behavior, he might keep things more lively at home. The aunt said that she and her husband were so busy worrying about others that they had no time to worry about their own problems. There was a veiled hint that this excitement over the boy's misdemeanors might have kept the aunt and uncle together. However, she added, she was looking forward to the time when the children left home: "My mothering days are over," she said.

In the next session the aunt said Roy had begun to take more interest in school work. We also learned more about the family's home life. There was little family discussion. The aunt did most of the housework while the others watched television. It appeared that she was quite obsessional about tidiness. Roy's room was untidy. He shoved everything under his bed, but more recently he had stuffed his belongings into a wooden crate that he and his sister named the "coffin." This naturally led to some discussion of the murder.

Roy had been told about it by his sister, when he was younger, at the time when he had asked her why he did not call his aunt his mother. At this point, when for the first time in the session he revealed some immediate anxiety, he started to blow his nose. (In the original individual assessment, Roy had said that he often wondered what his mother was like. He had seen pictures of her that made him cry and he wondered when he looked at them, "Is that my mother?")

We discussed Roy's wish for a mother and how it contrasted with the aunt's original plan to have the children for a limited time. We also looked at her current feelings of being tired of being his "mother." There were subtle indications that the aunt wished that we would take over the parenting, or at least become the "grandparent figures."

We were able to discuss fairly openly her problem of being an aunt and the lack of the usual incest taboo that exists between mother and son. They revealed some sadness about some of the closeness that had been missed in their relationship. The aunt felt that Roy's relationship with his father spoiled the possibility of a good one with her. When he turned to his father, she withdrew from him.

The last session of this phase, before a vacation, began with silence and difficulty in talking, which, when interpreted, led to fears of what might happen if the sessions went any further. There was also a fear of showing anger, particularly toward us, with the aunt flattering and appeasing us with gifts. What was apparent now was a split in the couple's relation to us and the real father. The therapists were idealized as good and the real father was seen as the mean parent who deserted his children. The children's split was in reverse, with the real father held as ideal and the therapists as nonunderstanding and unforthcoming. In both instances, these splits prevented the children and the couple from experiencing their anger with us for deserting them for our vacation.

Comments on the Introductory Phase of Therapy

Roy's relationship with his aunt was somewhat improved in these sessions, but the family was difficult to treat, both because of the members' shared memories of a horrific past and because of their current "knife-edge" balance; the family seemed to have erected various precarious defenses against intolerable anxiety related to their knowledge of the past. No doubt any family would have to be exceptionally united and understanding to deal with such strong pressures from memories of actual violence.

What was clear was that this family had difficulty in talking about tender and depressive emotions. Both in the past and in their present relation with us, they suffered from the absence of someone like a mother who they could feel would bear their distress and their complaints. This was indicated in the aunt's own remarks concerning her mothering days being over and also by her remarks about what a bad upbringing the children had had and her denigration of mothers, suggested by her reference to her own mother as "a geriatric."

Roy, the presenting patient, seemed to be carrying the delinquent, pornographic, murderous phantasies regarding the mother for the others, thus relieving them of the burden. The murderousness was stuffed under his bed like the contents of the wooden crate that he called "the coffin." The father, with whom Roy strongly identified, seemed to be the idealized, criminal father, who was also carrying projections. Roy referred with pleasure to the "open-air prison," a contradiction in which, in Roy's view, his father was enjoying his stay in prison rather than being punished there. Idealizing his father seemed to occur partly through equating breaking the law with strength. Presumably this was done to hide the absence of a functioning father in reality. The uncle was a weak substitute father, while the real father was rarely present. The need for a capable father was particularly present in the family's intense leaning on the male doctor/therapist.

In this phase, the aunt revealed her excitement in the relationship with Roy, which was unfettered by the normal incest taboo. This lack of an incest taboo and the absence of a strong father were perhaps factors destructive to the building of affectionate bonds. She fanned up Roy's conceit and his narcissism to create "the strong, sexual man" whom she desired but perhaps had not found in her husband.

There were various allusions implying underlying murderous phantasies, for example, the killed-off geriatric grandparents, the killing of affection, the coffin under the bed, and the wish of the aunt to ". . . the female teacher." Also their ignoring of the female therapist's comments was a way of killing them. The exaggerated focus on the male therapist and their pointed disregard for the female therapist made it seem that there was no place for a live mother or for a couple to work together.

In the family, the father's place, and with it the symbolic father's law, was not present. As Roy put it, he had not received his father's letters from prison. He was mystified as to where the letters had gone. Although his aunt insisted that in reality he had received and read them, at a symbolic level it made more sense, for it suggested that he was unconsciously aware that he lacked a good internalized father to whom he could relate and with whom he could identify. The fact that he had not "received" letters from a criminal father was also perhaps a sign of hope. His confused sexual identity later illustrated this lack of an experience of a father, either his real one or his uncle, relating to the "mother." Thus, although in reality Roy had received the father's letters, he had not remembered them. His denial of the reality of a communication from his father reflected his feeling of the lack of a father. That is, he had denied the letter of the father's law, what Lacan calls the symbolic "name-of-the-father." "It is in the name of the father that we must recognize the support of the symbolic function which, from the dawn of history, has identified his person with the figure of the law" (Lacan 1977, p. 67). In addition, as his father was a criminal father, perhaps Roy's forgetting and his putting him in phantasy into a "holiday-camp prison" was also related to a wish to deny his father's criminality and to absolve him from blame. Thus, there was the conflict between the wish to identify with his father, to receive the father's letters and to respect his father's name, and his anger with him, which was split off into his relationships with his aunt and uncle "who didn't give enough."

PHASE OF ABANDONMENT AND HORROR COVERED BY CONFUSED SEXUALITY

The first session after the break, the aunt had phoned us to say she had flu. The two children came alone for a few sessions. Roy, as he often did throughout the therapy, placed a newspaper with the headlines uppermost on the table nearby. After some initial embarrassment, Jill bombarded us with her talking, making it difficult for us to insert a word. The family had been talking about the murder. There was then some criticism of the children's aunt and uncle: Did the couple just foster the children out of guilt, or only to stop the children being separated, because their father could only cope with one of them? Jill talked about how it was she who had to look after Roy. "Yes, I'm the baby," he replied jokingly. She felt guilty about "corrupting" him by her complaints against the aunt. Then, when Roy tried to speak, Jill spoke over him. This was partly to make up for the fact that we knew Roy well, and she wanted to tell us about herself. But also there seemed to be a confusion between them, between who felt what. It was clear that they needed to feel the same and to be very close. Finally, we discussed their fears about all of us meeting together. Jill was worried that no one would say anything. We commented that perhaps just the opposite was worrying them, that they feared too much would be said.

In another session, Jill said that she was relieved that the family was not together because of her fear of what might happen, but she was also afraid that the therapists would "tell on them." We took up some of their concerns about us and the difficulty they had in saying what they felt about us. Then she talked about how at home, the aunt and uncle would send them away when they wanted to discuss things. She added that they would have tried to keep her from knowing about her mother, but "I was there." Roy added that he was also there, in the cot.

Jill also blamed the aunt and uncle for allowing the murder to happen. She said that her mother had telephoned them the night of the murder saying that she was afraid and unwell, but they never did anything. Next, she talked about how abandoned she had felt soon after, when she and Roy were sent to boarding school. From then on she felt she had to look after herself. Roy asked quietly why he had to go with her. We linked what they had said to their feeling abandoned by their absent uncle and by us in the session.

Then, Roy quickly spoke in defense of his aunt, saying that things were much better. He was "on the right side of her now." He was not getting into trouble, and was working harder at school. But Jill soon commented that Roy should ask when taking things. Roy grinned sheepishly, saying, "But I don't take things, apart from your make-up." Jill explained that this went back to when Roy was a certain age (the time he learned of his mother's murder). Jill had come into her room and had found Roy "with everything on." His nails were polished, and he had on lipstick and mascara. Now, whenever she loses things, she goes to Roy complaining, "Are you the one who took my mascara?" Roy replied jokingly, "I only take your bubblebath." Jill added that he was always in her purse. Later, they said that when they returned home from the session, their aunt and uncle would cross-examine them. "Did you find out anything? Who's mad then?" We interpreted how they might feel we were like policemen coming to investigate their private lives, to which they agreed.

Subsequently in the same session, with all the family together, the aunt and uncle, for the first time in years, said they were just about to go off on vacation alone. The uncle was quite jovial and pleasant, and said he'd had a stiff whisky before coming. We were complimented rather too much about Roy's progress. There was a holiday atmosphere, like a going-away party. The aunt felt that the children's seeing us did a lot of good. She added, "They can spit off a lot of venom." Having acknowledged the presence of the uncle, we wondered if he had felt left out of the sessions. He began talking about himself, explaining that his memory was bad, though he remembered a particular year. We wondered if this was when they married. He said it was, and the uncle and aunt exchanged affectionate confidences, while the children were obviously embarrassed. Jill mentioned how little they knew of their aunt and uncle. But she was then attacked by the aunt for not knowing things, for her naiveté and babyishness. Near the end of the session, the aunt said that she had told various people involved with the family to get in contact with the male therapist if anything went wrong with the children while they were away.

In the following session, without the aunt and uncle, Jill and Roy seemed very tired. Jill complained about Roy, saying he would do nothing to help her clean up. She said that she felt like her aunt, working all the time at home. Jill accused Roy of being deaf to what went on, and complained that he just watched television. Roy mentioned that their aunt and uncle were glad to have a vacation. Jill said they were probably glad to get rid of them. They were quite taken aback when we pointed out how much they might be missing their aunt and uncle, but they then agreed that they were. They seemed quite depressed at this point, but soon changed subjects by referring jokingly to sexual difficulties, with some vague allusions to menstruation. They did not turn up for the next couple of sessions, at first telephoning excuses, and then failing to let us know.

Comments on the Second Phase of Therapy

The children were clearly left in the therapists' care, which we found somewhat disconcerting. We were to become the caretakers, and to provide a place where they could, as the aunt said, "spit off venom," which might refer to her envy of us which was split off into the children. It seemed that the children could be treated as bad foreign parts which had to be expelled from the family. The infantile part, represented by them, was pushed around in the family and then attacked. One can see this in the aunt's attacking of Jill's naiveté. At this point weakness in the children cannot be understood or supported. It can only be criticized by parents.

Now, our easing some of the difficulties between Roy and his aunt may have created the possibility for her to feel more concern for the children and, thus, guilt about her destructive attitude toward them. Perhaps too, as she became more maternal toward the children, she may have feared taking the place of the mother because the mother had been murdered. Also, the aunt's own unconscious wishes to "take the life out of" her own mother, indicated in her reference to her as the "geriatric," made it difficult to identify with her own mother and to mother the children.

In the sessions with only the children, their feeling of being abandoned was evident. They seemed to cope with loss by a conspiratorial confusion of roles, in which Jill partly identified with her aunt. Sexual excitement and perversion were also involved, as is shown in Roy's transvestism. This latter sexualized feminine activity began after he learned of his mother's death. It could be indicative of identification with her, a way of keeping her alive, and also might show his dilemma as to how to assume his sexual role. This might help to understand his passive attitude to his aunt and sister, in which he let himself be nagged and seduced in a sadomasochistic relationship.

A striking element was the children's preoccupation with "being there" at the murder of their mother. This fixation at an early stage of their sexual development permeated their sexual phantasies, their interest in pornography being evidence of this. It helped divert them from mourning. Whereas normally death is an experience to expect in the future, their lives were preoccupied with death and destructiveness from the onset.

The family situation is somewhat reminiscent of the children in Henry James's short story "The Turn of the Screw." There, the two children, Miles and Flora, are left in the charge of their uncle after the death of their parents. They are then put in the care of a governess, but are haunted by the ghosts of the previous governess and the valet, both of whom in life had probably been involved in some kind of perverse and dangerous sexual game. The governess is particularly sensitive to the children's plight, and it is she, perhaps like the therapists, who first names the ghosts. The ghosts exert a terrifying power over the living. They beckon the children to come to them. Tragically, Miles succumbs, though the little girl, who refuses to be taken over by the ghosts, is saved. With the family, one can see the dilemma of how to deal with a horrific past event — does one stick to it, like headline news and be continuously excited by it, or does one try to face the painful consequences?

PHASE OF SOMATIZATION AND FLIGHT

The family met all together with us only twice after the aunt and uncle returned. The uncle wanted to make the children apologize for not coming. We pointed out that it seemed that we were to be the caretakers, but the children didn't come. The uncle replied jokingly that the male therapist was a lousy stepfather. Taking up this projection, we interpreted that maybe we were rejected so that the children did not have to face their own feelings of being rejected by their aunt and uncle. Jill said she had difficulties in their absence similar to those her aunt had with Roy, while Roy dealt with their absence by truanting. This might be seen as Roy's comment on the aunt and uncle's vacation. As the aunt and uncle had packed their bags, so too he had packed his bags and truanted.

At the end we were earnestly invited to come back home to see how things were there and to help the family talk. In the next session, the aunt was rather defensive when her husband, who was busy at work, did not show up, saying that business was, after all, very important for them. She was sitting in pain on some cushions we had offered her because of inflamed hemorrhoids, for which she was soon to have an operation. We discussed the fact that we would be taking a vacation during the usual time. This came as a surprise to them. Soon the aunt mentioned that Roy had once truanted this week. We commented on the family's truanting, not all coming, and mentioned the question of our "truanting" at vacation time.

A little later, the aunt said that each evening after the session, she examined her feelings, thinking of what she did right or wrong, adding that she would like to be criticized by us. We briefly discussed the dates of the forthcoming holidays before Roy broke in to discuss his own plans. The aunt continued discussing how she found it difficult to understand Roy. He added that he wished his uncle were here to "brighten things up." We talked a little about Roy's sadness. The aunt mentioned Roy's father, to whom he felt close. The children had a closer relationship to him, even though the aunt and uncle had raised them. She said that maybe it would be better if Roy lived with his father, a "blood relative" who must certainly love him more.

Just before the break, the aunt began by focusing on Roy and what to do with him. She was very frustrated by him. When we tried to understand the whole family, she replied that it did not do any good trying to understand him. He did not want to do things he was expected to do. She added that soon the children would be growing up and leaving home. Then she talked about her husband doing things separately. She took care of the old ladies while he enjoyed himself. If he did not do what he liked, he was unpleasant. One therapist said that it sounded like she did the work while he got the pleasure. She replied that they shared work. We took up that maybe they had wondered whether we did things together on vacation. They were astonished. One therapist said that there seemed to be a block on phantasies. But Jill added that she thought of us as interrogators who asked questions and gave nothing in return. The aunt said we were like brick walls, not forthcoming. She added that when she left the sessions, she felt as prickly as a porcupine.

We soon asked how she would feel if she discussed her coming operation, which was perhaps worrying her. She thought we would be bored. Roy added that he had a stomach ache and went out to the toilet. Finally, the aunt, in his presence, said that he was now doing well at school and he added that he now wanted to stay on and study to be a navigator, which surprised everyone. As they left, the aunt showed us her bloodshot eye, which we had not taken up in the session.

During the holiday, the aunt suffered a near-fatal complication after rectal surgery. When she had recovered from the acute crisis, she telephoned the male therapist and in a very distressed way told him what had happened, and that she would be convalescing with her husband, though the children would come to the clinic. It turned out that the first session after this event was to be the last. It was a flat and rather dead session. We sympathized with their aunt's trouble. Jill said that now she had to be the "mother" again. The uncle was irritable, angry, and was drinking. We took up Jill's mothering of Roy, and of his being the baby. We also discussed some of the past—how difficult it was for them when their aunt had been in such danger especially in view of their having lost a mother. Jill said in a dry, mechanical way that she felt lost and empty because she had never found the right mother in her aunt. She added that she did not trust us, and said that the skin condition from which she occasionally suffered, was flaring up. We talked about the anxiety they must have felt with their aunt's illness, and compared it to the deadness of feelings in the session.

There was then a strange embarrassment about naming these feelings. The female therapist mentioned that their sadness about being left by the aunt and uncle was not being named. The children giggled a little in a sexually seductive way. They then talked together about Roy's attitude to food. He had once had food allergies when they were left alone, and Jill had felt in need of help. Roy only liked the food Jill made, and not the spicy food his aunt made. We interpreted their sticking together, turning away from us and not wishing to accept "our food," which involved some pain and less excitement. Jill ended the session by criticizing our supposed lack of response.

Soon after, we received a letter from the family thanking us for our help, but saying that they felt they could not return. We encouraged them to have at least one session to discuss this, but without effect; and so we left it open for them to return in the future if they wished.

Comments on the Third Phase of Therapy

In this phase we felt particularly that we were dealing with a precarious balance of forces, once Roy became less of a scapegoat, and the pathology was redistributed. Death was ever-present, though often unnamed. Unfortunately, the aunt became a victim. She felt we should be criticizing her, no doubt to make her feel less guilty. There also arose a strong wish to be cared for, especially on her part when she handed our phone number to friends when she and her husband went on vacation. Also, they wanted to bring us into their home. But we were criticized as being brick walls and uncaring, while the aunt felt like a porcupine after sessions. Presumably this was in part related to the problem of the breaks, and their sense of hopelessness about caring unless it was continuous over these periods. The situation reached a crisis with the aunt's illness. Her near fatal medical complication could have been bad luck, but we felt that it had some further meaning. One could describe her anal symptoms as being related to the way in which an obsessional person might deal with loss (cf. Abraham 1924, p. 426). It was as if losing became painful, irritating, produced violent pressure in her rectum, and was mixed up with blood loss. Also her symptom perhaps revealed that there was something painful being torn away, that "needed to be operated on." Unfortunately, for reasons of confidentiality, we cannot describe how closely her symptom resembled those of the dying mother.

The somatic symptoms seemed to have been a piece of repetition. Freud (1913) said that

> occasionally it is bound to happen that the untamed instincts assert themselves before there is time to put the reins of the transference on them, or that the bonds which attach the patient to the treatment are broken by him in a repetitive action. [p. 154]

It seems that the life-risking complications indicated a psychosomatic symptom whose etiology related to the problem of mourning. The depressive current could not be developed in this family because of the overwhelming persecutory guilt over the past, which involved a traumatic murder, and also because of the intense hopelessness, associated with the absence of mothering re-evoked through our absences. It seems that the aunt's symptom symbolized in a concrete way, by a process of projective identification, her identification with the dead mother. Because she could not imagine the death of the mother she became, in a very concrete way, a nearly dead mother.

In short, one could say that what cannot be mourned may be identified with. Her symptoms followed on her becoming more sympathetic to the children and being more aware of depressive feelings and alive to the children's needs. It might be that there was something about this family that exposes a member, particularly the aunt, who recognized and named depressive feelings, to great risks. It is possible that this was an effect of the murder trauma or was already built into the family structure before the murder, or perhaps both these viewpoints have some truth.

Maybe we could have avoided the unfortunate turn of events, but the great problem was the extreme forces with which we were dealing, recalling Book Eleven of Homer's *Odyssey* in which Odysseus conjured up the shades of the underworld by a blood sacrifice. This was done within the context of a symbolic ritual that allowed him to withstand the horror of what he was seeing although at the end even he had to run away. So too, in the family therapy, various shades of the underworld were conjured up. It was with great difficulty that we and the family were able to deal with them in view of the family's weak capacity for symbolization. They seemed to either act out the experiences that they began to have, for example, Roy and Jill dramatizing their confused sexuality, or to somatize and then face severe life-risking complications.

DISCUSSION

There are many threads in the history of this family. We will try to unravel some of them, including two main areas—the effect of the trauma of the murder on the family and the possible light this family sheds on what conditions predispose to murder.

We were very concerned about the family when they were referred. It seemed important to intervene in some way. As the aunt expressed it, she was afraid that Roy would turn out like his father. He had already begun delinquent acts. We were also afraid that the original murdering situation could be repeated at some later date.

From the sessions, the following family dynamics can be observed: in a sense, the family we saw was not a family; the aunt was not the children's mother, and so on. The children showed that they wished their aunt and uncle had been more like real parents. After having some therapeutic experiences the aunt responded a little to their wish, though the uncle did not. So, initially, the place for real live parents of the children was vacant. This ambiguity made it hard to work with them. The resentment over the lack of real parents interfered with their appreciation of what was available. Both the uncle and his brother, the real father in name only, are enigmatic figures; perhaps they hold an important key to the understanding of the family. There were several hints from the aunt and uncle that they wished the father dead, that they were sorry he was not the convicted murderer, and blamed him for spoiling any relationship they might have with the children.

There had already been a split in the family between the brothers—one, the good businessman, irascible and a former stutterer, the other, the bad but rather ineffectual criminal, the family liability. There was always bad feeling between them. All we know of the paternal grandfather is that he was strict and intimidating, and constantly fought with his wife, and that the uncle was glad when he died. There was a certain amount of criminality in the family, which might be related to the harshness of the grandparent figure, and in the next generation to the splitting of fathers so that neither can function fully as a father. We have already mentioned the aunt's mothering difficulties (though to be fair, and we emphasized this in the therapy, the aunt and uncle were loath to give themselves credit for a tough job) while the paternal grandmother and the dead mother seemed to be rather passive, perhaps perfect victims for their partners' aggression.

It is one thing to have death wishes, another to murder. Once can only speculate whether there was something inherently murderous in the family, but what arose from the therapy was a clear current of latent murderous phantasies. Indeed, at times, it seemed as if the murder had just occurred. Some of these phantasies were directed toward fathers, as in the usual oedipal structure, but most were directed toward mothers, who became the victims. It seemed that the fathers kept themselves safe by being absent, as with the father during the murder and the uncle during therapy. Indeed, the events in the course of therapy were disturbingly reminiscent of the original murder of the mother. The uncle was nearly always absent, either at business or enjoying himself, as the aunt put it. The therapists were outsiders, perhaps similar to the soldier and the au pair girl having an affair. The aunt nearly died, leaving the children abandoned.

The murdering constellation had remained latent in the family, and a murdering type of situation arose once memories of the past, and with them guilt and remorse, were revived. The family had fended off these memories and feelings in various ways: the murderousness and delinquency were projected into Roy and into the absent father relieving the rest of them of the burden. It is as if there were an encapsulated, split off, and murderous part in the family (Williams 1964).

There was also a general difficulty in showing affection, as if it was too dangerous to handle. Roy in particular showed an "evacuation" of feelings (cf. Bion 1962a) for example, in his mindless watching of television and his inability to hold onto feelings in the sessions. As well as this difficulty in expressing affection, there was a failure to mourn the dead mother and absent father, so that the murder remained "unmetabolized." Perhaps Roy's display to us of the newspaper headlines indicated that the murder was still headline news. The murderousness was kept going, through talking about the murder and father's criminality because it had not had a chance to be properly worked through. Roy, who was an infant during the murder, that is the nonverbal child, carried the unmetabolized projections. Roy also carried the sexual excitement. Such excitement between the children, the aunt, and Roy in their relationship seemed to prevent an adequate process of dealing with loss and also interfered with the giving of care. There seemed to be a general tendency not to talk or think much about what was important, but rather to act. This suggests a rather weak family capacity to symbolize. The aunt's anal symptoms and collapse might be evidence for such a tendency toward nonverbal communication.

There is another main theme, that of the murder of mother love and of the life link between mother and child. As is well known, separation from the mother during vulnerable phases of infancy puts children at risk, particularly of developing a character disorder and of developing an antisocial tendency (Winnicott 1965). The children, especially Roy, showed such features. Perhaps this could only have been prevented if the caretaker parents had been exceptionally good parents, and not just "good enough." However, the aunt had great difficulties, for reasons of her own, in dealing with the children's understandable angry attacks on her mothering capacity.

Jill was overtly hostile to the aunt and to the possibilities of a new mother–child link, though she also desperately wished for this link. Roy attacked the aunt by not accepting, in a rather passive way, what she gave him. Also, the aunt was not helped by the father's managing to absolve himself from blame in the children's eyes. She was also hampered by her husband's weak fathering capacities. The fact that he was a stutterer may indicate that he also had a tendency to make phantasized attacks on the mother–child link, the maternal tongue being cut up in the stuttering. Perhaps these attacks on the link between mother and child are related to more general questions of attacks on linking and the ability to symbolize. Traumatic experiences may remain undigested when there is a limited capacity for symbolization. Bion (1959) writes:

> attacks on the linking function of emotion lead to an overprominence
> in the psychotic part of the personality of links which appear to be
> logical . . . but never emotionally reasonable. Consequently the links
> surviving are perverse, cruel and sterile. [p. 20]

Such mechanisms may account for the repeated examples of mindlessness, deadness and denial encountered in the therapy.

No doubt there are murderous phantasies in every family, as this is basic to the Oedipus complex, but normally they are not acted upon. Perhaps one should ask what it is that stops people from murdering, rather than what makes them murder. One can see in this family elements that without intervention could possibly lead to such an act. These elements include: (1) a great sense of grievance indicated in the deep and mutual feeling of resentment between the children and the aunt and uncle; (2) the absence of a named real father to lay down the law, which in the family can create a tendency toward criminality; (3) problems in dealing with a traumatic loss, real or imagined, which may include problems in symbolization due to murderous-type attacks on the life link between the primal object and the child, on the link between the mother and the father, accompanied by no symbolic father, and on linking functions in general; the use of perverse sexual excitement to deal with the loss; intense fear that acknowledging depressive feelings may lead to some internal catastrophe; and (4) an economic factor, say for example, a constitutional disposition to an excessive amount of destructiveness or envy.

Family therapy probably could not have resolved the effects of the murder or have completely taken the danger out of the family situation. However, we consider it a necessary preliminary when, as in this case, individual therapy is not accepted by the referred patient. This series of family sessions began the process of bringing the family to a point where the murder could be experienced as a natural rather than a fantastic event. The family was moved toward mourning the loss of the mother. This was particularly true for the children. The mourning process, however, brought its own difficulties which were: the danger of reenactment of the original trauma in some way; the tendency to somatize when hitherto denied impulses are uncovered but not recognized; and their feeling of being persecuted by the painful emotions discussed by the therapists. Their own preoccupation with the gory details of murder, in lieu of viewing their emotional experience, affected us at times. Indeed, there is truth in their accusing us of being police investigators. After all, as Freud (1906) pointed out, there is a parallel between the psychoanalytic search for the truth and the process of crime detection. Our capacity to experience deeply the effects of the mother's death was necessary to challenge repetition in the sessions of the family's relation to the horrific crime of the mother being killed.

Use of an Ending to Work with a Family's Difficulty about Differentiation

NONIE INSALL

This chapter describes the planned ending of therapy with a family where treatment had become a way of life, and where the family was unable to imagine itself existing without contact with an outside agency. By thinking with the family about the actual experience of separating from us, we hoped to work on the central dynamic that prevented them from functioning more independently.

BACKGROUND

I first became involved with the Daleys when Rosanne, a young teenager, was referred for inpatient treatment to the unit where I was working, by a psychiatrist with whom she had been in contact for several years. He described her as a severely disturbed, solitary girl who was unable to get to school, and who did not seem to have benefited from outpatient treatment. He wondered whether her illness was a severe hysterical one, perhaps having psychotic features. She was said to be more concerned with her love–hate relationship with her mother, from whom she could not bear to be apart, than with her peer group, for whom she had little interest. She had been severely disturbed at the time of her younger brother's birth, and recently had been in psychiatric treatment for some months, ostensibly because of her refusal to go to school.

The psychiatrist mentioned Mrs. Daley's history of chronic depression since a breakdown following Rosanne's birth, during which time Rosanne had been looked after by her paternal grandparents while Mrs. Daley had been hospitalized. Since that time, there had always been an intense hostility and rivalry between Rosanne's mother and paternal grandmother, particularly over Rosanne. Mrs. Daley had been in continuous psychiatric treatment until the time of Rosanne's referral to us. Neither John, the 10-year-old-son, nor Mr. Daley had had psychiatric treatment.

The apparent precipitating factor for Rosanne's referral had been a visit to the home of a French pen-friend some fifteen miles from where her family was on vacation. After a couple of days she had had to return to her family, feeling very ill. Later in the summer she went to stay with the girl who had been her next-door neighbor, but again, after three days was so ill she had had to return home. Since then, about five months prior to this referral, she had been sick and unable to get to school. We later learned that during this summer Mrs. Daley had been taken into the hospital for a minor operation, and that this too had added to Rosanne's disturbance.

Mr. and Mrs. Daley visited Rosanne a few days after she had been admitted to the unit, and Rosanne told them she would not stay on the ward any longer. Her parents were very confused about how to handle this situation, quite unable either to be firm with her and insist she stay, or to agree with her and remove her from the ward. The psychiatrist in the unit and I suggested that we should all meet to explore the issue. After some discussion, Rosanne said she would stay on the ward, and we agreed that we should continue to meet all together, while Rosanne was an inpatient. When she was discharged four weeks later, we agreed to carry on with these sessions at three-weekly intervals. The family lived almost 100 miles from the unit, but despite the effort involved in traveling there, they seemed keen to continue contact with us, attending about five or six sessions. During this time Mrs. Daley was admitted to the hospital for a further minor operation. Rosanne appeared to cope well with this situation, being able to remain in school despite her anxiety about her mother and also with the added setback of knowing she was to be left back a year at school because she had missed so much time there.

When I left the unit to work at another clinic, my colleague and I began to think about transferring the Daleys to the clinic. There were various complications, one being that we would only be able to work together with them for about four months, as my colleague would then be starting a new job elsewhere. We had to decide on this basis whether it was appropriate to arrange the transfer for such a short time, and if so, how best to use that time. The Daleys were eager to transfer, though they were quite understanding that this might not be possible, and overtly were not worried when the arrangements took longer than anticipated.

CLARIFICATION OF THE FAMILY'S PROBLEMS

We were considerably influenced by the Daleys' motivation to transfer and continue family sessions. However it gradually became clearer that this "motivation" could well be seen as part of the family's unacknowledged assumption of dependency—that the hospital or the clinic or someone would always be there for them. It represented their great difficulty in registering and experiencing loss or separation. They would easily miss sessions without reference to them afterwards; but then assume there would always be someone to see them later. Further, we had been made to feel very important, indeed indispensable, and had been unwittingly drawn into the family's institutionalized way of functioning. Their dependence on us, far from being the sort that could be used in aid of some growth toward separateness and independence, was of a much more parasitic kind, assuming someone to draw on indefinitely. We realized that by simply taking the family with us to the clinic, we were colluding with this assumption. In avoiding the experience of separation with all its conflicts and anxieties, they would also miss the chance of becoming more independent and self-reliant. However, although we had not worked on this crucial aspect in the previous unit, the recognition of it now enabled us to rethink our work with them.

We decided to provide a clear framework within which we could pay more attention to the family's experience of the boundaries, both of the sessions and of their contact with us, in order to enhance the process of differentiation. It was no surprise, in retrospect, that the presenting problem had become most acute when the first child, on the verge of adolescence, faced the real possibility of growing up separately. At the age of 13, she had become unable to leave home, either to go to school or to stay with friends. The thought of actual separation and all the feelings that this stirred up had become too threatening, both for her and for her family.

INITIAL PHASE

Some time after their last appointment at the previous unit, Mr. and Mrs. Daley brought Rosanne, though not John, to the clinic. We suggested that we could all meet for four sessions until the holiday break, and during that time, we could think about the possibility of meeting for eight further sessions. On their first visit they appeared to be very preoccupied with Rosanne's attendance at school. They wondered if they should force her to go, even if she was not very well and asked how they could know whether she really was ill. Rosanne talked about the difficulties at school, about how she had to be the joker, to make herself out to be something she was not, "so that people in my new class would accept me; they wouldn't want to know what I was really like."

This led Mrs. Daley to talk about how she had to hide what a failure she was, and gradually she began to tell us about her admissions to a psychiatric hospital. She became increasingly distressed as she unfolded the events—how she had been told it would be a vacation for her, but the reality was rows of disturbed people, doors with no handles. It was terrifying. She never talked about it, but she constantly thought about it; she was so ashamed of it. Rosanne talked about her own particular shame: her isolation, as if she too had felt locked away. In primary school, she had been isolated because of severe eczema on her hands, and no one would hold hands with her. Recently, someone had said her hands were like a grandmother's, but although she had laughed, she had been desperately upset, and could not show it.

After the session we felt flooded by this deluge of emotions. Rosenfeld (1965b) talks about how "any disturbing feeling or sensation can immediately be evacuated into the object without any concern for it, the object being generally devalued" (p. 171). The family had not been able to acknowledge the gap in our contact, or the uncertainty about the resumption of meetings; it seemed as if the reality of a possible separation had been obliterated. Now by pouring out all their distress, they were showing us how much they needed somewhere to put their pain.

John, Rosanne's brother, stayed at school for the first session but at our request they brought him to the second session.

Second Session

My co-therapist, was ill and unable to come. When the issue of the long gap before transfer came up, and now the weekly appointments, Mr. Daley denied the gap had any particular significance to them. They had noticed it at the time, but now it was over. Rosanne agreed, saying she knew at least that sometime she'd be coming back. She had come to accept that it was part of her life. Clearly, there was no sense of possibly losing us. This had been avoided by minimizing the significance of the delay. We were like pieces of furniture in their lives that would always be around.

"When the object is omnipotently incorporated, the self becomes so identified with the incorporated object that all separate identity or any boundary between self and object is denied" (Rosenfeld 1965b, p. 170).

Third Session

In the third session there was increasing talk about Rosanne's sexuality, whether she could have boyfriends and go to parties. She wanted to be more sociable than she had ever been before, but her anxiety was whether she could actually make friends. Mother was anxious about how Rosanne would behave, especially with regard to the emergence of her interest in her sexuality. There was a long interchange about how, when, and whether one could let teenagers be responsible for themselves, and the dilemma facing parents about how to cope with this. Mr. Daley said that they just had to take the risk, while Mrs. Daley said Rosanne was too young. When Rosanne was 17, she would let her go to parties because by then she, her mother, would not be able to do anything about it. Mrs. Daley seemed to have no idea about accepting Rosanne's need to grow and be independent. Separation could not only be an unavoidable event or a forced ejection, and this echoed their feelings about our ending therapy.

Fourth Session

At the fourth session Mr. Daley wanted us to tell him whether they should come for further sessions after the break, but he said he knew we would not. Immediately, there ensued a discussion about how interfering his parents were. We linked this to us and wondered whether they really wanted us to make the decision for them. Rosanne said she would like to continue coming after the break because she would miss it. She would feel empty inside without it. Here, the family had a chance to think more deeply than they would at home. Mr. Daley said he too would miss that opportunity to think deeply. Although acknowledging these positive feelings, they could not allow any negative feelings to be expressed. The conflicts and fears about coming back emerged when the children started to talk about their fear of their mother's anger. Mrs. Daley spoke of her own dread of its potency. She feared it could even kill her parents-in-law. She told us she would just walk out of the room, rather than let it come out. We said we thought this was linked to their wish to walk out of our room, rather than face both what they felt about coming here, and their fear of what might come out when they were here. At the end of the session, there was a mutual decision to continue coming weekly for eight further sessions after the break.

GRADUAL AWARENESS OF THE PROBLEM ASSOCIATED WITH SEPARATION

Fifth Session

After a three-week gap, the family returned. They were uncertain why they were here. They had been so busy that it did not seem like anything more than a week between sessions; and several times John called the previous session, "last week." Again, they were obliterating the experience of what it meant to do without something. It was as if we had been there all the time. I became aware of how they all seemed to be in uniform. Rosanne and John were both in their school uniforms; father wore a green army sweater and mother a navy blue sweater. I commented that I felt like a teacher in front of a class. Rosanne took this up, saying that it was like reporting back to a teacher; that's what they came for, in the hope we would be able to do something with their reports. We said it seems as if they were dependent on us to do all the work in the sessions, just as they felt they could not do anything without their grandmother's support. Straight away they denied that we were anything like the grandparents. They said we were not important, we were too far away, and there could be no repercussions from anything they told us. It did seem they needed either to idealize or to denigrate our contributions. It was difficult for them openly to acknowledge dependence on us when they actually had no power to control whether we would be there or not. It meant they would have to get in touch with their feelings both about our meaning to them and the consequent fact of losing us. According to Rosenfeld (1965b),

> Awareness of separation would lead to feelings of dependence on an object and therefore to anxiety. Dependence on an object implies love for, and recognition of, the value of the object, which leads to aggression, anxiety, and pain because of the inevitable frustrations and their consequences. [p. 171]

Sixth Session

At the start of the sixth session my co-therapist and I were aware that whatever we said was refuted. Then John said that his mother had asked him to remind her to say she was frightened of being independent. Mrs. Daley said she had forgotten she had said that. Rosanne then said that Mrs. Daley had also asked her to tell us that it would be as difficult for her to accept if her parents-in-law were to be as positive to her as they were currently negative to her. Mrs. Daley seemed to be using John and

Rosanne as her message carriers, as her memory, in relation to the therapy, while she herself was apparently turning her back on it.

We could link the fear of independence that they were expressing, and their uncertainty about the paternal grandparents' attitudes with their ambivalence about what they wanted from us. After a silence, they said they would not really be losing us. Just as, in the gaps, they hadn't noticed they were not coming, so we would still be in their minds and only slowly fade out and it would be au revoir, not goodbye. Rosanne had been silent throughout this, but now said she didn't mind leaving us. She then began to talk about her new boyfriend, Nicholas, and said she dared not become too involved with him because "he will be hurt" when he left the area. We felt she was also speaking of her own fear of getting involved with us, and being hurt by the end of the therapy.

In this session, Rosanne produced two letters from Nicholas that she wanted us to read. She made it very obvious though that she would not allow her parents to read them. This raised two related issues. First, it felt like a flaunting of Rosanne's private relationship with us (and with Nicholas) to the exclusion of her parents. It linked with Rosanne's relationship with her grandmother, which was a frequent topic, and which sometimes had a similar quality, that of flaunting a relationship with someone other than Mrs. Daley. A genuine, warm, caring relationship with another person — and there is no doubt that Rosanne was genuinely close to her grandmother — got distorted, so that it was used in a destructive way and was felt to be very provocative.

Second, it raised the whole issue of what could be kept private in this family. Could privacy be allowed, or was it an aggressive exclusion of another person? Privacy threatened the whole idea of fusion in a relationship, as it implied someone's commitment to separateness. There was little tolerance of anyone's privacy therefore and things could only rarely be kept private. Instead there was a pseudo-openness, with no acknowledgment of appropriate boundaries within and between relationships.

Eighth Session

When they came to the eighth session, after missing a session, Mr. Daley tried to justify their absence, denying they had made a choice about not coming. The family seemed to fear that any move away from us on their part would be met with anger and hostility, as if we too could not let them go.

During this session Mrs. Daley became very angry with me, saying "you tell us we don't get angry with you — but you never get angry with us. You don't tell us what you think about us. You don't tell me I'm to blame, that I'm a bad mother. You don't tell us we're a pathetic family." As she continued in this vein, Mr. Daley supported her, saying that they wanted to know what we thought, whether or not they had made progress. They knew they had to assess themselves and felt that some things had changed, but we must have thoughts and feelings about them, and we never told them. They were clearly persecuted by what we kept private. We took this up, as not only our sending them away without answers, but also their feeling that we had all sorts of thoughts we were not prepared to share with them. They were feeling us to be omniscient, withholding parents. We linked their fear of what we thought about them with their concern about what Mr. Daley's parents thought of the family. We also described how hard it was to free themselves from this constantly perceived criticism, as if they had no way of thinking about themselves other than by what was felt to be an external critic.

Mrs. Daley then told us that Rosanne had telephoned her grandmother from a telephone booth in secret. Mrs. Daley felt Rosanne had been disloyal, but more than that, that Mr. Daley's mother was subverting Rosanne, trying to regain, or possibly keep, control of Rosanne. Mother found it very hard to accept that both children wanted to keep in touch with and visit their grandparents. Mr. Daley said he could not understand why it worried Mrs. Daley so much, as he just ignored them. Mrs. Daley appeared relieved when I pointed out that she cared enough for two, as if she had to feel his feelings for him.[1] She was also bringing in the shared notion of a harsh controlling mother who would never let go, and could only be gotten rid of by total expulsion or rejection. The underlying fear was that the rage this object evoked would only be expressed in such a violent way that the object itself would be killed off. We were reminded of Mrs. Daley's fear that her anger could kill her mother-in-law, and of their fear of our reaction should they choose to do something as a family and miss one session. We also recalled their fear of our reaction right at the beginning of our contact with them when they had been so anxious about taking Rosanne home from the inpatient unit.

There seemed to be a preoccupation throughout this session not only with what would happen to them at the end of treatment but also about why we were sending them away. Was it to do with what we thought of them? Was it because they were such a hopeless family? How did parents make decisions? It was also noticeable how powerful I felt in this session. We later thought this had to do with their feelings of utter powerlessness in the face of being thrown out, and also with their need to have a strong

---

[1] For a discussion of the concept of shared objects in marital relationship, see Teruel 1966, and Chapter 9, this volume.

controlling object. Similarly, my colleague seemed to be untypically authoritarian at the end of the session. The parents had asked if John needed to come to the next session because he wanted to do something else, and my colleague found himself saying unusually firmly that we would expect them all. It seemed as if temporarily we had enacted the projection of being the powerful controlling object.

During this session, Mrs. Daley said with great emotion how frightening it was to change but also how she did not want to stay the same. She was beginning to have some notion that she could not be different, something that she had steadfastly denied before. She had constantly told us that all the troubles were her fault, and that she could not change; therefore, nothing could change. As we finished the session, Mrs. Daley looked at me and asked if I knew a particular woman. She fired the question at me like a bullet. She said that this woman, who she thought had been treated here, had committed suicide two months previously. I could only acknowledge, as the family were going out of the door, that it felt like a dangerous place to come to, if it could have that effect when one left.

MOVES TOWARD DIFFERENTIATION IN THE FAMILY

Ninth Session

They all duly came to the session, John lurking behind a duffle coat with which he covered himself, as he sat in the chair Rosanne usually sat in. He told us it was next week, and not this week that he did not want to come. He wanted to go to a disco. He became increasingly embarrassed as he and Rosanne sparred about boyfriends and girlfriends. This was a change in the family. Always before, John had been very denigrating about Rosanne's interest in boys, and had joined their parents in saying she should not stay out late at night, should behave herself, and so on. Now he was sitting in Rosanne's chair and having to acknowledge openly that he too had similar interests to Rosanne's. It looked as if he was now beginning to negotiate his own entrance into adolescent sexuality. The question in his mind was whether he would succeed where Rosanne had had so many difficulties.

Rosanne told us that yesterday she had participated in gym for the first time and she felt very proud of herself. For a couple of years she had refused to join in. Now she had, but she still had not been able to take a shower in front of the others. There was some acknowledgment that Rosanne was feeling better than a year ago, and she agreed. Mrs. Daley then recalled that John had had some nightmares in the past week, and it now seemed that John was being presented as the patient with problems, so that we should not terminate treatment.

I raised the issue of the patient who committed suicide after ending treatment at the clinic and maybe they were very frightened of what would happen to all of them. Mr. Daley said he was not frightened. They then told us about a family who was being thrown out of treatment, and who had asked for the treatment not to end. "They were thrown out for fighting, for not cooperating; maybe they were untreatable. The psychiatrist had said there was nothing more to be done," we were told. As we related this to their fears about why we were terminating our sessions, Mrs. Daley became more miserable, feeling she would probably continue to be like this for life. Rosanne talked about her own difficulty of going away (ostensibly to stay with friends) and I said that she seemed to be expressing the whole family's problem: how do you go away?

Mr. Daley said he could not leave his family of origin because he was still working in the family business and had an investment in it. After interpreting this, my colleague noticed that Mrs. Daley was very tense and so he asked her what she was holding on to with her closed fists. She was just thinking, she said. "Of what?" She began to weep gently, saying she just wanted to keep her children cuddled up tight and safe and let no one in. "How do you let children grow up?" she asked with desperation.

Later on though, when talking about the children being separate, Mother said she thought she was a recluse, a hermit, who did not want anyone else around. Rosanne was very tense at this moment and I found it so unbearable that rather than take up her feelings, I cut across them and went back to how Mrs. Daley wanted to cuddle the children tightly. Rosanne said at school she would never say she hated her mother like other girls; she was loyal to her.

I had responded to Rosanne's tension by action, rather than acknowledging how Rosanne herself could not accept it when her mother talked of separation and how she hated her at such times. It must have felt difficult for Mrs. Daley to think about letting the children go because the hostility, in this instance from Rosanne, was so great, and this immediately would stir up in Mrs. Daley her feeling she was not the real mother of Rosanne and that Rosanne might return to the grandmother.

Tenth Session

They arrived at the tenth session from Somerset where they had been for the funeral of an uncle of Mrs. Daley. We were shown two Valentine cards that the grandmother had sent Rosanne by Mrs. Daley, who wanted us to interpret the meaning of the words the grandmother had written inside.

However, any comments we made about what was going on were ignored or denied. Mrs. Daley then told us of a recent panic attack, saying she had not had one for a long time. This week it was she who was being presented quite explicitly as the patient. John was sitting very close to his mother, quite unlike the John of last week who had been big and independent. Today he looked small and vulnerable. Throughout the session, especially when it got tense, he touched her knee or her coat. There was much talk about Rosanne wanting to be with her grandparents, but how Mrs. Daley felt she was disloyal if she went. Mrs. Daley returned to the subject of the Valentine cards, and Mr. Daley became very irritated with her.

My co-therapist commented on how a lot of things seemed to be out of their control: John being told to come for today's session, the cards being sent, the funeral, as well as our finishing the sessions. Mr. Daley denied anxiety, saying that that was all right as long as it did not affect other people's happiness. In contrast, Mrs. Daley wondered what would happen after death; nothingness. It was terrifying, but also she sometimes thought she would prefer oblivion. Again this was linked to the end of therapy, and their fears of what would happen. They were beginning to grapple with what it would be like to experience an ending.

As the discussion about Rosanne going to her grandmother's home continued, Mrs. Daley became increasingly distraught. My colleague commented that it was difficult to let people go if you were never sure you had them. Rosanne continued that despite wanting to remain in contact with her grandparents, it did not mean that this need affect her relationship with her mother.

Suddenly Mrs. Daley stood up, saying, "I'm not going to listen to this any more," and stormed out of the room. Mr. Daley needed help from us to be able to go after her, while the children remained huddled and silent. Rosanne said her mother would not come back, that she had done this before. I felt very angry with Mrs. Daley for using such a powerful weapon to control her children's attempts at independence and, perhaps in some identification with the children, found it hard to think about what she was expressing for the family. Rosanne said her mother would not talk to her now, that her mother had always wondered "if she loved her grandmother." I thought Rosanne was going to say, "more than her" and Rosanne did not disagree when I said that. There were only about three minutes left of the session when Mr. Daley returned with his wife. Mrs. Daley, standing by the door, said it was time to end but she reluctantly came in and sat down. Rosanne apologized to her mother in a very flat way. John again huddled very close to his mother, and Mrs. Daley's hand was on the couch beside him, suggesting a wish to hold John's hand. John held his hand on his mother's coat. Rosanne and Mrs. Daley were now weeping quietly. Mrs.

Daley said that they were back to the beginning again: whose child was Rosanne? This presumably was not only a reference to the grandmother, but also to the relationship of Rosanne to us.

At the end of this session, we noticed a difference between how we both felt; my colleague felt more anxious about Mrs. Daley than I did. We thought this may have been because he was carrying Mr. Daley's anxiety about having to look after his wife, but maybe too the family was beginning to see us as separated and differentiated people, and thus were able to arouse differing reactions in us.

Eleventh Session

At the start of the eleventh session Rosanne told us that she had been able to spend the night away from home with an aunt. She now intended to spend a night at her best friend's house at the end of the following week (one night after we would have had our last session). When I said that Rosanne felt she had achieved something, Mrs. Daley said that one step was not the whole way. We commented that they seemed to feel that although some progress had been made, they were not sure whether they could make further steps. Mrs. Daley said that, if it were not for herself, everything would be all right, but both children became very annoyed with her. They recalled last week's session and how furious Mr. Daley had been with his wife for walking out of the session. She said he had told her she had no right to behave like that, but that she felt that maybe that was how she was. She was asserting that she did not have to be controlled by other people, and this was a shift from her automatic reaction of blaming herself. Anger was felt to be less dangerous now.

At times we suggested they seemed to feel that we had all the capacities and they had none. They could make us very powerful but the more they did so, the more impotent they became. They described us as a safety valve. We wondered what would happen when we were not around. Rosanne said she thought we would not miss them as much as they would us — we would be seeing other people in their place and would wipe the slate clean of them. We would have other people to talk to. For them, on the other hand, it was more important, and they would have no one in our place.

They were now struggling with and recognizing that there was to be an imminent separation, as if they really had some notion of the loss of us as specific people. The quality of this goodbye was very different from the goodbye at the previous unit. Now they were aware they would miss us, though concerned that we would not miss them, a concern that suggested that they expected us to be unable to experience the loss of them, just as previously they had been unable to experience any sense of loss of us. There was still an uncertainty about whether it was possible for the memory and significance of people to be retained, for objects to be internalized.

Last Session

They arrived a little late for the final session. Rosanne was wearing a large badge, saying "Join the lovable losers" and John was carrying a small child's toy. The atmosphere was sad. Mr. Daley eventually said that John would be glad not to come again; he did not like the car journey. John initially agreed but then went on to say that it was upsetting too. They had been coming for ages and now it was a dead end. This attempt by Mr. Daley to put his feelings about the ending onto John was not taken up by John. John seemed able to hold his own separate feelings. There was some talk about the expectations they had had from coming here, and their disappointment that we had not given them prescriptions for action. It was a more realistic appraisal of us; we were neither perfect nor irrelevant. During the last two sessions there had been confusion about which of us was leaving and now Mr. Daley tried to clarify the situation. My colleague commented that maybe Mr. Daley was wondering who they would be able to get in touch with again. He initially denied this but then agreed.

Rosanne said she would like to know if she could come back. She often thought of things she would like to say to the doctor and they never spoke as deeply at home as they did here. She could not say the things she said to us, to anyone else, or she would be told she was silly, so she wanted to stay in touch. Her eyes were red. She seemed to feel that this was a place where her distress and anxieties were taken seriously, without arousing too much fear.

Mr. Daley cut across this and asked his wife what she thought. I wondered why he had interrupted what Rosanne was saying. Rosanne angrily said he was the culprit, but she too was seeming to expect perfect parents and, like all the family, found it hard to accept that even if things were not perfect, there may be other things (about her father in this instance) that could be valued. Mrs. Daley now began to cry, saying she was terrified. She was holding on to John's hand and his mascot. Mr. Daley said he hoped that coming here would somehow have relieved him of his responsibilities and Mrs. Daley said that she now knew no one could help her, that she had to do it all herself. Rosanne said that she was intending to go to her friend Helen's home tomorrow night and would not be able to tell us how it had gone. She said that she might lose courage, knowing she would not be able to tell us. We tried to point out again how they were putting all the power for change in us, and here again Rosanne was saying she could only do this particular thing if she knew we were around. She still was not certain she had enough strength inside herself to do it alone, a remaining uncertainty about the degree to which we could be internalized. There was also a sadness in her thought that she would not be able to share the next step with us.

The family told us that there were now more fights than before, so things were not all right. We acknowledged that they had expected that the ending of our sessions should prevent any disagreements and because it was not like that, they felt disappointed. However, to us the important part of this communication was the greater capacity of the family to tolerate fights, which were now no longer felt as annihilating. The family could fight and not be overwhelmed, and this seemed to us a significant shift. They could test out their mixed feelings with less fear. Mr. Daley then brought up the possibility of coming back, asking if they could come back if things went disastrously wrong. We had wondered about the possibility of a follow-up and had decided to suggest it, hoping it would not be used as an avoidance of an actual ending. Now, in fact, it was Mr. Daley who raised it. We said that maybe they could come back to let us know how things were going anyway, and not wait for a disaster. Mr. Daley wanted exact dates. Both he and Rosanne seemed relieved they could come back, though Mrs. Daley and John were rather noncommittal and acknowledged the mixed feelings.

The ending was sad and they filed out of the door, looking dejected, but we felt they had worked up to the end about the meaning of leaving us as specific people for whom substitutes could not so easily be made.

FOLLOW-UP

At the follow-up three months later, John went straight to the chair that Mr. Daley had occupied throughout the earlier sessions, Rosanne sat in her usual chair, and for the first time, Mr. and Mrs. Daley were seated beside each other on the sofa. After a long silence, I said it was three months since we had met. John said it did seem a long time. Mr. Daley said he didn't think it was very long, and it was just as if he had never left. Gradually, Mr. and Mrs. Daley began to tell us about all the ways in which Rosanne had not improved, implying they were back to the beginning again. Although Rosanne had managed to stay away from home on a few occasions, there had been a fight the previous week about Rosanne going away, and Rosanne had ended up telephoning the Samaritans.[2] Furthermore, Rosanne had taken a couple of days off from school, as she was feeling ill, and, in retrospect, the family felt that she had not been ill; there was obvious concern that she was reverting to the earlier symptoms that had led to her referral.

We then heard about the local boys' school, and how the boys from it would come and see Rosanne constantly, using the house so often that Mr. and Mrs. Daley felt like doormats. Both parents felt exploited by Rosanne's expectations that these boys should be able to visit whenever they wished, but they denied that they felt envious of Rosanne's apparent enjoyment these days. While Mr. Daley said he felt proud of her, Mrs. Daley expressed concern about Rosanne's relationship with the various boys, but it was apparent that both parents were very uncertain about how to handle Rosanne. It was obvious that there was a double message from the parents to Rosanne. On the one hand, they expected her to be able to go away from home, to stay with friends (this was what the fight had been about last week), and on the other hand, they seemed unable to let her join in the activities that would give her the confidence to be able to stay away from home.

We were also in receipt of a double message. Initially, we had heard how badly things were going, that things were as bad as ever. Now we were hearing that things were actually changing. Rosanne was becoming much more outward looking. This was the crisis the parents felt ill-equipped to face, but the one around which we had been working.

We were very aware of the family's anxiety about how things were going, and of Mrs. Daley's anxiety about Rosanne's increasing independence. Certainly, at the end of the session, I was left feeling very unsure about how the family would get along. My co-therapist felt far less concerned than I did about them and may have been reflecting Mr. Daley's greater capacity both to be able to let Rosanne grow up, and to let his wife be responsible for her own feelings. Mrs. Daley, despite her considerable anxiety, appeared more able to think for herself, and to realize that things were not necessarily catastrophic when they had to rely on their own resources.

There was an acknowledgment from Rosanne about how difficult it was to talk to friends about things that mattered, and how much safer she felt when she could talk to us, for she felt we would not divulge what she had told us. We wondered if she was asking for more treatment in her own

---

[2] The Samaritans are an emergency telephone help service available for people feeling desperate or suicidal.

right, and made it clear that if, in the future, she felt she wanted something for herself, we would be able to see her to discuss this possibility. She was very tearful at the end and seemed to be the one who felt most upset about leaving.

Despite all the anxieties, however, it was obvious to both of us that the family had made considerable moves toward independence. Rosanne's social life and school life seemed to have improved considerably; certainly in our sessions she had been much more able to stand up for herself. John was continuing his interest in an adolescent social life, and Mr. Daley seemed to feel less responsible for his wife. Mrs. Daley was less in the grip of a controlling object. Although she felt rather abandoned by us, and at a loss to know how to cope with Rosanne's increasing sexuality, she had some idea that she did not need us around all the time. She had said, as if suddenly realizing she might change, "if no one else will change, you have to yourself." This acknowledgment of some possibility of change on her part, though grudging and somewhat defiant, was a new element and gave us some hope that there had been a significant shift for them. Similarly the fact that she was also far less preoccupied with world disasters, a theme that had arisen frequently, seemed to corroborate our feeling that she had made the corresponding psychic shift so that her internal world did not constantly feel in imminent danger of catastrophe.

DISCUSSION

In thinking about this family, we were aware that we were felt to be omniscient but withholding parents who could have given them all the answers if only we had wanted to. We were supposed to sustain the fantasy that there was someone who could enable them to be a harmonious family where there was no pain. At times, early on, we acceded to their pressure, unaware of what they were requiring of us. We were made to feel very powerful and helpful, and colluded with the myth of there being such an all-powerful, all-providing object. It flattered us that they came so far to see us, and wanted to continue seeing us despite various obstacles.

The other side of this type of dependent relationship became clear when we questioned or challenged it. We were then seen as persecuting, controlling people who were critical of all aspects of the family. They felt that if we really said what we thought, we would be telling them what failures they were, and confirming their experience of themselves as devoid of all capacities. At such moments their response would be again to deny our significance, make us useless, obliterate any sense of gap there had been between sessions, and so on. We realized that we would need to try to understand with them how they saw us, and the difficulty they felt in functioning separately and without the institution of the clinic.

As they began to realize, toward the end, that they too could lead a separate life, there was a presentation of different patients, as if in order to remain attached to us. Once Rosanne had begun to look outward from the family, John evoked concern because of his nightmares. Significantly this was in the session when he had begun to display his own adolescent interests. Then Mrs. Daley presented herself and her renewed panic attacks, perhaps as she realized she too might be able to be separate. She wasn't sure she wanted to be, or could deal with it, nor was she at all sure how to let the children negotiate their own increasing separateness. Each member of the family, in double messages, repeatedly showed ambivalence about going it alone, both wanting it and terrified of it. Rosanne was both pleased with and scared by the progress she made; John at times identified with controlling parents, disapproving of Rosanne's activities, and at other times identified with the more outward-looking Rosanne.

Both parents found it hard to know how to let Rosanne become independent gradually, and found themselves either pushing her out too quickly to stay with friends before she was ready, or stopping her going to parties and other activities appropriate to her age. In the countertransference, we as co-therapists, felt the same ambivalence: were we pushing them out too soon, toward disaster, or if we continued to see them, were we holding them too tightly and never wanting to allow them to grow away?

The idea of working in the way we did, using the external reality as a boundary, grew from a clearer understanding of how this family functioned, using the ending to work on the particular kind of difficulty the Daleys had in achieving separateness. In our work with them, we hoped to provide them with a space where each member of the family could have an experience of ending, could have the accompanying conflicts and anxieties acknowledged openly. This permitted them to separate, an experience that previously had been abandoned constantly because of the terror of catastrophe.

At the end of the therapy, and later on in the review, both children were beginning to negotiate adolescence with some confidence, and they neither looked so young nor felt so infantile. The parents were more in touch with their own anxieties, and had less need to project these into the external world. There was more notion of sharing both the responsibilities and pleasures of being a couple and of being parents.

Through the work we did on the family's relationship with us, there was a shift in their notion of dependence from that of a parasitic one to one of healthy dependence. There could now be an idea of us having something to give and of them being able to receive. We could work together toward an ending, where they felt that they could use their capacities to function as an independent unit, with the pains, anger, and anxiety this aroused. Also the sharing and cooperation within the sessions gave each member the knowledge that he or she could function both separately and as part of a family. In the parasitic relationship, any attempts at separation arouse fantasies of expulsion, rejection, and death. The family's way of dealing with this by a lack of differentiation between external people had been largely replaced by a positive, task-oriented dependence without acknowledgment of our importance to them.

Epilogue: Change

SALLY BOX

Thinking about the concluding chapter of this book, my mind is beset by a variety of competing concerns that seem to need acknowledging or addressing in some way. I am aware, for instance, of a number of relevant issues that we scarcely touched upon, and of others that raise new paradoxes and new problems. But many of them are related to a central preoccupation about the nature of change or, perhaps I should say, of different kinds of change since it is clear that the notion implies so many different dimensions and there are so many unspoken assumptions about it. Does one mean, for example, a change in behavior, change in attitude, in a state of mind, or something else?

In her discussion of the paper by Madanes and Haley, Susan Carvalho highlights some of the contrasting approaches, for instance, between the interest in behavioral or symptomatic change, on the one hand, and in the growth and development of the whole family on the other. Such contrasts are clearly important and involve corresponding differences in method. At the same time, some of the polarities that develop around them may be misleading and the significant differences not necessarily the most obvious ones. Perhaps the most interesting questions arise from considerations of the relationship between these different sorts of change.

For instance, when a mother successfully learns techniques from the therapist for handling her child, does she in the process have an experience of being held and understood, and does this, however minimally, increase

239

her own capacity to provide such an experience for her child? Alternatively, as the pattern of behavior in a family changes, when is there an accompanying shift in the members' perception of each other, a greater capacity, for example, to appreciate each other's point of view and be more responsive to each other's distress, and when, in contrast, does the change seem to represent simply a more competent way of exporting the tensions and conflicts out of the family?

These sorts of issues cut across traditional differences of methodology and sometimes involve factors that are very difficult to define. Who can measure the therapist's state of mind, for example, and his available resources for being himself contained? Yet these are relevant, whatever the proposed approach. Another important issue is the relationship between changes in one or two individuals and changes in the culture as a whole. When is one person's change another one's burden? Or when is it such that a more positive cycle is set in train?

It is clear that the problems we have struggled with and attempted to discuss in relation to families can be seen to some extent in every institutional group or community. What are the irrational processes that prevent good ideas and agreed plans from getting implemented there? What is the role of the outsider (like therapist or consultant) in relation to the change process? Over and over again one sees an apparently enlightened idea founder for lack of interest or support, and the line between a healthy skepticism and an apparently obdurate refusal or incapacity to entertain something new is very often difficult to draw. The tendency of living organisms to move in established pathways and to revert to them has been variously referred to at different times and in different contexts. From the point of view of stability and steady continuity of individual and cultural life the biological principle of conservatism (or homoeostasis, as similar processes have been named) is absolutely functional. The phenomenon of resistance, or at least discrimination, is a natural and even necessary one. Gregory Bateson, in his book *Mind and Nature* (1979), identifies the paradox in terms of the apparently contradictory needs for stability and innovation.

Britton, discussing it in Chapter 6, in terms of the "constancy" principle, draws on Freud to suggest what it is about man that conflicts with this tendency to revert back to a "dynamic equilibrium" and provides the impetus to let go of old patterns in favor of something relatively new and unknown — of new life, in fact. He shows how an apparently new initiative may actually be serving the purpose of restoring the status quo and avoiding substantial change, and he draws the important distinction between change as an "alternative to realization" on the one hand, and as a consequence of it on the other. The examples demonstrate that without such "realization," it is all too easy to become involved in reenacting old patterns in the name of something new. It is clear that the term *realization* in itself implies here a complicated process including the capacity to manage the anxiety and pressures toward enactment sufficiently to recognize them and reflect upon the situation relatively independently of them. It is also possible that an individual's capacity for such realization expands without his being very specifically conscious of it. For instance, as his capacity to contain anxiety develops, he is capable of more reflection.

Most of the chapters of the book have been oriented toward discussing the more technical problems involved in coming to grips with the emotional obstacles to this sort of realization so that family members have more freedom to make independent choices. It is clear that the kind of change being valued throughout is of a radical kind, a change from the roots that implies some involvement of the whole being and integration in its system. It is also clear that this is not wholly or necessarily a function of the length of the therapeutic encounter. There are some families, like the Langs described by Margot Waddell, who can, in just a few sessions, reach some new awareness that enables them to develop more fruitful patterns on their own; and others, like the Browns in Beta Copley's chapter who, rigidly ensconced as they were, still seemed able to gain a little flexibility and new perspective from their brief experience with her.

I think by this stage of the book a fairly clear idea will have been gained of the kind of criteria that we have used and found relevant for evaluating where different families are in these terms and for gauging different levels of functioning. For instance, the value attached to the capacity to suffer experience and learn from it as a measure of healthy functioning is quite explicit, and the effect of the level of persecutory feelings prevailing in the family is frequently referred to. Linked with this, a number of contributors have demonstrated the relevance of the particular ways that each family uses the processes of projective identification and the importance of the therapist's countertransference experience as a clue to this. One might add the specific suggestion that a major criterion of difference between the families is their way of dealing, individually and collectively, with the demands of containment that are made upon them, not only by the direct thoughts and feelings of each other but also by those that find expression in indirect ways such as projective identification and by the therapist's interpretations during the sessions. Again his experience of their response may provide an important clue to this.

For instance, in some families, such as the Johnson family described by Gianna Williams in Chapter 10, or the Dun family in Chapter 8, there is considerable sensitivity to each other's feelings, but the more painful aspects of these are felt to be so intolerable that great efforts are made to dispel them. They stay to some extent within the family, increasingly located in one member—perhaps the one most open to them or most vulnerable at the time—and tend to become more and more exaggerated, taking on the characteristics that Gianna Williams describes as pathological depression and evoking ever more frantic moves to counteract them. The struggle to contain anxiety in these particular families took the reciprocal form of a sponge-like response in the identified patient and an unporous barrier of efforts to cheer up, advise, and generally engender hope on the part of the other members of the family. These efforts represented faulty, though somewhat complementary forms of containment. But the roles were not too rigidly fixed and could be seen to change in each family during its treatment so that there was already some sense of space, despite the continuing tendency for persecutory feelings to take over at times of stress.

In other families, by contrast, such as the Stones (Hyatt Williams, Chapter 11), the Garcias (Dartington and Magagna, Chapter 9), or the Browns (Copley, Chapter 4), thoughts and feelings have relatively little currency and seem to have become quite divorced from awareness. The focus is much more on behavior and what people do to each other. There are suggestions, in the more extreme cases, of causing concrete physical damage, such as ulcers, heart failure, and even death. Distressing feelings not only find no place but are liable to be forcibly returned with interest, as it were. Projective identification is rampant and, in some of the families, such as those described by Hyatt Williams and Kennedy and Magagna, is manifested in quite primitive expressions of sexuality or violence.

With these families there tends to be far less space anywhere, including in the therapist's mind, for reflection, and the problems of containment are relatively obvious compared to the more subtle forces at work where enactment takes more intricate verbal forms. In fact, in many of these cases, it may be more accurate to speak of containment of non-anxiety since it is the difficulty these families have in entertaining their anxiety at all that makes it so hard to work with them. They incidentially exemplify—in rather an extreme form—the kind of vicious circle that ensues when excessive feelings can find no container, tending in consequence to become ever more excessive and to provoke a correspondingly negative response. But the phenomenon is present to some extent in all these families and can be seen to threaten especially when the containment provided by the treatment is interrupted.

Relating this sort of situation to the model of mother and baby, Bion (1962b) says: If the mother cannot tolerate these projections the infant is reduced to continued projective identification carried out with increasing force and frequency. The increased force seems to denude the projection of its penumbra of meaning (p. 114).

A much less obviously uncomfortable pattern of projective identification (from the therapist's point of view) is found in another group of families where the ubiquitous problems associated with separation are dealt with by unconscious phantasies of fusion. These families, like Nonie Insall's Daley family or the Manners described by Copley, often seem unusually eager initially to engage together in the therapy and take its continuation for granted. But they apparently differentiate very little between one therapist and another and movements towards differentiation on anyone's part tend to be met by more or less violent reactions. This kind of pattern and the gradually increasing capacity to allow differentiation between each other and between the therapists can be traced in the treatment of those two families. Again there are signs of some shift in the particular roles or aspects of the family dynamics represented by its different members.

These three examples of different patterns found in different groups of families are not, of course, intended to be conclusive or exclusive. They are ways that may be useful and may stimulate others to modify or add to them. As with the rest of the book, if they serve in any way to take other people's thinking further and provoke new ideas, they will have served a useful purpose.

The emphasis throughout is clearly on change in the internal dynamic of the family rather than in the externally observable structure, but perhaps the notion of role serves to bridge the two to some extent. There has been discussion of the shared internal object and one can see how a shared internal relationship may also be enacted in the family with different members playing the complementary roles in it. In the Dun family, the reciprocal aspects of the unsatisfactory feeding relationship were played out in different ways; similarly, in the Johnson family, the feelings of being the one left outside the door contrasted the relatively comfortable and self-satisfied "insider" feelings. These internally determined relationships are often reenacted by the family as a group in relation to the therapists—hopefully with a different response—and the process constitutes the nub of the therapeutic activity. Eventually the whole pattern may be modified, but often a significant step on the way seems to be marked by a change in the reciprocal roles, so that someone else in the family begins to represent the problems originally carried by a presenting patient, as when young John Daley began to demonstrate similar fears as those he had previously scorned in his sister (Chapter 14). In these instances, steps toward integration seem to go along with little increases in the repertoire of roles available.

In the family sessions described in this book, the therapists were as questioning about attitudes of glib acceptance to what they had to offer as about those of adamant refusal. Perhaps an important quality that links with the kind of change that occurs as a consequence of realization is that of discrimination, in contrast to a relatively unthought of reaction of submission or resistance. It implies sufficient internal freedom to make an evaluation and a decision about the relative values of alternative possibilities. An important aspect of the therapist's task seems to be to embody the possibility of such discrimination without somehow trying to impose his views of the implications of it. It brings us back to the question of values and raises another apparent paradox. For notwithstanding all these signs of change that we may recognize and welcome, as well as our obvious values in terms of growth and development, we have also indicated the efforts made to eschew the entertainment of specific wishes or goals for the family being treated, and to emphasize rather the struggle to provide the opportunity for its members to establish their own directions. The paradox in the juxtaposition of these two stances is evident and may lead to charges of inconsistency and even hypocrisy. "How can you pretend you don't have goals and aims?"

Bion (1970) has reminded us how, in work with individual patients, even the wish for signs of progress and the pleasure in it have to be disciplined. And this holds true of our work with families and represents one of its most taxing requirements. This principle also has a quite practical value as well as its significance as a principle in itself: if the underlying attitudes in a family contain elements of human perversity, the therapist may find that even his unexpressed wishes become food for their resistance to feed on. The preoccupation with specific symptoms and specific goals for the family may preempt in a quite practical sense the space for them to think for themselves. In view of its relevance to current debates about technical problems it may be worth dwelling on this matter a little further.

Presumably everyone in the field of human relations, whether with individuals, families, or other institutions, has to struggle with the phenomenon of negativism and perversity, in themselves as well as their clients—the tendency, for example, to do the very opposite of what the voice of authority, from inside or out, suggests would be for the best, or the readiness to deify objects or qualities that are essentially anti-growth or anti-life.

It is this phenomenon, I surmise, that leads to the use of techniques such as the "paradoxical injunction," which are designed to beat the perverse characteristic at its own game, so to speak, and get the members of the family to change their behavior in spite of themselves. In terms of the book, these tendencies are examples of the kind of emotional obstacles referred to earlier that must be understood and dealt with if people are to be freed from the pressure simply to react.

From our experience with families we can see especially clearly the link that such tendencies have with the fear of experiencing a position of unwanted dependence on another human being, particularly one who is in a parental role and whose physical and emotional presence is in any way unpredictable or felt to be outside his or her control. If, in such cases, the object representing the much-needed source of supply is unable to tolerate the powerful feelings engendered by its absence, or is otherwise unable to help with them, then the dependency situation must become more or less insufferable, and awareness of it to be resisted at all costs. There is what must feel to the child a fearful conflict provoked by his utter dependence on an object whose frustrating quality is not matched by the kind of opportunities for relief and satisfaction that usually serve to mitigate it. To express hatred and frustration or terror openly may in such cases imply the danger of losing even what source of supply there is or being even more erratically treated by it.

In this sense a so-called perverse reaction can be seen as one form of resistance to powerful forces that cannot be confronted directly. Whatever its precise etiology, any possibility of its modification depends upon the way that the hidden attitudes and internal relationships involved can emerge and be engaged with through the medium of other relationships. Moreover, in the relationship of the therapy it seems particularly important that every effort is made to avoid any exploitation of the dependent situation involved to impose specific goals and intentions of our own. So there is a sense in which the effort to free the mind of such intentions — at least during the sessions — is a crucial part of the therapist's task.

Waddell comments on the way the most relevant concepts in thinking about these processes and in actually working with families turn out to be strikingly similar to those prevailing in early infancy, and she reminds us of Bion's emphasis on the relevance of these same processes in the way that groups function. Again we can see how the family, as the place where the group becomes also the institution, can provide a valuable focus for observing and experiencing in detail the enormous influence of these primitive processes in the life of the institution and the community in general, and we can also attempt to study there what enables them to be harnessed and worked with sufficiently to allow for new qualities of concern, thoughtfulness, and creative action to emerge of the kind that in this book have been associated with shifts toward the depressive position and the capacity to tolerate frustration, conflict, and ambivalence.

Bateson (1979) talks about the profound differences between a change in the characterological state of an organism and changes in that organism's particular actions. The latter is a relatively easy one, and the former is profoundly difficult.

The path to change is not always at all obvious or direct, and progress, like the pilgrim's, is fraught with unexpected blocks and pitfalls. We, as therapists, cannot chart it or predict it. We can only try to provide the space for the emerging conflicts to be lived out in the sessions and thought about.

Glossary

ERRICA MOUSTAKI SMILANSKY

The following pages describe relevant key concepts within a theoretical framework used in psychoanalytic work with individual patients and groups. The work with families discussed in this book draws on this framework, while at the same time providing the opportunity to explore and test out its specific applicability and relevance to family work.

The terms are organized alphabetically, each presented in a separate section. These begin with the meaning of the term, usually followed by reference to relevant historical and theoretical factors. Finally, the application of the term to family work is presented. Each section includes a brief bibliography of relevant literature.

CONTAINMENT

This concept originates in Bion's (1962a) model of container ($♀$) / contained ($♂$) and draws on Klein's (1946) description of the mechanism of projective identification. It is based on the model of the mother as a container for the infant's projected feelings, needs, and unwanted parts. This function is provided by means of a capacity that Bion has called *reverie*. It implies a particular state of mind in which the mother is open and ready to take in and reflect upon what the baby projects, and conveys back to him the sense that his anxieties and communications are bearable and have meaning.

It is the internalization of this process and the identification with mother's containing function that is regarded as enabling the emergence of the individual's capacity to be open to the emotional impact of new experience without being disrupted by it. This depends on allowing the experience to exist in his mind sufficiently for it to be understood and integrated into his view of himself and the world. That is, the individual can retain his knowledge and experience and yet be prepared to reconstrue past experiences in a manner that enables him to be receptive to a new idea.

Relating containment to our work with families

The therapist in the transference has to be able to tolerate the family's frustrations as well as his own, and to help the family modify rather than evade anxiety. In order for containment to occur, the therapist needs to retain his own sense of goodness or effectiveness, despite the family's projection of the opposite into him; he needs to tolerate the doubt that is being created, and like the mother with her baby, to hold the unwanted feelings until they can be relayed back to the family in a form that may be assimilable. This provides the basis for the family's growth and learning from experience through which the emergence of an internal container is hopefully achieved. While the containing function of the work with the family is essentially the same as with individuals, it is further complicated by the concurrent variety and power of the conflicting projections and identifications of family members. In co-therapy, the co-therapists need to provide some containment for each other's countertransference and frustrations, both in the sessions and in discussion between the sessions.

References

Bion, W. R. (1962). *Learning from Experience*, London: Heinemann.

Grinberg, L., Sor, D., and Tabak de Bianchedi, E. (1975). *Introduction to the Work of Bion*, trans. from the Spanish by Alberto Hahn. Perthshire, Clunie Press for the Roland Harris Educational Trust.

Klein, M. (1946). Notes on some schizoid mechanisms. In *Developments in Psychoanalysis*. London: Hogarth Press and Institute of Psychoanalysis, 1952.

Steiner, J. (1979). Psychotic and non-psychotic aspects of border-line states. Unpublished paper, Tavistock Library.

COUNTERTRANSFERENCE

This concept refers to the whole of the analyst's/therapist's feelings and unconscious reactions experienced in relation to his patient, especially to his patient's transference (Racker 1968).

There are three different views regarding countertransference. In the first, the therapist's reactions are regarded as part of his own pathology and therefore as something to be overcome. This view originated in the early days of psychoanalysis and still exists to some degree today. Countertransference was seen as a neurotic disturbance in the analyst, preventing him from getting a clear and objective view of the patient. It was seen as a source of danger and an unconscious interference with his work. As such it was associated with the analyst's transference onto the patient of his own unsublimated, regressive instinctual strivings (Ruesch 1961).

According to the second view, it is not inappropriate for the therapist to be stirred up by his patients and have feelings in response to them since that is an inevitable phenomenon in any contact between two people. The therapist is encouraged to share his reactions with the patient, without necessarily trying to understand their meaning in the transference.

In the third view, countertransference is seen not only as an inevitable process, but also as an integral part of the therapy, which, if understood, processed, and utilized properly can provide a source of valuable information about the patient's unconscious. This is the view described and drawn on in this book.

Although Freud in his earlier writings maintained the notion of the analyst's continuous efforts to achieve a benevolent neutrality, as early as 1913 he gives some cues about the value of exploiting the countertransference manifestations in a controlled fashion for the purposes of the analytic task. Freud's remark was that "everyone possesses in his own unconscious an instrument with which he can interpret the utterances of the unconscious in other people" (1913, p. 445).

Paula Heimann (1950), in her classic paper on the subject, carried further the notion that not only is countertransference useful, but that it also represents one of the most important tools for the analyst's work and involves a particular kind of relationship between two people. She maintained, in contrast to earlier views, that the aim of the analysis is not for the analyst to share his feelings as such or to produce interpretations on the basis of intellectual procedure, but to sustain the feelings stirred in himself by the patient in order to subordinate them to the analytic task, as opposed to discharging them.

Hanna Segal (1975) further elaborated on the distinction between the analytic relationship and other relationship stressing that while the analyst is opening his mind freely to his impressions, he also has to maintain distance from his own feelings and reactions to the patient, so that he can observe them and draw conclusions from them, but not be swayed by them. She draws our attention to the notion that the patient is in a constant nonverbal interaction with the therapist in which he acts on the therapist's mind, and thus the therapist is seen not as a mirror onto which the patient projects, but rather as a container. Segal also stresses that the therapist's capacity to contain instead of discharging the feelings aroused in him by the patient, is his means of processing the patient's projections into him, so that he can return them to the patient in a more acceptable, digestible form. (This is further elaborated under *containment*.)

Being aware of the countertransference highlights the power of the projections to which the analyst is exposed. The more disturbed the patient, the more pressure there may be on the analyst to identify with the patient's projections and be pulled into action, losing his capacity for containment. In this context, projective counteridentification is the term used by Grinberg (1962) to describe the analytic experience of being in the "grip of something." There is, of course, the danger that the countertransference concept, as Segal (1975) points out, can be abused if it is resorted to as a justification for failure to understand.

Relating countertransference to our work with families

A link may exist between the nature of the infantile feelings and phantasies that the parental couple find difficult to bear in themselves and the problems in the family. Other members of the family may have been assigned the role of carrying some of these for the whole family, and projections that they have carried hitherto may now be experienced by the therapist in the countertransference and made available for understanding. Countertransference is the tool with which one knows what is to be contained.

The use of the countertransference is particularly important in this approach to work with families. In co-therapy, each therapist may react differently to the countertransference experience in relation to the different family members and to the co-therapist. This experience can provide internal evidence to be used, together with external evidence, for understanding conflicts in the family. The therapeutic pair needs to sustain and bear the differences and work on them both within and between themselves, so that they can communicate to the family their understanding of the underlying anxieties. Understanding the projections experienced in the countertransference takes place partially during the sessions but it also requires thinking and discussions outside them. Thus, in this kind of family work, containment takes place in the field created through the therapist pair's relationship.

In the case of the single therapist, the functions fulfilled by the pair vis-à-vis the projections are now to be carried by some sort of internalized couple within the single therapist. He must look at his own reactions in order to provide the family with an experience analogous to that with a therapy/parental couple.

References

Freud, S. (1913). The disposition to obsessional neurosis. *Standard Edition* 5:445.

Grinberg, L. (1962). On a specific aspect of countertransference due to the patient's projective identification. *International Journal of Psycho-Analysis* 42:436–440.

Heimann, P. (1950). On countertransference. *International Journal of Psycho-Analysis* 31:81–84.

Laplanche, H., and Pontalis, J.-B. (1973). *The Language of Psychoanalysis* London: Hogarth.

Money-Kyrle, R. E. (1956). Normal countertransference and some of its deviations. *International Journal of Psycho-Analysis* 37:360–366.

Racker, H. (1968). *Transference and Countertransference.* London: Hogarth Press and Institute of Psychoanalysis.

Segal, H. (1977). Countertransference. *International Journal of Psychoanalytic Psychotherapy* 6:31–37.

Singer, E. (1965). *Key Concepts in Psychotherapy.* New York: Random House.

DEPRESSIVE POSITION (SEE PARANOID–SCHIZOID DEPRESSIVE)

IDENTIFICATION (PROJECTIVE IDENTIFICATION – INTROJECTIVE IDENTIFICATION)

PROJECTIVE IDENTIFICATION

This term refers to the phantasy of entering the object with the whole or part of the self, which may lead to an altered perception of the identity of the self and object in relation to each other. It was first described by Klein (1946) in her work on the emotional development in the first months of life, and is seen as being active from the beginning of life. Its usage has been further enlarged, clarified, and developed by such writers as Bion (1959, 1962a), Segal (1964), Rosenfeld (1965a, 1969), and Meltzer (1967).

This term may well be confusing as it is used to describe a whole range of purposes such as for primitive communication; to keep good parts of the self safe from internal harm, as well as to get rid of bad parts; to control, attack or destroy the object; and to avoid the experience of separation.

In "Attacks on Linking," Bion (1959) supposes there is a normal degree of projective identification which, associated with introjective identification, is the foundation on which normal development rests. He emphasizes the normal function of projective identification, when in conjunction with a containing object that modifies the intolerable projections, constitutes a stepping stone in human development, one of the main factors in symbol formation and thus in communication.

Segal (1964) draws attention to it as the earliest form of empathy and points out that the capacity to put oneself in another person's shoes develops through processes of projective identification.

For projective identification to take place, the projector must experience some temporary differentiation between self and object. However, the process of projective identification leads to a loss in the sense of self, hence a blurring of the boundary between the self and the other. It interferes with the experience of loss if the object is absent and consequently prevents the formation of a symbolic representation of the lost object. In excessive use of projective identification, phantasy and reality become confused and the patient's capacities for verbal and abstract thinking are crippled.

Segal describes the two most important anxieties liable to follow projective identification as

> the fear that the attacked object will retaliate equally by projection; and the anxiety of having parts of the self imprisoned and controlled by the object into which they have been projected. This last anxiety is particularly strong when good parts of the self have been projected. [1973, p. 36]

Projective identification in clinical work

Work in the transference may relieve the projections of their unbearable quality and make it possible for the patient to reintroject them. Three of the different forms of projective identification that are highlighted by Rosenfeld (1969) in his paper "The Importance of Projective Identification in the Ego Structure and the Object Relations of the Psychotic Patient," are graphically illustrated.

1. Projective Identification as communication. This he relates to Bion's work on the container/contained model. He writes about how a patient unconsciously projects impulses and parts of

himself into the analyst so that the analyst may feel and understand those experiences and be able to contain them, enabling them to lose their unbearable quality. If the analyst is able to interpret this experience, the patient may then learn to own and tolerate his own impulses and start experiencing feelings that were previously experienced as meaningless or too frightening to assimilate.

Bion (1962b) had suggested earlier that the degree of readiness of the receiver to contain the projections will finally determine whether projective identification could take the form of the communication. Readiness means that the receiver is open to taking in the projections, capable of surviving their impact, including any aggressive elements, and therefore able to provide an opportunity for the patient to differentiate phantasy from reality. If the intended receiver does not offer himself as a container in this way then there is a kind of boomerang effect in which the projected element may be returned to the sender in the form of "nameless dread."

2. Projective identification as a defense to get rid of unwanted parts. Here the mechanism is used for the denial of psychic reality. The patient splits and projects unbearable anxieties into the analyst in order to evacuate disturbing mental content. For instance, it can be used to defend against aggressive impulses that are sometimes an expression of anger related to separation anxiety, but can also have a distinctly envious character. When in the grip of this form of projective identification, the patient primarily wants the analyst to condone the evacuation and denial of his problems; he experiences interpretations as critical and reacts to them with resentment

3. A third use of projective identification is as a means of control. This is shown when the patient attempts to control the analyst's body and mind, and seems to be based on a very early infantile type of object relationship. The patient believes that he has omnipotently forced himself into the analyst and, as with the infant and mother, he is fused and confused with him, preventing the experience of separation, but at the expense of being tortured by anxieties relating to the loss of the self.

Any of these three forms of projective identification can occur singly or together in one patient and their distinction has important clinical implications both in terms of treatment technique and prognostic evaluation. In general, the more that either of the latter two predominate, that is, as a means of defense or as a means of control, the greater is likely to be the degree of disturbance.

Relating projective identification to our work with families

Box (1978) suggests that the

> concept of projective identification provides the major link between concepts such as role and unconscious process, between individual and group and between individual and family; and it is this concept which is most central in the approach to families being developed. [p. 119]

In much of this work we attempt to understand how unconsciously shared elements that cannot be tolerated by one or more of the family members are reallocated inside or outside the family in an attempt to avoid the experience of internal conflict. Often such families insist that the disturbance is all located in the index patient who may have unconsciously colluded with the family system that has "chosen" him to become a receptor. In a similar way that the disturbance is projected, other facets, say being the "good child," may also be located in one member to the detriment of his fuller life and general development. All the projections lead to a depletion of family members' individuality.

The therapists, in their interaction with the family by means of their countertransference experience, attempt to take the projective identification into themselves, find space for and try to understand the nature of the elements disowned by the family, and thereby provide some containment. They also need to remember that this may be a communication that the family does not know how to make in any other way. Where the projective identification is for the purposes of evacuation or control, the attempt at understanding may be so hated that there is great risk that the therapy may be broken off.

The attempt at unraveling this process can hopefully lift some of the burden that a particular family member or members may carry for the rest, and may therefore free family members to express parts of themselves that were locked and obscured by having carried particular roles for the family.

References

Bion, W. R. (1959). Attacks on linking. In *Second Thoughts*. London: Heinemann, 1967.

———— (1962). A theory of thinking. In *Second Thoughts*. London: Heinemann, 1967.

Box, S. (1978). An analytic approach to work with families. *Journal of Adolescence* 1:119–133.

Klein, M. (1946). Notes on some schizoid mechanisms. In *Developments in Psychoanalysis*. London: Hogarth, 1952.

Meltzer, D. (1967). *The Psychoanalytic Process*. London: Heinemann.

Rosenfeld, H. (1965). *Psychotic States: A Psychoanalytic Approach*. London: Hogarth.

———— (1969). Contribution to the psychopathology of psychotic states: the importance of projective identification in the ego structure and the object relations of the psychotic patient. In *Problems of Psychosis*, vol. I, ed. P. Dauret and C. Laurin. Amsterdam: Excerpta Medica.

Segal, H. (1964). *Introduction to the Work of Melanie Klein*. London: Heinemann; also Hogarth, 1973.

INTROJECTIVE IDENTIFICATION

This concept describes a process of taking in aspects, qualities, or skills of the object in such a way that they are gradually identified with and inform the character of an individual. Meltzer (1967) has drawn attention to the significance of the acknowledgement of separateness and the freedom to come and go as necessary preconditions for this process to occur.

Relating introjective identification to our work with families

There is some evidence of introjective identification having occurred when the family shows that it can metabolize and process experience and anxiety in the absence of the therapists with a clear sense of their separateness from them and acknowledgment of where the skill they have acquired has originated. Rather than mere instant imitation of the therapists' ways of functioning, painstaking, and therefore more lasting, internalization must take place for healthy development to continue.

This differs from the defensive type of projective identification in which characteristics of the object are surreptitiously taken over without a struggle with feelings of envy and competitiveness. Introjective identification not only involves allowing the therapists their freedom, but also involves admiration and respect for their qualities in the work of the sessions. Such admiration should be distinguished from indiscriminate idealization. In contrast to projective identification, introjective identification implies the emergence of the capacity for reality testing, and differentiating what belongs to the self and what does not. Hence, the case may occur where "bad" qualities of the object are introjected but are recognized as separate to the self.

References

Heimann, P. (1952). Certain functions of introjection and projection in early infancy. In Developments in Psychoanalysis, ed. M. Klein. London: Hogarth.

Meltzer, D. (1967). *The Psychoanalytic Process*. London: Heinemann.

INNER WORLD

The inner world is the world of figures formed on the pattern of the persons first loved and hated in life, which also contains aspects of oneself; these inner figures exist in phantasy, engaged in apparently independent activities "as real" or "more real and actual to the person in his unconscious feeling than external events" (Rivière 1955, p. 346). When the phrase *inner world* is used as a specific term, internal objects do not denote exact replicas of the external world, but "are always coloured by the infant's phantasy and projections" (Segal 1979, p. 64).

As Rivière (1955) points out, "the inner world" is exclusively one of "personal relations." Everything happening in it refers to the self, to the individual's own urges and desires toward other people and of his reactions to them as the objects of his desires. Our relation to our inner world has its own development from the inception of life onward, just as that to the external world has.

Relating *inner world* to work with families, the crucial part of work with families is to provide an opportunity for changes to take place in their inner worlds. What we attempt to do is to examine, in various ways, which predominant internal conflicts and relationships are shared by members of the family and played out among them. Our notion is that the experiences in each person's inner world provide the impetus for reenactment both in the external world and within the therapeutic setting.

The family therapy described is aimed at working with the shared inner world of the family through working with what is transferred to the therapists (see transference, glossary). At any particular time in the work, although communications may come from individuals and be regarded as such, they are also seen as linked to the family's unconsciously shared phantasies.

References

Rivière, J. (1965). The unconscious phantasy of an inner world reflected in examples from literature. In *New Directions in Psychoanalysis*, ed. M. Klein et al. London: Tavistock.

PARANOID-SCHIZOID/DEPRESSIVE POSITION

These terms, introduced by Melanie Klein, refer to different levels of mental development. The first is characterized by primitive mechanisms of defense such as splitting, idealization, and denial. The second is indicative of greater integration. It involves the capacity to bring together the feelings of love and hate in relation to a whole object of person rather than splitting them between separate parts. It is this capacity that enables the individual to experience concern for the object and survive its absence so that it can become symbolically represented in the mind and allowed a separate existence.

In practice, especially following the work of Bion, these two positions are seen to describe different states of mind that may fluctuate from moment to moment and are both more or less present for everyone at different times so that it is unlikely for anyone to be free of experiences and associated with the paranoid/schizoid position. The capacity to bear and contain the conflict this fluctuation implies is an essential feature of the depressive position.

These two positions can be described in more detail from a developmental point of view:

Paranoid-schizoid position

In the first few months of life the infant has relatively undeveloped perceptual powers and only very limited capacities to conceptualize; the mother or the person who looks after him is perceived not as a whole person, but in parts, such as eyes, breasts, hands, which are relatively unrelated to each other. At this stage also, a feature of normal development is the sorting out of experiences and objects into pleasurable experiences stemming from gratifying, idealized sources on the one hand and painful, frustrating experiences felt to be derived from bad, denigrated part-objects, on the other. The frustration and deprivation due to the absence of a "good" object are often experienced as if they were caused by the presence of a "bad" object. This phase is thus characterized by a prevalence of splitting of good and bad in the ego and in the object.

The depressive position

Gradually during early infancy, the child develops the capacity both to perceive the mother as a whole person and to sustain conflictual feelings toward her. While this state of mind prevails, the polarization between good and bad is bridged. The infant may, therefore, recognize that his hostile feelings and phantasies have harmed or destroyed the gratifying loved one, not just the depriving one. As a result of this integration, he begins to experience feelings of concern for the mother lest his hostile feelings should predominate over his loving ones. Some capacity to hold on to the painful anxieties at this phase, that is, some negotiation of the depressive position, is important for future growth and maturation. Without such negotiation the infant remains dominated by the more primitive persecutory anxiety, based upon a feeling of being attacked and threatened, which may lead to an abiding sense of grievance. If there is some success in dealing with the depressive position, depressive anxiety, which has to do with anxiety over harm done by the self predominantly to one's good object, is able to be felt and sustained. The tolerance of this kind of anxiety promotes feelings of responsibility, attempts at reparation for harm done, and the development of creativity.

The working through of the depressive position during the first year of life is never complete. There are various defenses employed to avoid such painful feelings, for instance, a lapse into a schizo-paranoid state of mind or a flight into a manic one. Renegotiation of the anxieties and relationships to do with the depressive position is necessary again and again, particularly at times of personal crisis and developmental change such as adolescence, the menopause, the midlife crisis in the thirties described by Professor Elliott Jaques (1955) and others.

In our work with families we attempt initially to provide an external containment of conflict that might help members develop an internal capacity to contain a depressive feeling. This in turn diminishes the pressure to project into others unwanted parts of the self or persecutory objects through the use of projective identification.

PHANTASY (THE KLEINIAN DEVELOPMENT OF THE TERM)

This concept refers to the primary content of unconscious mental processes and does not refer simply to a repressed fantasy.

> Phantasy is (in the first instance) the mental corollary, the psychic representative of instinct. There is no impulse, no instinctual urge or response, which is not experienced as unconscious phantasy . . . The first mental processes, the psychic representatives of libidinal and destructive instincts, are to be regarded as the earliest beginning of phantasies . . . All impulses, all feelings, all modes of defence are experienced in phantasies which give them mental life and show their direction and purpose. [Isaacs 1952, p. 83]

Hanna Segal (1964) highlights the important implications of this view for psychoanalytic thought about the development of the ego:

> Phantasy-forming is a function of the ego. The view of phantasy as a mental expression of instincts through the medium of the ego assumed a higher degree of ego-organization than is postulated by Freud. It assumes that the ego from birth is capable of forming, and indeed is driven by instincts and anxiety to form primitive object relationships in phantasy and reality. [pp. 2–3]

Phantasies are always inferred, not directly communicated as such. They are present and actively influential in every individual throughout life. They are not restricted to pathological processes, and what determines the distinction between normal and pathological is the nature and degree of the desire or anxiety associated with them, and the way they interact with each other and with external reality. There is evidence that disturbances in the capacity to symbolize in phantasy are accompanied by corresponding problems in development, talking, playing, and working.

Unconscious phantasy is in a constant interplay with external reality, both influencing and altering the perception or interpretation of it and also being influenced by it. It is to be distinguished from the popular concept of conscious fantasy used to describe a means of escaping from external reality, as in daydreaming, for example.

Although not necessarily defensive, phantasies may have a defensive aspect, such as phantasying gratification, or fulfilment of instinctual drives to deal with the external reality of deprivation; and/or phantasying as a defense against other phantasies, as when a manic phantasy serves to counteract the painful effect of a depressive one.

Relating phantasy to work with families

The significance attached to phantasy relates directly to our emphasis on the use of transference in work with families. To the extent that current and perennial difficulties in relationships are a function of these primitive object relationships in phantasy, it is the manifestations in the transference of those internal relationships that form the core of the material to be worked on in the sessions.

Bion has shown how group processes tend to mobilize primitive levels of mental life and basic human phantasies that are shared at an unconscious level. In institutionalized groups such as the family, these phantasies become crystallized into forms that are specific to that group and its particular life — aided presumably by the constant interaction of projection and introjection between the members. They have been termed *shared phantasies* and explored by Dicks (1967) in relation to marriages. It is this notion that forms the basis and rationale for the emphasis on interpretations made to the group rather than to particular individuals within it: the interpretations are intended to illuminate the current shared phantasies underlying the communication from the family.

References

Bion, W. R. (1961). *Experiences in Groups*. London: Tavistock.
Dicks, H. (1967). *Marital Tensions*. London: Routledge & Kegan Paul.
Isaacs, S. (1952). The nature and function of phantasy. In *Developments in Psychoanalysis*, ed. M. Klein et al. London: Hogarth.
Segal, H. (1973). *Introduction to the Work of Melanie Klein*. London: Hogarth.

TRANSFERENCE

Transference, in the context of therapy, refers to all that is projected into, and experienced in relation to the therapist and the treatment setting via the unconscious phantasies accompanying the patient/therapist experience.

The clearest early description of transference was made by Freud (1905) in the case history of Dora:

> What are transferences? They are new editions or facsimiles of the impulses and phantasies which are aroused and made conscious during the progress of the analysis; but they have this peculiarity, which is characteristic for their species, that they replace some earlier person by the person of the physician. To put it another way: a whole series of psychological experiences are revived, not as belonging to the past, but as applying to the person of the physician at the present moment. Some of these transferences have a content which differs from that of their model in no respect whatever except for the substitution. These then—to keep the same metaphor—are merely new impressions or reprints. Others are more ingeniously constructed; their content has been subjected to a moderating influence—to sublimation, as I call it—and they may even become conscious, by cleverly taking advantage of some real peculiarity in the physician's person or circumstances, and attaching themselves to that. These, then, will no longer be new impressions, but revised editions. [*Standard Edition* 7:116]

The Kleinian view emphasizes the importance of experiencing the revised editions in the here and now in the therapeutic setting. Transference not only refers to the unraveling of repressed feelings and traumata, but also to the whole set of internalized object relationships. Thus, the therapist comes to stand for the internal figures, and all that the patient brings contains elements of the transference even from the moment he enters the therapeutic situation. The here and now in the therapeutic setting is the meeting point of the past and the unconscious phantasy accompanying the past as it expresses itself in the present.

The latter way of thinking and use of the here and now may have a direct link with the function of transference in the task of containment. By the therapist's spelling out the content of the different projections or phantasies as they refer to himself, the patient may not only understand but may also have an experience of containment conductive to a modification of his inner world. This takes place by virtue of the therapist's recognizing and offering a contextual space including the clearly defined boundaries of the setting that enables the work in the transference to take place.

Hanna Segal (1973) says that

> a full transference interpretation should include the current external relationship in the patient's life, the patient's relationship to the analyst, and the relation between these and the parents in the past. It should also aim at establishing a link between the internal figures and the external ones. . . .

She modifies this view by saying that in actual practice an interpretation is hardly ever full nor can the therapist be in an active preoccupation as to how to achieve it. As H. Rey says, transference involves looking at "what, in what state, does what, with what motive, to what object, in what state, with what consequences?" (Steiner 1979, p. 9).

Relating transference to our work with families

Although it is the pathology of the individual patient with which we are presented, we feel that the individuals comprising the family have a meeting ground, which is their shared inner world, implying the existence of shared anxieties. We regard every communication as being linked to their common underlying anxiety. When we say we are working in the transference with families, we mean that in relation to the separate communications of different members, we concentrate on trying to understand what is the common transference, seeing each as part of a whole family system, engaged in an unconsciously joined interaction not only with each other, but also with the therapists. This relationship between individuals in the session springs from the relationships of their inner objects. Understanding this with the family provides the opportunity for each family member to recognize its specific relevance to himself as a separate individual and allows an internal process of modification to develop. Our attempt is to understand not only the content of the communications, but also how a particular communication is expressed.

References

Freud, S. (1905). Fragment of an analysis of a case of hysteria. *Standard Edition* 7. *1917 Introductory Lectures on Psycho-Analysis,* 27th and 28th Lectures, *Standard Edition* 16.

Laplanche, J., and Pontalis, J.-B. (1973). *The Language of Psychoanalysis.* London: Hogarth.

Segal, H. (1973). *Introduction to the Work of Melanie Klein.* London: Hogarth.

Steiner, J. (1979). Psychotic and non-psychotic aspects of borderline states. Unpublished paper, Tavistock Library.

References

Abraham, K. (1924). Development of the libido. *Selected Papers of Karl Abraham*. London: Hogarth.

Ackerman, N. (1966). *Treating the Troubled Family*. New York: Basic Books.

Bartlett, F. H. (1976). Illusions and reality: R. D. Laing. *Family Process* 15:51–64.

Bateson, G. (1979). *Mind and Nature*. London: Wildwood House.

Bateson, G., Jackson, D., Haley, J., and Weakland, J. (1956). Towards a theory of schizophrenia. *Behavioural Sciences* 1:251–264.

Beels, C. C., and Ferber, A. (1969). Family therapy: a view. *Family Process* 8:280–318.

Bentovim, A. (1979). Family interaction and techniques of intervention. *Journal of Family Therapy* 1:321–343.

Berne, E. (1964). *Games People Play: The Psychology of Human Relationships*. New York: Grove.

Bertalanffy, L. von. (1968). General system theory—a critical review. In *Modern Systems Research for the Behavioral Scientist*, ed. W. Buckley, pp. 11–30. Chicago: Aldine.

Bion, W. R. (1953). Notes on the theory of schizophrenia. In *Second Thoughts*, pp. 23–35. London: Heinemann, 1967.

———— (1959). Attacks on linking. *International Journal of Psycho-Analysis* 40:308–315.

———— (1961). *Experiences in Groups*. London: Tavistock.

———— (1962a). *Learning from Experience*. London: Heinemann.

———— (1962b). *A Theory of Thinking*. In *Second Thoughts*, pp. 110–119. London: Heinemann, 1967.

———— (1965). *Transformations: Change from Learning to Growth*. London: Heinemann.

———— (1967). *Second Thoughts*. London: Heinemann.

———— (1970). *Attention and Interpretation*. London: Tavistock.

—— (1974). *Bion's Brazilian Lectures*. Rio de Janeiro: Imago Editora.

—— (1984). *Learning from Experience*. London: Maresfield Reprints.

Boszormenyi-Nagy, I., and Spark, G. M. (1973). *Invisible Loyalties*. New York: Harper & Row.

Bowers, M. (1961). Family psychotherapy. *American Journal of Ortho-Psychiatry* 31:40-60.

Bowlby, J. (1949). The study and reduction of group tensions in the family. *Human Relations* 2:123-128.

Box, S. (1977). *Problems of Parents with Difficult Children*. Document no., NT1719. London: Tavistock.

—— (1978). An analytic approach to work with families. *Journal of Adolescence* 1:119-133.

Byng-Hall, J. (1973). Family myths used as a defence in conjoint family therapy. *British Journal of Medical Psychology* 46:239-250.

—— (1988). Scripts and legends in families and family therapy. *Family Process*, vol. 27, June.

Camus, A. (1946). *The Outsider*. (*L'Etranger*, 1942). London: Hamish Hamilton.

Chasseguet-Smirgel, J. (1985a). *Creativity and Perversion*. London: Free Association.

—— (1985b). *The Ego Ideal*. Trans. P. Barrows. London: Free Association.

Copley, B. (1991). Exploration and theory in family work. In *Extending Horizons*, ed. R. Szur and S. Miller, pp. 47-64. London: Karnac.

Dare, C. (1981). Psychoanalysis and family therapy. In *Developments in Family Therapy*, ed. S. Walrond-Skinner, pp. 281-297. London: Routledge.

deCarteret, J., and Whiffen, R. (1982). Evolution of supervision: overview. In *Family Therapy Supervision: Recent Developments in Practise*, ed. R. Whiffen and J. Byng-Hall. New York: Grune and Stratton.

Deutsch, H. (1942). *Psychoanalysis of Neurosis*. London: Hogarth.

Dicks, H. V. (1963). Object relations theory and marital status. *British Journal of Medical Psychology* 36:126-129.

—— (1967). *Marital Tensions*. London: Routledge & Kegan Paul.

Eliot, T. S. (1919). *Hamlet* in *Selected Prose of T. S. Eliot*, ed. F. Kermode. Boston: Faber and Faber.

Fairbairn, W. R. D. (1952). *Psychoanalytic Studies of the Personality*. London: Routledge & Kegan Paul.

Flugel, J. C. (1921). *The Psychoanalytic Study of the Family*. London: Hogarth.

Freud, S. (1905). Fragment of an analysis of a case of hysteria. *Standard Edition* 7:116.

—— (1906). Psychoanalysis and the establishment of the facts in legal proceedings. *Standard Edition* 9:99-114.

—— (1909). Analysis of a phobia in a five year old boy. *Standard Edition* 10:3-149.

—— (1913). The disposition to obsessional neurosis. *Standard Edition* 12:445.

—— (1914). Remembering, repeating and working through. *Standard Edition* 12:147, 156.

—— (1917). Introductory lectures on psychoanalysis, 27th and 28th lectures. *Standard Edition* 16:431-463.

_____ (1918). From the history of an infantile neurosis. *Standard Edition* 17: 7–122.

_____ (1920). Beyond the pleasure principle. *Standard Edition* 18:7–64.

_____ (1930). Civilization and its discontents. *Standard Edition* 21:59–151.

Frude, N. (1980). Methodological problems in the evaluation of family. *Journal of Family Therapy* 2:29–45.

Gibran, K. (1926). *The Prophet*. London: Heinemann.

Goffman, E. (1961). *Asylums: Essays on the Social Situation of Mental Patients and Other Inmates*. New York: Doubleday.

Grinberg, L. (1962). On a specific aspect of countertransference due to the patient's identification. *International Journal of Psycho-Analysis* 42:436–440.

Grotjahn, A. (1929). *Arzte als Patienten Subjektive Krankensgeschichten in Arztlichen selbstschilderungen*. Leipzig: Georg Thieme.

Gurman, A. S., and Kniskern, D. P. (1978). Technolatry, methodolatry and the results of family therapy. *Family Process* 17:275–282.

_____ (1979). Research on marital and family therapy progress, perspective and prospect. In *Handbook of Psychotherapy and Behavioural Change*, 2nd ed., ed. S. L. Garfield and A. S. Bergin. New York: Wiley.

Haley, J. (1977). *Problem Solving Therapy*. San Francisco, CA: Jossey-Bass.

Heimann, P. (1950). On countertransference. *International Journal of Psycho-Analysis* 5 (31):81–84.

_____ (1952). Certain functions of introjection and projection in early infancy. In *Developments in Psychoanalysis*, ed. M. Klein, et al. London: Hogarth.

Henderson, R. E., and Williams, A. H. (1974). *An Essay in Transference*. Document no. NT1729. London: Tavistock.

Isaacs, S. (1952). The nature and function of phantasy. In *Developments in Psychoanalysis*, ed. M. Klein, P. Heimann, S. Isaacs, and J. Riviere. London: Hogarth.

Jackson, D. D., ed. (1968). *Therapy, Communication and Change*. Palo Alto, CA: Science and Behavior Books.

Jaques, E. (1955). Social systems as a defence against persecutory and depressive anxiety. In *New Directions in Psychoanalysis*, ed. M. Klein, P. Heimann, S. Isaacs, and J. Riviere. London: Tavistock.

Jones, M. (1952). *Social Psychiatry: a Study of Therapeutic Communities*. London: Tavistock.

Joseph, B. (1975). The patient who is difficult to reach. In *Tactics and Techniques in Psychoanalytic Therapy*, vol. 2, ed. P. Giovacchini, pp. 205–216. New York: Jason Aronson.

_____ (1978). Different types of anxiety and their handling in the analytic situation. *International Journal of Psycho-Analysis* 59:223.

Kafka, F. (1925). *The Trial*. London: Victor S. Gollancz, 1935.

Klein, M. (1932). *The Psychoanalysis of Children*. London: Hogarth.

_____ (1935). A contribution to the psychogenesis of manic-depressive states. In *Contributions to Psychoanalysis*, pp. 282–310. London: Hogarth.

_____ (1940). Mourning and its relation to manic-depressive states. In *Love, Guilt and Reparation*. London: Hogarth, 1975.

———— (1945). The Oedipus complex in the light of early anxieties. *International Journal of Psycho-Analysis* 26:11-33.

———— (1946). Notes on some schizoid mechanisms. In *Developments in Psychoanalysis*, pp. 292-320. London: Hogarth.

———— (1955). On identification. In *New Directions in Psychoanalysis*. London: Tavistock.

———— (1957). *Envy and Gratitude*. London: Tavistock.

———— (1975). *Envy and Gratitude and Other Works 1946-63*. London: Hogarth.

Lacan, J. (1977). *Ecrits*. London: Tavistock.

Laforgue, R. (1936). La névrose familiale. *Revue Française de Psychanalyse* 9:327-355.

Lagache, D. (1964). La méthode psychanalytique. In *Psychiatrie*, ed. L. Michaux et al. Paris:

Laing, R. D., and Esterson, D. (1964). *Sanity, Madness, and the Family*. London: Tavistock.

Laplanche, J., and Pontalis, J. B. (1973), *The Language of Psychoanalysis*. London: Hogarth.

Lawrence, G. (1979). Exploring boundaries. In *Exploring Individual and Organizational Boundaries*. New York: Wiley.

Madanes, C., and Haley, J. (1977). Dimensions of family therapy. *Journal of Mental and Nervous Diseases* 165:88-98.

Magee, B. (1978). *Men of Ideas: Some Creators of Contemporary Philosophy*. British Broadcasting Corporation.

Martin, F. E. (1977). Some implications from the theory and practice of family therapy for individual therapy (and vice versa). *British Journal of Medical Psychology* 50:53-64.

Medawar, P. (1969). *Induction and Intuition in Scientific Thought*. London: Methuen.

Meltzer, D. (1967). *The Psychoanalytic Process*. London: Heinemann.

———— (1973). *Sexual States of Mind*. Perthshire, Scotland: Clunie.

———— (1978). *The Kleinian Development, Part III*. Perthshire, Scotland: Clunie.

Meltzer, D., and Harris, M. (1986). Family patterns and culture and educability. In *Studies in Extended Metapsychology*, pp. 154-174. Perthshire, Scotland: Clunie.

Menzies, I. E. P. (1970). *A Case Study in the Functioning of Social Systems as a Defence against Anxiety*. London: Tavistock.

Minuchin, S. (1967). *Families in the Slums*. New York: Basic Books.

Money-Kyrle, R. E. (1956). Normal countertransference and some of its deviations. *International Journal of Psycho-Analysis* 37: 360-366.

Palazzoli, M. S., Boscolo, L., Cecchin, G., and Prata, G. (1978). *Paradox and Counter-Paradox*. New York: Jason Aronson.

Parsons, T. (1967). *Sociological Analysis and Politics: The Theories of Talcott Parsons*, ed. W. C. Mitchell. London: Prentice-Hall.

Racker, H. (1968). *Transference and Countertransference*. London: Hogarth, 1974.

Rice, A. K. (1975). Selections from systems of organization. In *Group Relations Reader*, ed. A.D. Coleman and H. W. Bexton, pp. 52-68. Washington, CA: Grex.

Riviere, J. (1955). The unconscious phantasy of an inner world reflected in examples from literature. In *New Directions in Psychoanalysis*, ed. M. Klein et al. London: Tavistock.

Rosenbleuth, A., and Wiener, N. (1961). Purposeful and non-purposeful behavior. In *Modern Systems Research for the Behavioural Scientist*, pp. 232–237. Chicago: Aldine.

Rosenbluth, D. (1965). The Kleinian theory of depression. *Journal of Child Psychotherapy* 1 (3) 20–25.

Rosenfeld, H. (1965a). *Psychotic States: A Psychoanalytic Approach*. London: Hogarth.

_____ (1965b). The psychopathology of narcissism. In *Psychotic States: A Psychoanalytic Approach*, p. 169. London: Hogarth.

_____ (1969). Contribution to the psychopathology of psychotic states: the importance of projective identification in the ego structure and the object relations of the psychotic patient. In *Problems of Psychosis*, vol. I, ed. P. Dauret and C. Laurin, pp. 115–128. Amsterdam: Excerpta Medica.

_____ (1971). A clinical approach to the psychoanalytic theory of the life and death instincts: an investigation into the aggressive aspects of narcissism. In *Melanie Klein Today*, ed. E. Bott Spillius, pp. 239–255. London: Routledge, 1988.

Ruesch, J. (1961). *Therapeutic Communication*. New York: W. W. Norton.

Sartre, J-P. (1944/1982). *No Exit (Huis Clos)* In *Three Plays*. Penguin Harmondsworth.

Satir, V. (1967). *Conjoint Family Therapy*, rev. ed. Palo Alto, CA: Science and Behavior Books.

Schank, R. L. (1954). *The Permanent Revolution in Science*. New York: Philosophical Library.

Scharff, D., and Scharff, J. S. (1987). *Object Relations Family Therapy*. Northvale, NJ: Jason Aronson.

Scharff, J. S., ed. (1986). *Foundations of Object Relations Family Therapy*. Northvale, NJ: Jason Aronson.

Scott, R. D., and Ashworth, P. L. (1969). The shadow of the ancestor: an historical factor in the transmission of schizophrenia. *British Journal of Medical Psychology* 42: 13–32.

Segal, H. (1964). *Introduction to the Work of Melanie Klein*. London: Heinemann.

_____ (1973). *Introduction to the Work of Melanie Klein*. London: Hogarth.

_____ (1975). Countertransference. *International Journal of Psychoanalytic Psychotherapy* 6:31–37.

_____ (1979). *Klein*. London: Fontana.

Shapiro, R. L. (1967). The origin of adolescent disturbances in the family: some considerations in theory and implications for therapy. In *Family Therapy and Disturbed Families*, ed. G. H. Zuk and I. Boszormenyi-Nagy. Palto Alto, CA: Science and Behavior Books.

Singer, E. (1965). *Key Concepts in Psychotherapy*. New York: Random House.

Skinner, B. F. (1953). *Science and Human Behavior*. New York: Macmillan.

Skynner, A. C. R. (1969). Indications and contraindications for conjoint family therapy. *International Journal of Social Psychiatry* 15:245–249.

———— (1976). *One Flesh: Separate Persons*. London: Constable.

Slipp, S. (1984). *Object Relations: a Dynamic Bridge between Individual and Family Treatment*. Northvale, NJ: Jason Aronson.

Slipp, S., and Kressel, K. (1978). Difficulties in family therapy evaluation: I: a comparison of insight vs. problem-solving approaches. II. design critique and recommendation. *Family Process* 17:409–422.

Steiner, J. (1977). The borderline between the paranoid schizoid and the depressive position in the borderline patient. *British Journal of Medical Psychology* 52:388–391.

———— (1979). Psychotic and non-psychotic parts of the personality. In *Borderline States*. Tavistock Clinic Document no. LT3245. London.

Stierlin, H. (1977). *Psychoanalysis and Family Therapy*. New York: Jason Aronson.

Strachey, J. (1934). The nature of the therapeutic action of psychoanalysis. *International Journal of Psycho-Analysis* 15:127–159.

Sussal, C. M. (1992). Object relations family therapy as a model for practice. *Clinical Social Work Journal* 20 (3): 320–331.

Teruel, G. (1966). Considerations for a diagnosis in marital psychotherapy. *British Journal of Medical Psychology* 39:231.

Turquet, P. (1974). Leadership: the individual and the group. In *Analysis of Groups: Contributions to Theory, Research and Practice*, ed. G. S. Gibbard, J. J. Hastman and R. D. Mann, pp. 349–371. San Francisco, CA: Jossey-Bass.

Walrond-Skinner, S. (1976). *Family Therapy: the Treatment of Natural Systems*. London: Routledge & Kegan Paul.

———— (1979). *Family and Marital Psychotherapy: a Critical Approach*. London: Routledge & Kegan Paul.

Watzlawick, P., Weakland, J., and Fisch, R. (1974). *Change: Principles of Problem Formation and Problem Resolution*. New York: W. W. Norton.

Wiener, H. (1968). Cybernetics in history. In *Modern Systems Research for the Behavioral Scientist*, pp. 31–36. Chicago: Aldine.

Williams, A. H. (1964). *The Psychopathology and Treatment of Sexual Murderers in the Pathology and Treatment of Sexual Deviation*, ed. I. Rosen. Oxford, England: Oxford University Press, 1979.

Wilson. C. (1956). *The Outsider*. London: Victor Gollancz.

Winnicott, D. W. (1965). *Maturational Processes and the Facilitating Environment*. London: Hogarth.

Wynne, L. C., Ryckoff, I., Day, J., and Hirsh, S. (1968). Pseudo-mutuality in the family relations of schizophrenics. In *The Psychosocial Interior of the Family*. London: Allen & Unwin.

Zinner, J., and Shapiro, R. (1972). Projective identification as a mode of perception in families of adolescents. *International Journal of Psycho-Analysis* 53:523–530.

Index

Abandonment, murder's aftermath
treatment phase, 209-212
Abraham, K., 215
Ackerman, N., 15, 17
Ackerman Institute, 16
Action
family therapy and, 21-22
reenactment and, 89
Adolescence, 67-77
case discussion, 70-72
case example, 69-70, 73-77
individuality and, 133
overview, 67-68
as temporary outsider role, 92-94
therapeutic task, 72-73
violence and, 106-107
Aggression, schizophrenia and, 26
Albee, E., 38
Anorexia
adolescence and, 107
family and, 5
Anxiety
containment, family dynamics, 33-35
countertransference and, 82
defenses against, 87
group dynamics and, 38

parents and, 134, 139-144
psychic pain and damage, 158, 162
Ashworth, P. L., 3
Assessment
murder's aftermath, 205
parents and, 132-138
transference, 187-188
to treatment transition, 135-138
Avoidance, of frustration, 4-5

Baby-battering, family dynamics, 33
Bartlett, F. H., 16
Bateson, G., 15-16, 240, 245
Beels, C. C., 17, 18, 19, 20
Behavioral science, environment and,
14
Bentovim, A., 20, 192
Berne, E., 72
Bertalanffy, L. von, 88
Bion, W. R., 4, 6, 9, 14, 30, 34, 47,
59, 63, 68, 71, 81, 82, 84-85, 87,
94, 108, 115, 148-149, 187, 191,
199, 217, 242, 244, 247, 251,
252, 253, 257
Borderline patients, session dynamics,
117